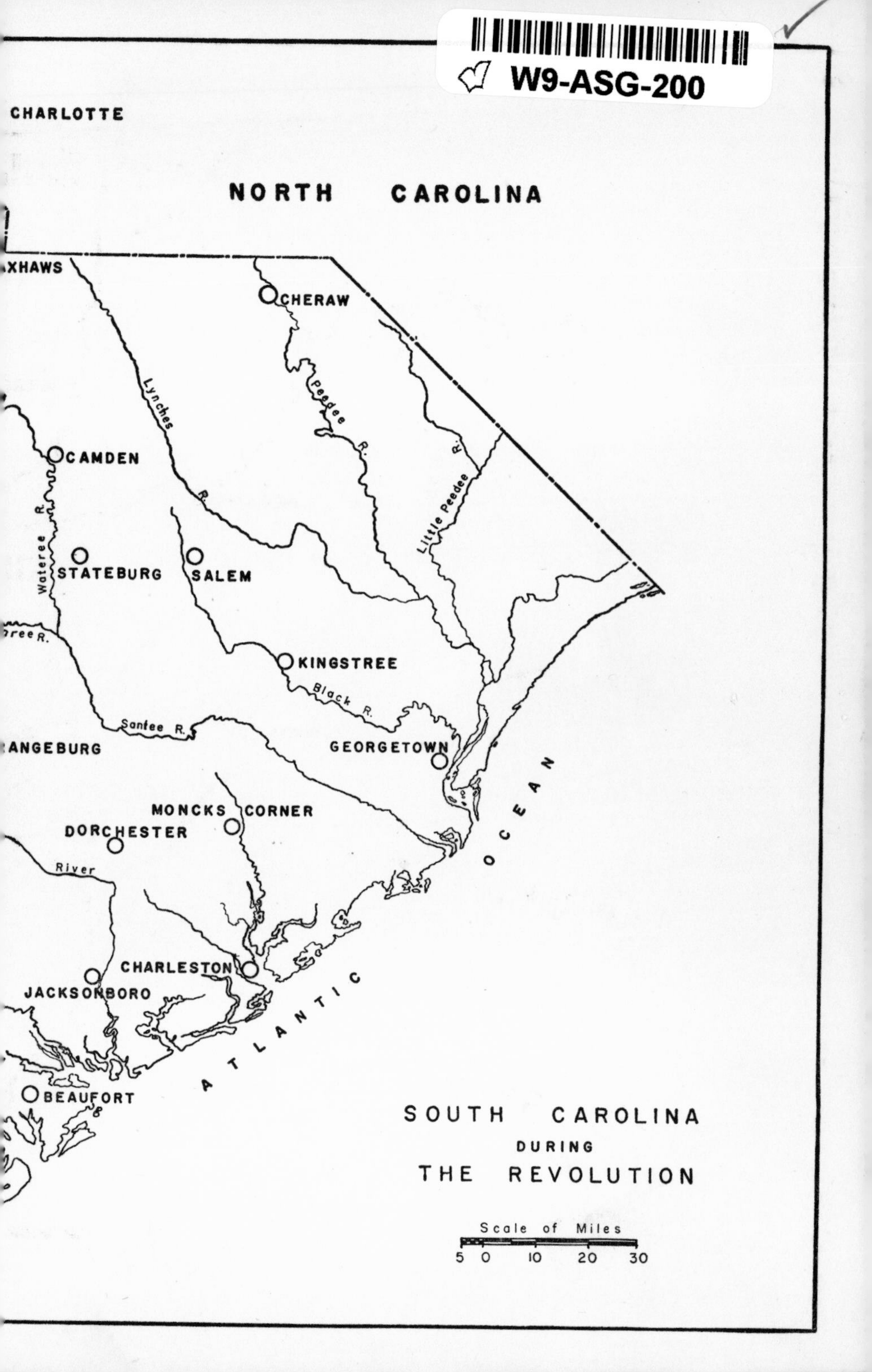
CHARLOTTE
NORTH CAROLINA
XHAWS
CHERAW
Lynches
Peedee
R.
Little Peedee
R.
CAMDEN
Wateree R.
STATEBURG
SALEM
ree R.
KINGSTREE
Black R.
Santee R.
ANGEBURG
GEORGETOWN
MONCKS CORNER
DORCHESTER
River
OCEAN
CHARLESTON
JACKSONBORO
ATLANTIC
BEAUFORT
SOUTH CAROLINA
DURING
THE REVOLUTION
Scale of Miles
5 0 10 20 30

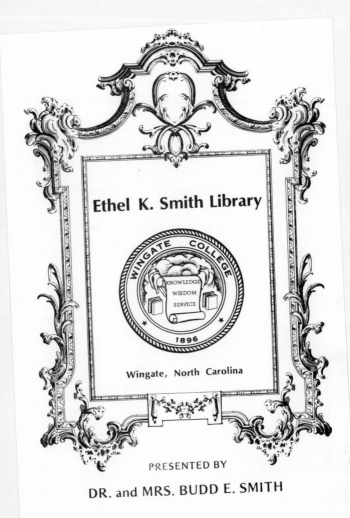

GAMECOCK

Books by the same Author

The Green Dragoon: The Lives of Banastre Tarleton and Mary Robinson
Swamp Fox: The Life and Campaigns of General Francis Marion
Gamecock: The Life and Campaigns of General Thomas Sumter

Illustrated with maps and photographs

By Robert D. Bass

The Life and Campaigns
of General Thomas Sumter

Holt, Rinehart and Winston New York

Published simultaneously in Canada by Holt, Rinehart and Winston of Canada, Ltd.

First Edition

Library of Congress Catalog Card Number: 61-10732

80831-0311

Printed in the United States of America

To
Robert and George
with a father's esteem

Acknowledgments

Many individuals, groups, and organizations have given me help and encouragement during the writing of *Gamecock*. To all of these I express gratitude.

I acknowledge indebtedness to the Historical Society of Wisconsin for use of the large collection of material about Thomas Sumter made by Lyman C. Draper. I also acknowledge my debt to Dr. Anne King Gregorie for use of her research into the finances, property, and litigation of the Sumter family and especially for use of the splendid bibliography in her *Thomas Sumter*.

For use of microfilm copy of the Draper Collection and for much kindness and tolerance, I am indebted to Dr. Robert C. Tucker, Librarian of Furman University, and to Miss Alice B. Adams, Miss Rachael S. Martin, and Miss Margaret T. Weaver, of his staff. Mr. Herbert Hucks, Librarian of Wofford College, has provided help and encouragement. Mr. J. W. G. Gourlay, Librarian of Clemson College, and his staff have done me favors. And I also thank Mr. Alfred Rawlinson, Librarian of the University of South Carolina, and his staff for aid.

For help in locating material I am indebted to members of the staff of the Library of Congress, especially to Dr. C. P. Powell and Mr. John de Porry of the Division of Manuscripts. I am likewise indebted to Dr. Vernon D. Tate, Librarian of the United States Naval Academy; Dr. Howard V. Peckham, Director of the William L. Clements Library; the directors and staffs of the New York Historical Society and of the New York Public Library. Dr. Harold Easterby, Secretary of the South Carolina Historical Commission, and his staff; and to Miss Katherine M. Jones, of the Greenville Public Library.

I am grateful to Dr. Newton Jones, of the Department of History at the Presbyterian College of South Carolina, for reading the manuscript and making many valuable suggestions.

I am obligated to President John L. Plyler and to Dr. Francis W. Bonner, head of the Department of English, for providing me with time for research and writing and for making available the facilities of Furman University.

To Lord Braybrooke and to the Director of the Public Record Office in London I am under obligation for use of the unpublished correspondence of Lord Cornwallis; and to Mrs. Helen M. Fagan for the unpublished letters of Sir Banastre Tarleton.

For permission to reproduce pictures I am obligated to the Division of Prints of the Library of Congress; the Print Room of the New York Public Library; the National Gallery; and the National Portrait Gallery.

To Mr. Green H. Giebner, friend and former student, I am indebted for preparing the maps. To Mrs. Beulah Harris, my editor, I am grateful for counsel and guidance in all phases of publication.

And, finally, to Virginia Wauchope Bass, my wife, now advanced from critic to typist, I shall be forever indebted for help in research, copying material, and typing, and for her loving care in preparing the manuscript of *Gamecock*.

ROBERT D. BASS

Furman University
Greenville, South Carolina

Contents

GAMECOCK

Prologue

In the spring of 1780, while Lord Cornwallis was marching through eastern Carolina, a veteran Continental named Thomas Sumter galloped from his home in the High Hills of Santee. Among the Whigs in the Up Country he recruited a band of guerrillas. Then boldly emerging from secret bases, he hovered around the advancing enemy, ambushing and bushwacking them at the fords and ferries along the Catawba. Fearless and inexorable, like a gamecock he struck with fiery gaffs, leaving death and carnage at every pitting.

In gory fighting at Hanging Rock, Sumter drove Carden from the field and destroyed his Prince of Wales' Regiment. But too bold and incautious, while resting from the August sun at Fishing Creek, he was surprised and routed by Tarleton. Surprised again at Fish Dam Ford, in wild night fighting his men defeated and captured Wemyss. Then at Blackstock's later in November, on a rain-swept bluff above Tyger River, even though left bloody and unconscious, Sumter defeated Tarleton and his Green Horse.

Highly imaginative, the Gamecock was always the grand strategist, instinctively using both men and terrain to baffle the enemy. He was a daring tactician, leading raw militia in hand-to-hand fighting with British regulars. Powerful and tireless, he fought in berserk abandon, reckless of his own life and prodigal with the lives of his men. So enamored of victory was he, said Light Horse Harry Lee, that he would wade through torrents of blood to achieve it.

Sumter was a genius at arousing, organizing, and leading irregular troops. During his campaigns from Rocky Mount to Quinby, he embodied ten regiments of volunteer militia. While there was no governor, legislature, or judiciary in South Carolina, he assumed dictatorial power and raised six regiments of State Troops on Sumter's Law.

Stern, aloof, and taciturn, the Gamecock treated his men like peers, but he courted no familiarity. He was a lonely and rugged Partisan, self-reliant and proudly independent. To Nathanael Greene he seemed a glory fighter, a Carolina freebooter, a backwoods *condottiere* subsisting his private army by plundering Tories. But to the hungry, ragged, unpaid militia, he was a hero, a Galahad bearing the oriflamme of liberty.

After the Revolution no Parson Weems romanticized the life of Thomas Sumter. But the veterans never forgot the fighting and suffering of the Gamecock. They sent him to the General Assembly. They elected him to Congress and followed him into the party of Thomas Jefferson. They elevated him to the Senate of the United States and then offered to make him governor of South Carolina.

A venerable patriot, after a life of public service, he retired to the benign High Hills. Rich, vigorous, and greatly beloved, he lived to be ninety-eight, the last surviving general of the Revolution. Then the proud Carolinians erected a monument of brick, steel, and honor, circled it with flame, and named it Fort Sumter.

Chapter 1 SERGEANT FROM PREDDY'S

THOMAS Sumter was born on July 14, 1734, in the Preddy's Creek settlement of Louisa County, Virginia. His parents were William and Patience Sumter; he was the second of their four children: William, Thomas, Patience, and Anne.

William and Patience Sumter were respectable folk, poor but hard-working. Patience, the daughter of genteel English parents, was headstrong and willful enough to repay a good education by eloping and sailing to the New World with a man beneath her social class. Upon his death, she married William, another English emigrant, and they moved to the frontier in search of free land. Stopping at Preddy's, east of Piney Mountain in the foothills of the Blue Ridge, they raised a cabin, cleared a few acres, and began farming. Soon afterward William built a small gristmill on the north fork of the Rivanna.

Like their pioneer neighbors, the Sumters struggled to make a living, attended church, and gave their children a common-school education. As soon as Thomas was old enough to begin earning his keep, Patience set him tending sheep in the meadows along Preddy's Creek. She cherished this lad with soft blue eyes, curly brown hair, and soaring imagination. At night she told him all she remembered of men and women and manners in the Old World. Tom listened with rapt admiration. "It took a strong-willed woman," he said lovingly in after years, "to raise a strong-willed boy."

When Tom reached adolescence, William took him into the mill. High-spirited and nimble, he went singing about his work, dancing around in his leather breeches and leading his friends in swimming, wrestling, and playing a game of ball called fives. Upon the death of William, Patience bound the mettlesome lad to Benjamin Cave. Like another of Cave's plowboys named Lucas, Tom owned a single shirt. On Sundays they washed these in Cave's Creek, hung them on bushes, and spent the afternoon playing marbles or pushpin.

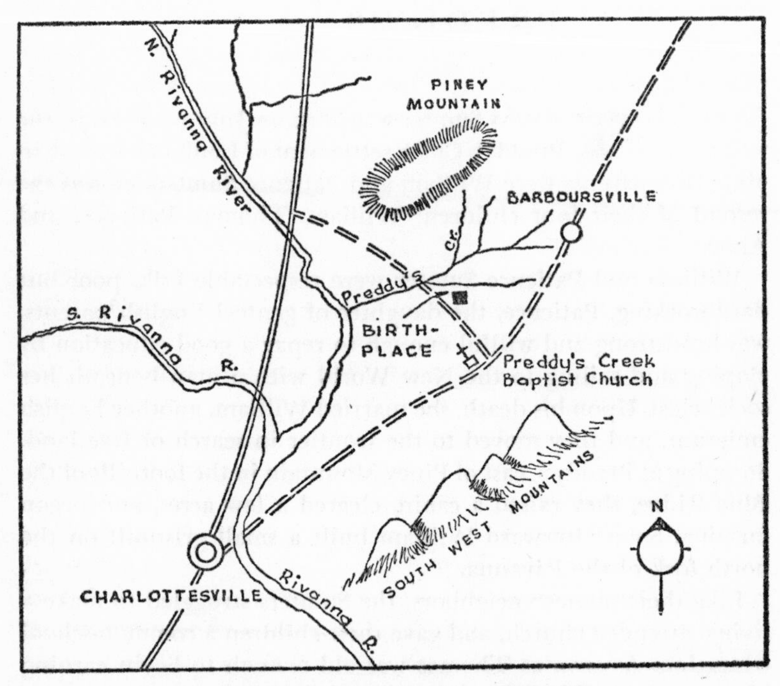

BIRTHPLACE OF THOMAS SUMTER

The men along Preddy's were small farmers, woodsmen, and Indian fighters. Rough, shrewd, and often illiterate, they spent their leisure in fox chasing, bear hunting, and cockfighting. Tom early developed a love for blood sports. He raised a flock of game chickens and fought his stags against those of Lucas.

As young Sumter came to manhood, he was slender, muscular, and wonderfully quick and powerful. Of medium height, he admired towering Joe Martin and Ben Cleveland. With them he joined the militia under Colonel Zachariah Burnley, who lived at Somerset, and then he began running around to the frolics, dancing, flirting, and exhibiting a knack for deviltry. Soon whispers were going around that Widow Sumter's younger son was a wild buck, devoted to gambling, cockfighting, and horse racing. When he tried to court a pretty neighbor, she tossed her head and flounced off.

While Thomas Sumter was becoming notorious, the new frontier beyond Preddy's was in turmoil. The French attempt to seize the Ohio Valley spread into the French and Indian War. In 1755 General Edward Braddock, with British regulars and Virginia militia, marched toward Fort Duquesne. After the French and Indians had ambushed and defeated Braddock, Lieutenant Governor Robert Dinwiddie entrusted the defense of Virginia to Colonel George Washington.

The following spring the Indians came surging along the Blue Ridge, murdering, scalping, and burning. Dinwiddie called out ten regiments to support Washington. Burnley mustered his troops, marched into the wilderness, and spent the summer hiking, camping, and training his militia. Then home again he came, parading his sunburned men through the settlements like heroes. As Private Sumter swaggered through Preddy's, he did not condescend to glance at the belle who had spurned him.

But at last Thomas had found his vocation. He enjoyed the activity, excitement, and routine of military life. When General Forbes began preparing his campaign against the French, Sumter and Martin joined the regiment commanded by Colonel William Byrd. Then like water seeking its level these turbulent young men headed toward the Ohio. They were with the troops who captured Duquesne and renamed it Fort Pitt, a post soon encompassed by Pittsburgh.

Colonel Byrd moved on through Ohio. Before the end of the campaign, Thomas Sumter, because of his leadership, prowess, and willingness to take hazardous assignments, was proudly wearing the chevrons of a sergeant. And because he was now steadier and more moderate, he had won the confidence of Lieutenant Henry Timberlake.

When Great Warrior Oconostota led the Cherokee Indians on the warpath in 1760, the General Assembly of Virginia recalled Colonel Byrd and sent him against the Over Hill Cherokees. After crossing the Blue Ridge, Byrd encamped for the winter near the settlement of Samuel Stalnakres, west of the cabin of John Holston at the head spring of Holston River. Although Dinwiddie and Lieutenant Governor William Bull of South Carolina had decreed a co-ordinated drive against the Cherokee nation, Byrd remained at Stalnakres' during the spring and summer.

In the meantime Colonel James Grant, with British regulars and Carolina militia commanded by such staunch officers as Lieutenant Colonel Henry Laurens, Captain William Moultrie, and Lieutenants Isaac Huger, Francis Marion, Andrew Pickens, and Andrew Williamson, had marched up from Charleston and begun carrying fire and sword to the Middle Towns of the Cherokees.

So terrible was the Carolinians' destruction of food, villages, and warriors that in July old Kanagatucko, Emperor of the Cherokees, with Chief Attakullakulla as his spokesman, came up to Byrd's camp and sued for peace. After sending the Cherokees back to arrange a truce with Grant, Colonel Byrd turned his regiment over to Lieutenant Colonel Adam Stephen and headed for Westover. Colonel Stephen soon moved down the Holston to Long Island and began erecting Fort Robinson.

At Fort Prince George on Keowee River in the Lower Towns, the Cherokees overtook Colonel Grant. After rejecting Grant's demand that he surrender four warriors to be put to death, Attakullakulla hurried down the Cherokee path to Charleston. In an oration of pathos and great power he told the Council that Chiefs Oconostota, Ostenaco, and Standing Turkey had repented of starting the war. Upon concluding a severe but honorable treaty with Governor Bull, he again started for Virginia. At Fort Robinson, on November 19, Chief Kanagatucko signed a similar treaty with Colonel Stephen.

Old Kanagatucko then asked that a Virginian carry the document to Echota, the peace town of the Cherokees. When Stephen hesitated to order a man on such a dangerous mission, Sergeant Sumter and Lieutenant Timberlake volunteered for the perilous journey to the Over Hill Towns in the shadow of the Great Smoky Mountains.

Despite attempts of Chief Ostenaco to dissuade him, Timberlake decided to make the journey by water. To finance the trip

Sumter borrowed £60 from Alexander McDonald. With this he bought a large canoe, provisions for ten days, and about £20 worth of goods to swap for horses. And on bitterly cold November 28, accompanied by interpreter John McCormack, they shoved off down the Holston. Scarcely had they lost sight of Long Island before they ran into shallow water. "Sumter the sergeant leaped out," said Timberlake admiringly in his *Memoirs,* "and dragged us near a hundred yards over the shoals, till we found deep water again."

Seeing a hunting party of Cherokees, they enquired the distance to Echota. On high water, the braves replied, a canoe might cover the distance in six days, but since a great drouth had lowered the water the trip would take much longer. They warned Timberlake against difficulties and dangers, especially against Northern Indians who hunted the territory in winter. They invited the three men to their supper of dried venison dipped in hot bear grease.

During the following nineteen days the three emissaries suffered great hardships. They had to drag their canoe for several hours each day, sloshing down the river while ice hung to their clothes. And because of their slow descent, they ran out of provisions.

Both Sumter and McCormack carried muskets. On December 6 Timberlake tried to shoot a turkey with McCormack's gun, but it misfired and blew off the hammer and firing pin. About a mile farther along they saw a great bear waddling down to the river. "Sumter, to whom the remaining gun belonged, took it to shoot," said Timberlake; "but not being conveniently seated, he laid it on the edge of the canoe, while he rose to fix himself to more advantage; but the canoe giving a heel, let the gun tumble overboard."

Failing to locate the gun with a long pole, they began to talk of drowning themselves. But recovering from despair they went ashore and built a fire. While Sumter was gathering wood for the night, several black bears invaded their camp. With trembling fingers Timberlake rigged a firing mechanism on their lone gun, and McCormack began following a large, fat male. After a long chase he fired. Timberlake, who had been drying his socks, sprang up and raced barefoot through the woods. The interpreter had missed. On the next shot, however, McCormack killed a male weighing about four hundred pounds. After feasting on broiled bear steak, they loaded as much meat as they could in the canoe and resumed their journey.

Next day the three men saw a large cave opening on a ledge about fifty feet above them. Mooring their boat hastily, they climbed the rocky bank, entered the cave, and began examining the stalactites. Suddenly they noticed their canoe drifting downstream. "Sumter scrambled down the rock, and, plunging into the river, without giving himself scarce time to pull off his coat, swam a quarter of a mile before he could overtake her," said Timberlake.

After building a fire to thaw Sumter's freezing clothes, the men decided to encamp. Little did they sleep. Wild animals penned in the cave by the flames screamed and howled throughout the night.

On December 11 they heard guns booming on both sides of the Holston. Believing that they had run into a hunting party of hostile Northern Indians, they sped downriver and hid in a thicket. Afraid to build a fire, they tried to sleep in their cold, wet blankets. After their miserable experience, the following night they penetrated into a dense canebrake and built a fire. About midnight they were awakened by footfalls around their camp. Yelling that they were beset by Indians, McCormack ran down to the river, sprang into the boat, and tried to shove off. But Timberlake seized and held the canoe.

"I imagined it some half-starved animal looking for food," said Timberlake in his *Memoirs*. Then he continued in admiration of his fearless sergeant: "Sumter had been so certain of this, that he never moved from where he lay; for when, in an hour after, I had persuaded McCormack to return to the camp, we found Sumter fast asleep."

Reaching the great falls on the Holston, Timberlake tried to carry the ammunition around, while Sumter and McCormack shot the rapids. Finding the route overland impossible, he called them to the shore and boarded the canoe. "We scarce advanced a hundred yards, when we ran with such violence against another rock, that Sumter, breaking his pole in attempting to ward the shock, fell overboard."

The *voyageurs* waded ashore and built a fire. But as it was alternately raining, hailing, and snowing, they wrapped their sopping blankets around them and lay on the wet ground, exhausted and shivering. Next morning they found the river frozen from bank to bank. After breaking a passage through the ice, they moved slowly downstream until they reached French Broad River.

Two days later, when in sight of Little Tennessee River, they heard a shout from the shore. Looking up, they found themselves under the leveled muskets of a party of Indians.

"To what town do you belong?" shouted the leader in Cherokee.

"To the English camp," replied interpreter McCormack. "The English and the Cherokees have made peace. We are carrying the treaty to the Cherokee nation."

Chief Slave-Catcher of the Tennessee invited the Virginians to his camp. He treated them with great friendliness and gave them a supper of dried venison, honey, and boiled corn. Next morning he guided them to his village opposite the mouth of Tellico River. After a feast and a powwow, he sent them on to Tomotley.

Having heard nothing from the Virginians since leaving them at Long Island, Chief Ostenaco was surprised to see them walk into Tomotley. Extremely hospitable, he invited them to stay in his cabin during their sojourn among the Over Hill Cherokees. After summoning the other chiefs, he accompanied Timberlake and McCormack to a powwow at their great town house in Echota.

While his companions called upon the Indians along the Little Tennessee, Sergeant Sumter remained at Tomotley to guard the property of the expedition. Always eager to increase his education by observing the manners and customs of people, he watched and talked and listened. He noted the facial markings and delicate tattoos of the Cherokee warriors, their lines enhanced by white and vermilion paint. He noticed their curious dress, ornamented with beads, shells, and feathers.

As a soldier, he marked their pride in weapons, their care of bows and arrows, and their delight in firearms. He listened to their war songs, watched their war dances, and heard the death hallo of a party returning with scalps. After viewing their athletic contests, especially their ball games, Sumter decided that he could outrun, outwrestle, and outshoot any brave among the Cherokees.

Like most men reared among the Indian traders on the Southern frontier, Tom Sumter knew many words of the Cherokees. During the peace negotiations he had learned the names of many of their chiefs. He now began to hear the names of their rivers, mountains, and towns. As he sojourned among them, listening and talking, he became moderately fluent in Cherokee.

After two months spent in visiting the Cherokee villages from the Tennessee to the Chattahoochee, Timberlake decided that he had completed his mission. With the goods brought for trading, the emissaries bought horses and began preparing to return to Virginia. Fearful that his guests might run into a hostile war party, Ostenaco declared that he would escort them home. On March 10 Timberlake, Sumter, McCormack, and Ostenaco, guarded by a hundred warriors, left Tomotley on the Indian path to Long Island in the Holston. When they arrived at Fort Robinson after a tedious march, Ostenaco begged to be allowed to continue on to Williamsburg.

Upon reaching the capital, Timberlake introduced Chief Ostenaco to Lieutenant Governor Francis Fauquier. For several weeks the governor entertained the Cherokees, and after he had distributed presents among them, they began preparing to return to Tennessee. But just before their departure, the Reverend James Horrocks invited Ostenaco to supper at William and Mary College. During the evening he showed the chief a portrait of young King George III.

"Long have I wished to see the King my father," exclaimed Ostenaco. "This is his resemblance, and I am determined to see himself. I am near the sea. Never will I depart from it till I have obtained my desires."

After much hesitancy and debate, Governor Fauquier agreed to send Chiefs Ostenaco, Conne Shote, and Wooe to London. He then engaged Timberlake, Sumter, and a skillful interpreter named William Shorey as their escorts. On the night before their departure, Ostenaco held a farewell ceremony. The townspeople, especially the students at William and Mary, came to hear his songs and prayers.

Thomas Jefferson, like the other students around Timberlake and Sumter, was profoundly moved by the eloquence of Ostenaco. "I was in his camp when he made his great farewell oration to his people the evening before he departed for England," said Jefferson in recalling his years in Williamsburg. "His sounding voice, distinct articulation, animated action, and the solemn silence of his people at their several fires, filled me with awe and veneration, although I did not understand a word he uttered."

At Hampton Roads the Virginians and Cherokees embarked in the *Epreuve,* a Royal frigate commanded by Captain Peter Blake. As the Atlantic became tempestuous, the passengers became violently seasick, and about mid-ocean Shorey died. On June 16 the survivors landed at Plymouth and took coach to London. Captain Blake introduced the visitors to Lord Egremont, Secretary of State. After promising to escort them to St. James's Palace, the Secretary sent them to lodgings in Suffolk Street.

All London became excited over the Cherokees. "They are full, well-made Men, near six feet high, dressed in their own Country Fashion, with only a Shirt, Trousers and a Mantle round them," said the *St. James Chronicle* on June 18; "their faces are painted of a Copper Colour, and their Heads adorned with Shells, Feathers, Earrings, and other trifling Ornaments."

Cherokees and escorts soon began a round of sight-seeing and visiting. On June 23 the troupe visited Kensington Gardens. Two days later they visited Westminster Abbey. Londoners thronged them. Realizing the sensation that their party of Indians was creating, Timberlake and Sumter bought red-coated uniforms and passed themselves off as officers of the British Army. "Two English officers who had seen service in America and learned something of their language accompanied them as interpreters," said the *St. James Chronicle.*

The visitors from America became the social rage. The Lord Mayor invited them to dine at Mansion House. The Earl of Macclesfield entertained them at Twickenham. Joshua Reynolds painted the three Cherokees in a group and then did a portrait of Ostenaco. Oliver Goldsmith visited their lodging, waiting three hours for the crowd to thin enough for his admittance. He gave Ostenaco a present, which the chief acknowledged with such an embrace that it left the poet's cheek smeared with vermilion paint. Finally the Cherokees and their escort were presented at St. James's Palace.

To impress the Indians with the might of the British Navy, Lord

Egremont sent them down the Thames to the naval depot at Woolwich. Mr. Montague, the Virginia agent, went with them through the Tower of London. They visited St. Paul's Cathedral. With the enthusiasm of experienced ballplayers, they watched the cricket matches at White Conduit House—while pickpockets worked the crowd. They visited Ranelagh, where they were followed by mobs. They supped at Vauxhall Gardens, where strangers crowded around their tables. They visited Sadler's Wells, and Ostenaco tried to get a tightrope walker to go with him to the wilds of Tennessee.

On their second visit to Vauxhall, the troupe was surrounded by ten thousand frenzied spectators. The Cherokees joined the revelry and amused the onlookers by sounding the organ, scraping upon violins, and clapping their hands to return the applause. All the while they were downing bumpers of sweet Frontiniac wine. As they started for their lodgings about three o'clock in the morning, Ostenaco lurched against a gentleman's sword hilt. In the succeeding brawl, the man drew his sword. Ostenaco seized and broke it in two. Holding up his bleeding hands, he howled long and wildly and then fell prone. After a struggle, his guardians tumbled him into a coach. "The coachman, by driving away, put an end to this wretched Scene of British curiosity and savage debauchery," said the horrified *St. James Chronicle.*

Timberlake denied Cherokee wretchedness and debauchery. In his *Memoirs* he wrote: "A bottle of wine, a bowl of punch, and a little cyder, being the ordinary consumption of the three Indians, Sumter, and myself."

The Beau Monde as well as the rabble began crowding into the Indians' lodging, and seeing an opportunity to make a few pence the servants began charging admission. "Some days after, Sumter, who had contracted some genteel acquaintance, some of whom he was bringing to see the Indians, was stopped by the servant," said Timberlake. "The young man, who had faced all dangers for the service of his country in the war, who had been so highly instrumental in saving us from the dangers that threatened us in going to their country, and had accompanied us ever since, received that affront from an insolent servant; but not being able to bear the insult, he took a warrior's satisfaction, and knocked him down."

Deciding that the time had come to get the Cherokees out of England, Lord Egremont arranged a private audience with King George. For this Ostenaco dressed in a rich blue mantle covered with lace. Against his throat he placed a gorget engraved with the arms of the King. Wooe and Conne Shote wore scarlet coats adorned with gold lace. Timberlake and Sumter wore their uniforms with gorgeous scarlet coats.

Upon arrival at St. James's Palace, Lord Eglinton presented them to his Majesty. Inspired by meeting the Great Father, Ostenaco made an eloquent speech, pledging friendship and alliance with the English. The audience lasted for an hour and a half. "They were received by his Majesty and their Behaviour was remarkably humble and meek," said *The Gazetter and London Daily Advertiser* of the Cherokees. "There seemed to be a Mixture of Majesty and Moroseness in their Countenances."

Erect and handsome, his swarthy features and light blue eyes enhanced by his scarlet coat, Sumter interpreted the speeches, occasionally growing confused and stumbling through the wild oratory of Ostenaco. He spoke softly, his eyes shifting from Cherokee to King and his ears catching every word of his Sovereign. As he stood before young King George III, Sergeant Thomas Sumter was a long way from Preddy's Creek.

Just before the departure of the Cherokees, in routine change of station the Admiralty ordered the *Epreuve* to sail to the coast of South Carolina; Lord Egremont decided to send the Indians home by way of Charleston. Ostenaco refused to sail unless through Hampton Roads. But ministers assured him that he would land safely in Virginia.

Lieutenant Timberlake also refused to go to South Carolina, pleading the expense of returning overland to Virginia. Undersecretary Wood declined to advance him any more money and began looking for another escort. "Sumter was immediately sent for by Mr. Wood, but he refused the employ till he had obtained my approbation," said Timberlake. "Sumter had too much honour to accompany them to my prejudice."

Sumter finally accepted the offer of £50 in hand and £100 upon arrival in Charleston, and Lord Egremont gave the Cherokees farewell gifts of muskets, scalping knives, axes, and peace pipes. He also gave them letters containing pledges of peace. After great formalities, on August 20 Sumter and his wards set out in coach and six for Portsmouth.

The return voyage of the *Epreuve* was uneventful until she reached American waters. After hailing the *Runner,* a New England vessel returning from the forbidden French West Indies, Captain Blake gave chase. Believing the vessel to be a French privateer, the Indians loaded their muskets for battle, but the little coaster meekly surrendered. As their share of contraband, Blake gave the Indians some coconuts and tobacco and a keg of gunpowder. On October 28 the *Epreuve* sailed along Sullivan's Island and entered the harbor at Charleston.

Sumter immediately called upon Governor Thomas Boone. After introducing the chiefs, he delivered a letter from Lord Egremont. The Indians reported that they had enjoyed their visit to London and sent messages of friendship to King George. Chief Ostenaco praised Sumter's attention during the voyages and their stay in England. "That gentleman has treated us exceedingly well," he told Boone, "and has been very good to us."

Ostenaco begged Sumter to escort the party back to Tomotley. Governor Boone furnished horses and wagons, and on November 10 the procession set off on the Cherokee path. They paused at Eutaw Springs, and Sumter listened to the murmuring water pouring from the crevice in the limestone. Moving up the Santee and the Congaree, they paused again at Congarees. From the Saluda they passed on to the Keowee.

Sumter stopped at Fort Prince George, adjacent to the Lower Towns. He invited the chiefs of these to a conference, and Ostenaco told them about seeing the marvels of London, meeting the Great Father, and viewing the terrifying power of England. Soon afterward the cavalcade passed through Rabun Gap and came again to the Over Hill Towns.

After a summer in London, Thomas Sumter enjoyed visiting Tomotley. He liked the Indians' simple manners and aboriginal customs. Joining in their games, he ran and jumped and wrestled, defeating all their braves except Saucy Jack. Because of his integrity, strength, and courage, the Cherokees invited him to remain with them, but toward the end of winter he began preparing to return to Virginia.

In late January, however, Baron des Jonnes, a lieutenant in the Canadian militia and veteran of the campaign against Braddock, came to the Over Hill Towns. Des Jonnes, master of seven Indian languages, set about learning Cherokee. In a short time he began telling the Cherokees in their own tongue that the French were winning the war. They would soon throw the English out of North America.

Realizing that Des Jonnes was making converts, Sumter asked permission to arrest him. But Great Warrior Oconostota was visiting the French in Alabama, and lesser chiefs hesitated. Finally they gave their consent with the proviso that Sumter arrest the Canadian singlehanded.

Sumter immediatley rode to Tokowee, found Des Jonnes, and seized him. With a show of strength and ferocity he told the Canadian that resistance meant death. The baron replied that he was not afraid to die. They grappled and fell to the earth. As they lay kicking and writhing, an excited warrior seized a chunk of wood and moved in to rescue Des Jonnes. A chief yelled, "Let the white men fight it out."

After a bloody struggle Sumter subdued the baron. Tying the prisoner on his horse, he mounted behind him and set off for Fort Prince George. Upon their arrival, Lieutenant Charles Taylor, the commandant, praised the sergeant for his skill and courage. He sent Des Jonnes on to Governor Boone, who immediately clapped him into the brig of the frigate *Nightingale* and rushed him to England.

Sumter rode leisurely down to Charleston, talking, questioning, and listening. He liked the people on the Carolina frontier. Many of them had come down from Virginia during the recent trouble with Indians, and some of them remembered Joe Martin, Ben Cleveland, and the Hendersons. After passing through Ninety-Six he rode along the tumbling creeks, noting splendid sites for dams and mills and plantation houses. Here was free land and wood and water of surpassing worth.

Tom Sumter again paused beside the murmuring springs of Eutaw. He loved the cool, dark gash in the earth, covered with brambles, dogwoods, poplars, and oaks, through which flowed Eutaw Creek. Of all the spots that he had seen between Preddy's Creek and the Thames this was one of the most pleasant. Three miles below the springs, at the fork where the road turned toward Nelson's Ferry, he stopped. "What a site for a store," he mused as he reined his horse toward Charleston.

Governor Boone admired the friendly young sergeant. Impressed with the capture of Des Jonnes, he invited Sumter to visit the Council Chamber and tell its members about his adventures in the Cherokee nation. He even sent a report of the talk to Lord Egremont and requested that Sumter be indemnified for his "expenses, time, fatigue, and risk." *The South Carolina Gazette* carried stories about the capture of Des Jonnes. By summer many of the people of South Carolina had read or heard of the strength and daring of Sergeant Thomas Sumter.

After having been paraded and toasted as a hero, Sumter left Charleston to return to Virginia. At the fork, as he turned toward Nelson's, he paused and again surveyed the site for a store. But he kept riding and without further adventure reached Preddy's Creek.

The past seven of Tom's twenty-nine years had been spent in military or Indian service. He now found the settlement on Preddy's vastly changed. Brother William, with sons William and John, was living on Piney Mountain. Sister Patience had married John Franklin, and upon his death, James Suddarth. She had two sons, William and James. Sister Anne had married Thomas Land. And Widow Sumter was now a skilled midwife, the beloved granny of the expanding settlements along Preddy's and the Rivanna.

Tom lingered at his mother's cabin, chatting, boasting, laughing. He related his adventures among the Cherokees, and she beamed over his physical prowess. He spoke affably of Governors Fauquier and Boone. He described the sights of London, and her eyes moistened from memories. He told her about his visit to St. James's Palace and confessed that he had stumbled and stuttered as he stood before King George. Patience Sumter's heart swelled as she gazed at her powerful, handsome son, neatly dressed in a scarlet coat with sergeant's stripes and talking familiarly of chiefs, governors, lords, and the King.

But Tom Sumter did not long enjoy his triumphal return to

Preddy's. He had never repaid Alexander McDonald the money he had borrowed for the trip down the Holston. The angry Scotsman had been waiting, and now he swore out a warrant for indebtedness. The jurors for the November term of court for Louisa County in 1763 found Sergeant Sumter cooling his nimble heels in jail. Friends arranged bond. Then Samuel Cowden and Company brought similar action. For want of a bondsman Sumter was thrown into jail at Staunton.

As Tom lay in his cold, bare cell, with little hope of paying Cowden and less of escape, Joe Martin rode into Staunton. After spending the day with Tom, the tall, powerful Indian fighter asked permission to spend the night. "In the morning, when he went out, he left with Sumter his tomahawk and ten guineas," said Martin's son William. "With one or both of these he escaped from prison."

Three weeks later, from Long Canes Creek, on the frontier between South Carolina and the Cherokee nation, Sumter wrote Martin: "Pray excuse my going away and Not leaving your money: but I greatly hope it ante make any great odds as I inter in again Very Early in the Spring." But he cautioned Joe, "What Ever is between you and me keep it to your selfe till I return and I am for Ever your Honest Friend."

Chapter 2 CAPTAIN OF MILITIA

IN THE little settlement on Long Canes Creek, an outpost on the border between Carolina and the Cherokees, Thomas Sumter pondered. Civilization or savagery—which should he choose? Which offered the most to an outlaw afraid to return to Virginia? Beloved by Ostenaco and respected by the Cherokee warriors, he could turn Indian trader and become rich. But he was as highly respected by Governor Boone and the people around Charleston. Low Country lawyers and merchants and planters had wealth and education and daughters. There was free land from the sea islands to the Blue Ridge. There were Eutaw Springs and the vacant site near the fork of the road below Nelson's. Perhaps Lord Egremont had sent the money for his "fatigue and risk."

Like a gamester watching the dice spin slowly into a double six, Sumter decided. After packing, he vaulted into his saddle and for the second time headed down the Cherokee path from Ninety-Six to Charleston. He rode leisurely through communities on the Saluda and the Congaree. Again he paused at Eutaw Springs and the vacant lot at the fork. In July, 1764, he reached Charleston and petitioned South Carolina for £400. The Council pointedly informed Mr. Sumter that the Province had not engaged him as an escort for Chief Ostenaco.

Lord Egremont was more generous. The British government paid Sumter £700. With this modest fortune he rode back to Eutaw. From the tract east of the fork he bought a lot, built a small store, and stocked it with items necessary and useful to the planters. Having fulfilled the dream of many retired soldiers and adventurers, he settled down to the life of a country merchant.

With an eye for strategy, Sumter located his store on the border between the Low Country and the Up Country. He was only sixty miles from Charleston, seat of the Royal governor, the legislature, the courts, and the army and the navy. And yet he was not too near the capital, with its aristocracy, its English educated lawyers, preachers, and doctors, and their snobbery. He was scarcely more than sixty miles from either Congarees or Camden, with their trade from the backwoods and Indian lands. And yet he was not too close to the frontier, with its democracy, poverty, ignorance, and crudity. At the fork in front of his store converged most of the traffic between the capital and the frontier. And a couple of miles behind it flowed the Santee, its surface dotted with canoes, rafts, and boats from the great central drainage basin of Carolina.

Around Sumter's store lived well-to-do, hospitable folk, mostly Huguenot or Scotch-Irish in blood, with large and fertile plantations, mansions and messuages, servants, and ranges filled with cattle, hogs, and sheep. Huguenot Tacitus Gaillard, a power in St. John's Parish, was Justice of the Peace. At Pond Bluff, four miles beyond Eutaw Springs, lived Francis Marion, a hero of the Cherokee War.

Among these neighborly people Thomas Sumter was busy, selling, swapping, buying, talking. And he prospered. Within a year he had accumulated considerable property. In June, 1765, he mortgaged three slaves, a pair of horses, and a new wagon to William Flud for £1,000. He then began dickering with Charles Cantey for two hundred acres of farm land near the Santee.

Cantey, famed for his seven beautiful daughters, was a member of the clan descended from Tiege Cantey, a penniless immigrant from Ireland. Now the Canteys were wealthy and powerful. William Flud had married a Cantey. Above Jack's Creek on the north side of the Santee lived Colonel Richard Richardson, a former Virginian, who had married Mary Cantey, accumulated property, and risen to influence in military and political affairs of the Province. Just below Richardson's, on a plantation of ten thousand acres, lived William and Mary Jameson. William was an Irishman who had migrated to Carolina, and Mary was a daughter of Captain Joseph Cantey, owner of Mount Hope plantation, some twenty miles down the Santee.

The Jamesons were wealthy. Their new mansion was filled with mahogany furniture; their table was laden with china, glass, and silver. Their lands were planted in corn, peas, potatoes, cane, and indigo. Their stalls were filled with splendid horses. Pastures fed droves of hogs and herds of sheep and cattle. And fifty-eight servants kept their house, ran their errands, tilled their land, and herded their livestock.

Life on the plantations along the Santee was usually pleasant, but sometimes the summers were hot and wet, with plagues of mosquitoes and epidemics of malaria and yellow fever. During the fever season of 1766 William Jameson died. In his will he divided his estate, evaluated at £19,000, between his wife and Agnes Stit, a sister in Ireland. Instead of returning to Mount Hope, Mary continued to live on her plantation, managing her home and extensive property.

Soon after settling in St. John's, Thomas Sumter had become acquainted with the Jamesons. As soon as he felt that it was proper, he turned his attention to Widow Jameson. He fascinated her with his talk of faraway places, of Indian chiefs and Royal governors and King George, and of the manners and customs of men from tribal Echota to imperial London.

Mary, eleven years older than Thomas, was a woman of average height, spare build, and strong features. In childhood she had suffered infantile paralysis, which withered her left side, leaving a game leg and shortened arm. But infirmity had so mellowed her disposition that she was gentle and amiable, and yet utterly fearless.

Mary liked handsome Tom Sumter, with his keen blue eyes, firm mouth, and curling brown hair. From neighboring gossips she had learned much about the Virginian. He was sober, honest, and hard-working. Agile and powerful, he could swim the roiling Santee, defeat any ballplayer in St. John's in a game of fives, or vault into his saddle without touching horse or stirrup. He had stirred the Province by his capture of Des Jonnes. And so, as she listened and spring blossomed into summer, she agreed to share her life and fortune with the thirty-three-year-old swashbuckler.

Thomas and Mary were married in the summer of 1767. They settled on her plantation on Great Savannah. Their mansion sat in a grove of live oaks and cedars, athwart an eminence directly above the Santee swamp and about a half mile below the road to Camden. Comfortably situated, surrounded by servants and flourishing plantation life, despite the difference in their ages, they were happy. On August 30, 1768, in her forty-fifth year Mary bore a son whom they named Thomas, Junior.

Affluent with Mary's property, Thomas Sumter began plunging. He sold his store at the fork and built a larger one on Great Savannah. Keenly interested in water power and machinery, a heritage

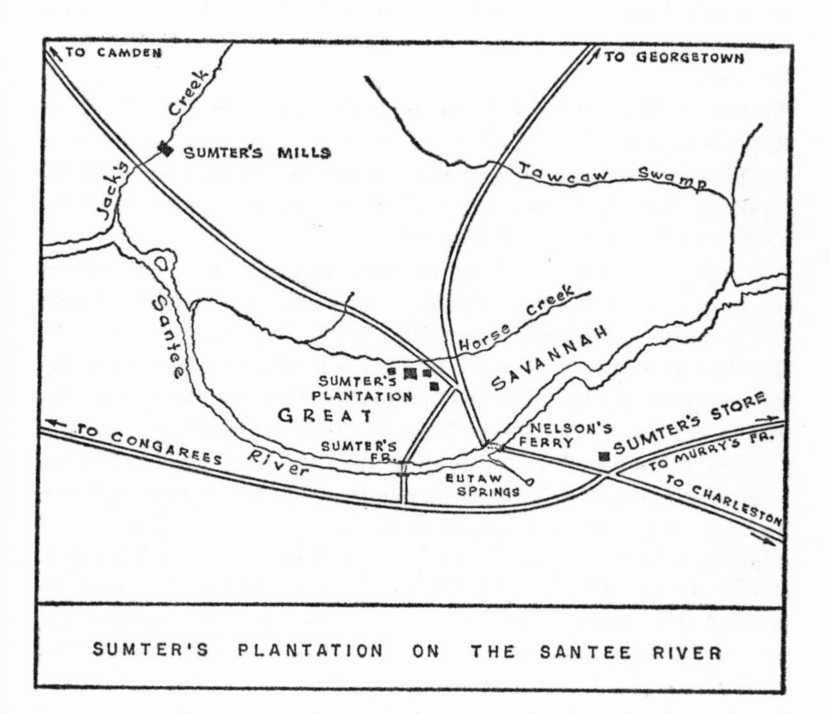

SUMTER'S PLANTATION ON THE SANTEE RIVER

from his days as millboy, he built a sawmill and a gristmill on Jack's Creek. With a pioneer's land hunger, he began buying and selling, speculating, and fighting lawsuits. But he remembered the jail at Staunton and kept in practice with Joe Martin's tomahawk.

In the summer of 1768, during agitation created by the Regulator's demand for additional courts, Deputy Sheriff John Wood rode into the back country with a wallet filled with writs and executions returnable to the Court of Common Pleas in Charleston. As he was returning with eight distrained slaves, on the night of June 27 five masked men waylaid him. They disarmed him, freed his prisoners, tied him over his horse, flogged him, and kept him in confinement until he escaped. Wood later identified the ringleader as Moses Kirkland. Curiously, one of the warrants was for Thomas Sumter.

During the ruckus over the manhandled deputy, Sumter formed a warm attachment for Kirkland. He liked the positive, direct action of the illiterate planter, politician, and militia leader from the settlement along Saluda River. As a champion of backwoods democracy Sumter backed Kirkland for a seat in the House of Representatives. And in 1768, at the height of the excitement over Regulators, new courts, and maladministration of justice, Kirkland was elected, the first representative from the vast Up Country ever to sit in the General Assembly.

During the early opposition to the Stamp Act, Sumter had been too busy to meddle in politics. As a man who had visited London and had attended an audience with King George, he was a Loyalist. But in the summer of 1766, while on a trip to Charleston for merchandise, he had heard Christopher Gadsden harangue the mechanics under the Liberty Tree. As the fiery liberal spoke on the folly of relaxing efforts or hoping that England would change, Sumter felt an aspiration for independence. As he wrote years later, he "first saw the effects of concerted and orderly associations of men, in resisting and restraining usurped power, and unconstitutional abuses of power." With the enthusiasm of a convert he entered the struggle and soon became a popular leader. He was appointed Justice of the Peace and in 1773 was a member of the Grand Jury for Camden District.

While riding and talking politics, Sumter continued to speculate and amass land. Between 1768 and 1773 he secured 4,450 acres in St. Mark's Parish through Royal grant. But just as his speculation, debts, and lawsuits were about to come to a balance, his clerk absconded with all the money he could draw from the store.

Overwhelmed, Sumter placed an advertisement in *The South Carolina Gazette* for March 19, 1774, offering for sale his plantation of fourteen thousand acres, with livestock, implements, and mills on Jack's Creek. Unable to find a buyer or get any accommodation from his creditors, he called in ten or fifteen of his most devoted servants, saddled his horses, and started toward the free land on the Western frontier. As his entourage was passing through the Blue Ridge, agents of his creditors overtook him. After arguments, accommodations, and adjustments, they persuaded him to return to his plantation on the Santee.

Since Sumter's personal struggles were only an index of the troubled times, he lost neither standing nor influence. When the leaders of rebellion called for the election of a representative assembly to deal with the Tories of Royal Governor Sir William Campbell, the Whigs in the district eastward of the Wateree, led by the powerful Cantey family, chose Sumter to represent them in the first Provincial Congress of South Carolina.

The delegates met in Charleston on January 11, 1775. From the parishes around the capital came Charles Pinckney, Henry Laurens, John Rutledge, and Christopher Gadsden. From the outer parishes came Charles Cotesworth Pinckney, William Henry Drayton, William Moultrie, and Francis Marion. And from the Santee and Up Country came Richard Richardson, William Thomson, Thomas Taylor, and Andrew Williamson. Here Thomas Sumter first became intimately acquainted with popular, rich, and dynamic leaders in the movement for independence.

The delegates unanimously elected Charles Pinckney the President of the Congress. They named Peter Timothy, publisher of *The South Carolina Gazette,* their secretary. Then they set to work. They listened to reports from the delegates to the Continental Congress in Philadelphia. They adopted the American Bill of Rights. After heated debate on the clauses dealing with nonimportation and nonconsumption of articles manufactured in England, and nonexportation to England, they adopted the Articles of Continental Association. Then they waited upon Sir William Campbell and presented an address in which they styled themselves loyal subjects of King George.

Sumter, as well as the other delegates from the Wateree, was named to the local committee for putting into effect the Continental Association. The committees were ordered to sit on the first and third Saturdays in each month in order to hear petitions and redress grievances under the Association. And although the members hoped for reconciliation and peace, the Congress recommended that the men of the Province gather on the muster fields and practice maneuvers and the use of arms.

Veterans of the Cherokee wars began forming companies of volunteer militia. As they drilled, on May 8 news reached Charleston that on April 19, 1775, the King's red-coated troops had fired on the Massachusetts militia at the village of Lexington. The General Committee summoned members to meet in Charleston on June 1 for the second session of the Provincial Congress.

While the Continental Congress was assuming command of the troops around Boston and appointing George Washington, a delegate from Virginia, commander in chief of the Continental Army, the Provincial Congress of South Carolina authorized the raising of two regiments of infantry and one of mounted rangers. On June 12, only five days before the battle of Bunker Hill at far off Boston, they elected Christopher Gadsden and William Moultrie to command the infantry regiments. And for colonel of the rangers the Congress chose William Thomson, of Belleville plantation on the Congaree. They selected sixteen captains, including Francis Marion, Isaac Huger, and Moses Kirkland. But the Carolinians offered no commission to the former sergeant from Preddy's Creek.

Provincial Congressman Sumter returned to his plantation on the Santee. During the political ferment he continued his planting, his merchandizing, his milling, and his speculating. He kept in contact with congressmen from the Up Country. He listened closely to the advice of Colonel Richard Richardson, the distinguished militia leader who lived across Jack's Creek. He served faithfully in carrying out the work of the Continental Association, but he was disappointed and restless. Having served for several years in the Virginia militia during the Cherokee War, he felt that he was qualified for an officer's commission in one of the permanent regiments of South Carolina.

As Sumter watched the election of officers by the Congress, he realized that family, political influence, and adherence to the Low Country ruling group, as well as military experience and ability, were factors in the selections. He knew that he had served longer on active duty than Captains Charles Cotesworth Pinckney, Francis Marion, or Peter Horry. And he also knew that in the heated political atmosphere of the rebellion in Carolina, a uniform with epaulettes would give a former millboy great social prestige.

While Sumter waited in disappointment, a row began smoldering among Thomson's rangers. During the formation of the permanent regiments the congressman from the Up Country voted for officers from the Low Country to command the infantry. But they felt that the commanding officer of the rangers should come from their section. Both Moses Kirkland and James Mayson became candidates for the colonelcy, and both were disappointed when the Congress compromised in the election of Lieutenant Colonel William Thomson, already colonel of the militia in Orangeburg. Kirkland became embittered when the Congress elected Mayson the major of the rangers. Nevertheless, he accepted a commission as captain.

Colonel Thomas Fletchall, commander of the militia regiment on the upper Saluda, shared some of Kirkland's ill will. He felt that the leaders in Charleston were going too far in their growing hostility to England. He was not satisfied with the policy of Continental Association. And when the Council of Safety instructed him to call his regiment together and have the captains read to each company the Act of Association, he disobeyed the order. After his militia refused to sign the Association, he allowed them to sign an association drawn up by Major Joseph Robinson.

While Fletchall was brewing trouble in the militia, Major Mayson learned that Indian agent John Stuart was inciting greater trouble among the Cherokees. As a precaution Mayson ordered Captains John Caldwell and Moses Kirkland to march their rangers to Fort Charlotte, a small post on the Savannah River some forty miles above Augusta. Then leaving Caldwell and his troops to guard the fort, Mayson and Kirkland began moving a large quantity of gunpowder back to Ninety-Six.

Jealous, smarting under Mayson's command, and out of sympathy with the actions of the Council of Safety, Captain Kirkland sent a courier to Colonel Fletchall revealing the transfer of gunpowder. Immediately embodying his regiment of militia, Fletchall sent Major Robinson and Captains Robert and Patrick Cunningham to seize the powder. Upon the approach of Robinson, Kirkland deserted the rangers, disbanded his troops, and carried away those of Captain Ezekial Polk.

In formally resigning his commission to the Council of Safety, Kirkland in good faith recommended that his friend Sumter be commissioned to succeed him as captain of the rangers. Alert for such opportunity and not realizing that friendship with Kirkland might taint him with treason, Sumter immediately applied to the Council for a commission. Fearing that the adopted Carolinian was involved in the schemes of Kirkland, the members hesitated and laid his application on the table.

The Council then began offering both intimidation and conciliation to Fletchall's men. As the first measure it ordered Colonel Thomson to march his rangers to Congarees. And as its second it commissioned William Henry Drayton, its most vehement legal spokesman, and William Tennent, a leading Presbyterian preacher, to go into the interior parts of the Province "to explain to the people the nature of the unhappy public dispute between Great Britain and her American Colonies."

The delegates set out for the Up Country in the heat of early August. Upon reaching the store of Kershaw and Chestnut at Congarees, they paused. Mutiny had broken out among the rangers encamped on Congaree Creek. The German militia leaders in Orangeburg were also disobeying Thomson's orders to call out their men. "We have engaged Colonel Thomson to order a muster of two Dutch companies in this neighborhood on Wednesday next," Drayton and Tennent wrote the Council of Safety on August 7, "and we have declared that if the officers disobey they shall be broke."

The Council had instructed its emissaries to inquire secretly into Sumter's loyalty, association with Kirkland, and fitness for a commission in the rangers. "We have consulted with Colonel Richardson touching Mr. Sumter's application to the Council," Drayton and Tennent reported. "The Colonel readily approved not only of the measure, but of the man, notwithstanding Kirkland recommended him as his successor in the company of Rangers, which he has so treacherously quitted and attempted to disband. The Colonel, nevertheless, from his seeming connection with Kirkland, purposes to keep a sharp eye upon Mr. Sumter's conduct."

Richardson's testimonial did not satisfy the Council. "We think it best to postpone a consideration of a military appointment for Mr. Sumter until your return or till we more clearly understand what duty he proposes to take upon himself and upon what consideration," the secretary replied, in rather summarily dismissing the application.

Richardson knew that Thomas Sumter was a leader, a veteran of the Virginia militia, and too valuable a Whig to be shunted aside. He suggested that the applicant forego the rangers and organize a company of local militia. Accordingly, Sumter called together the younger men of St. Mark's Parish and formed them into a company. In appreciation they elected him their captain. Soon afterward the Cantey family, friends, and militia elected Captain Sumter to represent them in the second Provincial Congress.

During the long, hot summer of 1775 Drayton and Tennent carried the message of the Council of Safety to the backwoods of Carolina. They rode from settlement to settlement, arguing and preaching. They met Fletchall, Robinson, and the Cunningham brothers in debate. In spite of fatigue, hardship, and constant danger, they succeeded. On September 16 Drayton signed an agreement with Colonel Fletchall.

Three weeks after the signing, however, Major Andrew Williamson, an able but semiliterate Scotsman who lived on White Hall plantation, upon a hint from Drayton dressed his Ninety-Six militiamen like Indian braves and surprised and arrested Captain Robert Cunningham. Fearing retaliation, Major Williamson hustled Cunningham off to Charleston. In spite of this precaution, Fletchall's militia rose. Captain Patrick Cunningham assembled his company to release his brother. In his angry foray he waylaid a convoy and seized a thousand pounds of gunpowder that the Council had sent the Cherokees.

Captain Sumter was in Charleston on November 1 for the convening of the Provincial Congress. He saw the aroused congressmen cast aside judicial and pacifistic Henry Laurens and elect fiery William Henry Drayton the President of the Congress. Determined to intimidate the Loyalists in the Up Country, President Drayton had Robert Cunningham brought before the Congress. He charged that Captain Caldwell had heard the prisoner make seditious statements. Cunningham did not deny the reported utterance. He protested that he did not consider himself bound by the agreement signed by Drayton and Fletchall. "I have behaved myself as peaceably as any man," he further asserted, "and, although I have opinions, I have not expressed them except when asked." The Congress expressed dissatisfaction with the prisoner's answers. Upon a warrant signed by Drayton, Sheriff Grimball remanded Cunningham to the Charleston jail.

While the Congress was debating the case of Robert Cunningham, Major Williamson embodied the Whig militia to retake the gunpowder. Captain Patrick Cunningham assembled his Tories. To prevent civil war, the Congress ordered Colonel Richardson and the militia of the Camden District to march immediately toward Ninety-Six. And on November 8, by a vote of fifty-one to forty-nine, the Congress ordered Richardson, reinforced by Colonel Thomson's rangers and Orangeburg militia, to arrest and bring in the leaders of the Tories. As Colonel Richardson prepared to march to the upper Saluda, he appointed Captain Sumter his adjutant general.

Before Richardson had crossed the Congaree, Major Williamson retreated and fortified the courthouse at Ninety-Six. Cunningham quickly surrounded the village, and his men began firing on the Whigs. For two days the battle dragged along, the Tories killing one man and wounding twelve, and the Whigs killing three and wounding twenty of the besiegers. Faced with a stalemate, on November 22 Majors Williamson and Mayson met with Major Robinson and Captain Cunningham. After secret negotiations they signed a truce. But for the first time during the Revolution blood had been spilled in South Carolina.

As civil war between Whigs and Tories flared around Ninety-Six, Colonel Richardson moved slowly westward to assert the power of the Provincial Congress. With a corps of five thousand men he marched into the Dutch Fork, the fertile, rolling country between the Broad and the Saluda. There he opened an aggressive campaign. From his camp on Duncan's Creek south of Enoree

River he dispatched Thomson ahead with the rangers. Crossing Tyger River, these horsemen swept along Fair Forest Creek until they reached the home of Colonel Fletchall. The mighty Nabob, as Drayton had contemptuously nicknamed the fat old Tory, had fled. But like beagles after a hare, the rangers unkenneled him from a cave above Fair Forest.

Working through Adjutant General Sumter, the strategist and one of the most indefatigable officers on the expedition, on December 21 Richardson sent a detachment of thirteen hundred men to bring in Patrick Cunningham. After a rapid night march of twenty-five miles, the Whigs fell upon the Tories at the Great Cane Brake on lower Reedy River. Awakened by their musket fire, Cunningham jumped out of bed and yelled for every man to save himself. Then, not even pausing to draw on his breeches, he sprang upon a horse without a saddle and galloped into the land of the Cherokees.

The detachment destroyed the Tory rendezvous and then turned back. "The next day they returned to camp, the snow set in, and continued for thirty hours without intermission," Richardson reported to the Council from Congarees on January 2, 1776. "Eight days we never set foot on the earth or had a place to lie down, till we had spaded or grabbled away the snow, from which circumstance, many are frost bitten, some very badly; and on the third day a heavy cold rain fell, together with sleet; and melted the snow and filled every creek and river with a deluge of water."

The Snow Campaign, as historians afterward called Richardson's expedition, was an ordeal for the militia. "I shall, while I stay, do everything I can for the good of my country," Richardson wrote the Council of Safety, "but the winter is advanced, the men from their precipitate collecting and marching, illy provided, no tents, shoes wore out, and badly clothed, make it very difficult to keep them here." The campaign, nevertheless, became a triumph for Captain Sumter. Trained for survival in the terrible voyage down the Holston, in which he had often slept in wet blankets and worn frozen clothes, the rugged adjutant general set a heroic example for the militia in the snow, rain, and ice along Saluda River.

Colonel Richardson had brilliantly accomplished the task given him by the Congress. He had shown the power of the revolutionary government to the rebellious Up Country. He had captured Colonel Fletchall, some ten disaffected militia captains, and one hundred and twenty of the most mischievous of the Loyalists. And so, upon reaching Congarees, Richardson turned these prisoners over to Sumter and his militia and disbanded his army.

"The prisoners I send in a boat from this place to Nelson's Ferry under the command and guard of Capt. Thomas Sumter," Richardson informed the Council in manifesting his esteem for the officer on whom he had promised to keep a sharp eye, "who on this expedition I constituted Adjutant-General, who has behaved very well and has been to me and the cause, of extra service."

Chapter 3 COLONEL IN THE CONTINENTALS

CAPTAIN Sumter lingered with Mary and his son for a few days, resting and looking after private affairs, and then rode on to Charleston. He found the capital floating with rumors. When the Provincial Congress met on February 1, 1776, its members were excited. Parliament had declared the American Colonies to be in a state of rebellion. British newspapers were filled with stories of a powerful force in the ports of southern England. Gossips, rumormongers, and intelligence sources declared its primary objective to be the capture of Charleston.

The Congress was bold and defiant. Having suppressed their internal dissidents, the Carolinians began preparing to meet their external foes. President Rutledge was already fortifying the approaches to Charleston. At his request Colonel Owen Roberts, senior artillery officer, was superintending the building of a fort of palmetto logs and sand on Sullivan's Island. The state would need additional regular troops to man her defenses. Cognizant that their action would likely mean war, the congressmen passed a bill establishing two regiments of riflemen, one of seven hundred and one of five hundred men.

On February 29, 1776, the congressmen began selecting officers for the new regiments. They unanimously named Isaac Huger the colonel of the First Regiment of Riflemen. Having chosen a Huguenot from the Low Country, after surveying the candidates for the Second Regiment, they decided to choose a colonel who would appeal to the sharpshooters from the Up Country. They knew that many former Virginians lived on the frontier. Fletchall had boasted that he could raise a thousand veterans of the Virginia militia. In Thomson's rangers, filled with emigrants from many countries, there were only fifty-two born Carolinians to one hundred and twenty-four former Virginians. On the next ballot the

Congress unanimously elected Thomas Sumter the lieutenant colonel, commandant, of the Second Regiment of Riflemen.

For major of the Second Riflemen the Congress chose William Henderson, a merchant, planter, and legislator from Pacolet River in the extreme Up Country. Captain Henderson, a veteran of Woodward's company of rangers, had distinguished himself in the Snow Campaign. Coming from the same stock and background in Hanover County, Virginia, the major had great admiration for his colonel.

The day after his selection, Lieutenant Colonel Sumter, energetic and restless, drew £3,000 from the state treasury and set off on a recruiting expedition among the settlers on the Wateree-Catawba. Riding through the Waxhaws, on through the Indian lands and the New Acquisition, and into Mecklenburg, with enthusiasm, banter, and a little swagger he began enlisting sharpshooting Carolinians and Catawbas. After filling his quota, he marched his recruits slowly downriver, paused at Great Savannah, and then moved on toward Charleston.

Encamping at Ten Mile Spring, in close proximity to the camp of Thomson's veteran rangers, Colonel Sumter began teaching his riflemen, most of whom had already served in the militia, the tactics of organized warfare. But as a veteran of the Virginia militia, he emphasized bravery and individual prowess, not the close-order fighting that had been fatal to General Braddock. He was not a disciplinarian, as were Moultrie and Marion, and the camp of the Second Regiment of Riflemen resembled a political gathering more than a field of Mars.

As the Carolinians rushed their preparations for defense, the British decided upon a two-pronged movement for crushing rebellion in the Southern Provinces. Their plans began revolving around an Indian attack along the frontier and an amphibious operation along the coast. As early as July 24, 1775, Lord Dartmouth had decreed that the Indians be induced "to take up the hatchet against his Majesty's rebellious subjects." In September, as soon as he had received Dartmouth's order, General Gage instructed Indian agent John Stuart to incite the Southern Indians "to take up arms against his Majesty's enemies, and distress them all in their power."

During the fall and winter Stuart worked among the Cherokees. His agents held powwows in important villages. Chief Ostenaco, still awe-struck from his voyage to London with Timberlake and Sumter, recited the story of his reception by King George and his view of the power of Great Britain. The chiefs decided to cooperate with the Great White Father.

While Stuart was inciting the Indians, Lord Dartmouth began assembling his forces. After the Admiralty sent Commodore Sir Peter Parker to command the fleet, Dartmouth chose Earl Cornwallis, with the provincial rank of lieutenant general, to command the expedition. He also ordered Sir Henry Clinton, second in command of the British forces in America, to move southward to lead the assault upon Carolina.

After a rendezvous at Cork, on February 12, 1776, Commodore Parker and Lord Cornwallis boarded the frigate *Bristol.* Sir Peter then hoisted sail, and after a long, rough, and somewhat irritating voyage his warships, with their convoy of troopships, dropped anchor off Cape Fear, North Carolina. On May 3 Cornwallis debarked his troops and for exercise marched them to Fort Johnson. Upon the arrival of Clinton, he embarked again, and the armada began its slow descent upon Charleston.

As soon as the chiefs of the Cherokees learned that the British fleet had reached the coast of Carolina, they deployed their braves along the Appalachian warpaths. In late June they struck the frontier from Georgia to Virginia. With tomahawk and scalping knife they ravaged the settlements, slaughtering both Whigs and Tories. In upper South Carolina they looted and burned and murdered, falling with savage fury upon the families of Patrick Calhoun at Long Canes and Anthony Hampton on Tyger River.

As quickly as possible Colonel Andrew Williamson called out the militia around Ninety-Six. Fearing to leave their families, his men came in slowly, and it was August before he had collected eighteen hundred men. After the Indian attacks, even Tories cooperated. Robert Cunningham, recently loosed from the Charleston jail, rode into camp and volunteered. "I have no doubt of Cunningham proving true to his declaration," Williamson wrote the Council of Safety, "but at present, it would be improper to confer any public trust on him."

On August 1 Williamson marched his Carolinians against the Lower Towns. As his men were crossing the Keowee near Essenecca, they fell into a night ambush laid by Alexander Cameron, deputy agent to Stuart. Stung by this initial attack, Williamson swept relentlessly through the valleys, his men slaughtering, scalping, and burning. With savagery equal to that of the Indians, they destroyed the houses, orchards, crops, and animals of Cherokees east of the Blue Ridge.

On June 1, 1776, the British fleet anchored off the Charleston bar, the only obstruction between the warships and the capital being the little fort near the southern end of Sullivan's Island. Instead of trying to force a passage, to be followed by amphibious assault upon the city, Sir Henry Clinton began landing troops on Long Island, just across a narrow channel from the eastern tip of Sullivan's. Among those going ashore was Cornet Banastre Tarleton, fresh from Oxford and the study of law in the Middle Temple.

Three days later General Charles Lee, second to General Washington in the Continental Army, arrived in Charleston. His presence was equal to a reinforcement of a thousand men declared Colonel Moultrie, who lay behind the ramparts of Fort Sullivan with his Second Regiment and a detachment of Continentals. Although expecting invasion, people in the capital were resolute, as Captain Thomas Pinckney wrote his sister on June 8, for Colonel Sumter and his riflemen were guarding the city.

General Lee countered Sir Henry's move by sending Thomson's rangers, Sumter's riflemen, and some scattering units of infantry and artillery to repel any crossing from Long Island. After brief skirmishing Clinton hesitated. Lee expected him to land troops upon Sullivan's Island directly from their transports, and to oppose such a landing, he pulled Sumter's marksmen nearer to Fort Sullivan. "The regiment to which I belonged," Charles Brandon wrote long afterward in his pension affidavit, "under the command of Colonel Sumter, was stationed some distance from the fort, to watch and counteract the British under General Clinton."

When Sir Henry abandoned his attempts to capture Sullivan's

General Lee recalled all troops from the island except Thomson's rangers and Moultrie's corps. The Virginians, North Carolinians, and South Carolina riflemen of Huger's and Sumter's regiments were scattered around Haddrell's Point, said Drayton in his *Memoirs of the American Revolution,* "and in advance parties to the left of it, opposite to Sullivan's and Long Island."

Deflected from the mainland by this formidable array, Sir Henry decided to level Fort Sullivan. On June 28, 1776, Sir Peter moved his warships into position, and about eleven o'clock the *Thunder* began lobbing shells into the fort. Soon the *Bristol,* the *Experiment,* and the *Solebay* joined in the cannonading. Moving into direct range at four hundred yards, the *Active* began pouring in solid shot, but they sank harmlessly in the soft palmetto logs.

A shot cut away the staff of the Second Regiment's blue flag with a silver crescent. "Colonel," exclaimed Sergeant William Jasper, "don't let us fight without our flag!" He then sprang from the rampart, seized the bunting, and returned unharmed through shot and shell. Tying the flag to a sponge staff, he hoisted it again above the fort.

While Sumter and his riflemen watched enviously, the defenders of Fort Sullivan, paced by Major Francis Marion, answered slowly and deliberately, conserving their powder and directing their shots with great effectiveness. Their shells wrought havoc, killing some two hundred sailors and wounding many others, including Commodore Parker and Lord Cornwallis. To silence the American batteries Parker ordered the *Acteon,* the *Sphynx,* and the *Syren* to round Sullivan's and enfilade the fort from the rear. But the pilot missed the channel and grounded the vessels. Baffled by the stranding of his auxiliaries, Sir Peter continued his frontal attack. About sunset, however, his defeated captains began slipping the cables of their ships and standing away toward Five Fathom Hole.

The *Sphynx* and the *Syren* floated free on the rising tide and rejoined the armada. But the *Acteon* was still aground, and on the morning after the battle her crew set her afire. After some Carolinians had boarded and stripped her of salvage, the burning frigate exploded, spewing flaming timbers and charred debris high above the shoal on which later would stand mighty Fort Sumter.

After Sir Henry Clinton had moved his force northward to reinforce General Howe in an attack on Washington's troops strung out around New York, the Southern states began a co-operative movement against the Cherokees. Colonel William Christian marched down the Holston from Virginia to attack the Over Hill Towns. General Griffith Rutherford marched his North Carolinians against the Middle Towns. And Colonel Williamson, his South Carolina militia augmented by Georgians, moved toward the Valley Towns beyond the Blue Ridge.

With Charleston secure, President Rutledge dispatched Sumter's riflemen to reinforce Williamson's militia. "As it is intended that Thomson's and Sumter's regiments shall soon be detached on a service which may separate them from the General for some time," General Lee said in his orders of July 30, "he takes this opportunity to return his warmest thanks to the colonels, to the officers and the men for the zeal, alacrity, and spirit which they have displayed on all occasions."

On August 12, Colonel Sumter drew £1,500 for recruiting and then set the Second Regiment of Riflemen on the long march to Keowee. As his troops slogged along, burdened with a thousand pounds of gunpowder and two thousand pounds of lead dispatched to Williamson, Sumter crossed at Nelson's, spent several days with Mary and Tom, and then rode on to the Waxhaws.

While Colonel Sumter loitered on the Catawba, offering the Scotch-Irish an attractive bounty to enlist for fifteen months, Williamson stood poised on the Cherokee border. Hearing nothing from Sumter, on August 25 he sent him two messengers, one on the road to Congarees and the other by the short route to Orangeburg. Hearing nothing from his messengers, Williamson began to fume. Next day he sent Captain Benjamin Tutt to bring in the tardy riflemen.

On September 3 Captain Tutt reported that Colonel Sumter was trying to collect thirty beeves and three thousand pounds of flour before advancing to the frontier. Eight days later Sumter reached Fort Prince George with the ammunition, beeves, and flour. But he had only three hundred and thirty men, "many of whom, by the fatigue of the march from Charleston rendered incapable to proceed into the nation, were left in the fort." With two hundred and seventy effectives on September 12 he marched into Williamson's camp at Essenecca.

Next day Colonel Williamson, with a corps of eighteen hundred men, opened his campaign by marching through the ruined Lower Towns. Passing the Oconee Mountains, he camped at Old Estatoe and then turned northward through Rabun Gap. As the column moved toward the Valley Towns, Colonel Le Roy Hammond commanded the left wing, Colonel Thomas Neal the center, and Colonel Sumter the right wing.

On September 17 they reached the narrows, a forbidding passage between the Noewee, a branch of the Little Tennessee, and the Cowee Mountains. Here in 1760 the Cherokees had ambushed Colonel Montgomerie. Near the same spot in 1761 they had ambushed Colonel Grant, only to be driven from their hiding places by Lieutenant Francis Marion. A veteran of Grant's expedition, Williamson approached the narrows with trepidation, but his troops passed through without seeing any Indians.

At the Noewee, Colonel Williamson turned northward to Connutee. But General Rutherford had already passed the village in his sweep of the Middle Towns, and Williamson turned down the Little Tennessee. On September 19, 1776, while creeping along the Coweechee, he stumbled into the Black Hole, a meadow surrounded by a ring of mountains, the formation resembling a gigantic horseshoe. Fearing an ambuscade he began advancing cautiously. He deployed Hammond toward the mountains on the left with orders to begin an enveloping movement. He then ordered Sumter and his riflemen to file toward the mountains on the right to guard the stores and baggage.

As Colonel Neal's militia stalked across the bowl of the horseshoe, Captain Edward Hampton spied Indians lurking among the trees along the rim. Still grieving for his massacred parents, Hampton opened the attack. Six hundred Cherokees returned his fire. For the next two hours the battle raged, the little valley echoing the roaring muskets of the Ring Fight.

As the shadows lengthened, Captain Hampton, powerful and courageous, charged into the Indian covert shouting, "Loaded guns advance! Empty guns fall back and reload!" The Cherokees fled, leaving the ground strewn with furs, stores, and ammunition.

But as Williamson strictly obeyed Rutledge's orders to use the riflemen only as a *corps de reserve,* although Sumter waited anxious and chafing, he did not get into the Ring Fight.

In Charleston, meanwhile, there was a change in the status of Sumter's riflemen. Requests had come from the Continental Congress that all South Carolina state regiments be put on the Continental establishment. And on September 20, 1776, the day after the Ring Fight, the Second Regiment of Riflemen became the Sixth Regiment of the South Carolina Continental Line.

At Hiwassee River, Williamson set his men ravaging the Valley Towns. With gusto the inflamed militiamen cut ripened maize, killed livestock, and burned log cabins. After razing Little Tomotley, they moved against the beautiful town of Little Tellicho. Thomas Sumter was in familiar country; he had passed through these mountain valleys in escorting Ostenaco from Charleston. But this was war, and he was merciless. He helped burn hundreds of acres of corn.

From the Hiwassee, Colonel Williamson marched into lovely Nacoochee Valley. While his militia were plundering and destroying, he ordered Sumter to visit Frog Town, a prosperous trading center on Chestatee River. Hearing rumors that several hundred warriors had assembled in the village, Sumter turned back with his riflemen. Next morning with three hundred mounted infantrymen he again set off on the sixteen-mile trip. In crossing the Blue Ridge near Blood Mountain, he led his horsemen along a fourteen-inch ledge of rock more than a hundred feet long, which rimmed a sixty-foot precipice above the Chestatee. Finding that the Cherokees had fled, he burned Frog Town and then destroyed the corn and peas throughout Frog Town Valley. After dark he returned undaunted across the dangerous precipice and rejoined the army at Nacoochee. Next day the Carolinians burned Chotee on the headwaters of the Chattahoochee.

After a conference with Neal, Hammond, and Sumter, Colonel Williamson turned back. Passing through Estatoe and swinging down Tugaloo River, on October 7 he marched into Essenecca. He was satisfied. He had defeated the Cherokees in five battles, burned thirty-two villages, and scorched their valleys. In co-operation with troops from the other colonies he had completely humbled the Indians.

With their corn destroyed, their cattle slaughtered, and their cabins burned, by midwinter the Cherokees were starving. In February, 1777, old Ostenaco led his chiefs down to Charleston. In return for a treaty of peace they ceded the victorious Carolinians some three million acres of land east of the Blue Ridge.

From Essenecca, Colonel Sumter marched his regiment to Fort Ripley, a post on Little River in the vicinity of Ninety-Six. For two weeks he rested and refreshed his riflemen. While they enjoyed their return to civilization, he went recruiting for more sharpshooters. After filling his vacancies, he moved on down the Saluda to Congarees. Finally he encamped on Tawcaw Swamp, a creek five miles below his plantation on Great Savannah.

The ground along the Tawcaw was high and dry, offering a splendid campsite, and there was plenty of wood and fresh water. In Williamsburg there was an abundance of provisions for hungry troops. After resting his men, Sumter marched to Dorchester, and for the next three weeks they guarded the magazine. Then he returned and settled down on the Tawcaw.

Sumter established headquarters at his home. At last he could be with Mary and Tom and devote some time to personal affairs. They needed attention, for on November 5 the presiding judge in Camden had fined him £10 for not having attended court and served as grand juror.

The British, however, were not long quiescent. General Augustine Prevost, commanding the garrison at Saint Augustine, ran short of provisions. In February, 1777, he sent his brother, Colonel Mark Prevost, to collect beeves from the Whigs in southern Georgia. He also ordered an advance guard under Colonel L. V. Fuser to cover the Americans at Sunbury, a village on the coast some twenty-eight miles below Savannah.

To meet Fuser's advance, General Robert Howe, commandant of the Continentals in Charleston, hurried off to Georgia, leaving orders for Colonels Marion and Sumter to bring down their regiments. Francis Marion immediately crowded six hundred men, equipment, ammunition, and provisions into several small vessels and sailed for Tybee. From his camp on Tawcaw Swamp, Sumter marched his riflemen down the muddy, wintry road to Purrysburg. There he commandeered all the boats on the river, embarked his regiment, and drifted down to Savannah.

Meanwhile Fuser was moving unhindered through Georgia. But at Ogeechee Ferry, fifteen miles from Savannah, Colonel Samuel Elbert and his Georgians turned him back. After retreating, Fuser demanded that Colonel Lachlan McIntosh surrender the fort at Sunbury. Replied McIntosh, "As to surrendering the fort, receive this laconic answer: Come and take it!"

Upon the retreat of the British, General Howe's expedition bogged down in a miasma of inefficiency and Georgia politics. Button Gwinnett, president of the Georgia Council, and Lachlan McIntosh, now commanding general of the Continental Line of Georgia, were in a struggle for power. Realizing his inability to accomplish anything without the co-operation of these leaders, Howe ordered Marion to return to Charleston and Sumter to occupy the fort at Sunbury.

Having secured the fort, Sumter marched his riflemen boldly through the open country on the trail of Fuser and Prevost. Leaving a detail to garrison Fort Howe on the Altamaha, he moved on to Fort McIntosh on the Satilla, where Fuser had surprised and captured Captain Richard Winn and his company of Thomson's rangers. While Sumter was on the Satilla, affairs in Georgia reached a climax, with McIntosh ultimately challenging and killing Gwinnett. In disgust General Howe ordered Sumter to bring his riflemen back to Charleston.

Seeing the Carolinians leaving for home, other Continentals began pulling out. "Colonel Sterk and Captain Pannil of the 2nd Georgia Batt'n are apprehensive they have influence sufficient to stop a Number of men late of the 1st Batt'n whose Times are out, and about to leave the State," Sumter wrote General McIntosh with characteristic decisiveness as he prepared to march; "in consequence of which I have thought it no way improper for them to go to Savannah for a few days as I judge there is no danger at present."

In early May, Colonel Sumter and his riflemen trudged back into Charleston. As they were tired from their useless marching and dispirited over the wrangling, Sumter furloughed those who wished to visit home and sent the others on to his camp on Tawcaw. On June 8 Captain Samuel Taylor and some officers and men from his company passed Chestnut's store at Congarees and rode on to their homes in the fork between the Congaree and the Wateree.

The bungled campaign and the killing of Gwinnett aroused the Continental Congress, and the congressmen invited Lieutenant Colonel Sumter to come to Philadelphia. On May 15, as soon as he had disposed his troops for the summer, he drew £812 and set off for the City of Brotherly Love. After pausing with Mary and Tom, he rode on his swift but uneventful journey. The Congress, having listened to him, appointed a committee of five members to hold a thorough inquiry. On August 6 they instructed Howe to relieve McIntosh of command and send him to Philadelphia.

Thomas Sumter never overlooked an opportunity. Having a private as well as a public reason for visiting the Congress, even before testifying he conferred with the delegates from South Carolina. Henry Laurens, now president of the Continental Congress, was an old friend from the Provincial Congress. His son, Colonel John Laurens, an aide to Washington, was also an old friend. And so, after conferring and testifying, on August 18 Thomas Sumter rode homeward a colonel of the Continental Line.

During Sumter's absence, Major Henderson commanded the Sixth Regiment. Since the enlistments of the riflemen had begun to expire, on May 18 Henderson drew £9,750 for recruiting. On July 2 he drew an additional £3,250 and set off for his home on the Pacolet. By midsummer batches of young recruits were sauntering into the camp on Tawcaw. About the time of Sumter's return from Philadelphia, Henderson began training the young riflemen. After a few weeks of intensive drill, he had them ready for the barracks in Charleston.

Colonel Sumter and his riflemen continued in barracks during the winter. His troops followed dull garrison routine of mounting guard and standing watch. Discipline among the idle troops was lax. To impress the young women of the capital, the soldiers began growing beards and long hair. Colonel Charles Cotesworth Pinckney of the First Regiment pleaded with his troops to keep their hair cut without a special order. Lieutenant Colonel Francis Marion of the Second Regiment ordered that his men who let their hair grow long enough to fall down their backs "must have it plaited and tied up." The cocky little Huguenot also threatened to dry-shave anyone who came on parade with a beard.

Gun polishing had even less appeal to the officers. Morale dropped, and they began resigning. On January 2, 1778, Captain Dan Jackson and Lieutenant Henry White resigned their commissions and left for home. Lieutenant Coit was promoted to captain, and Second Lieutenants Henry Hampton and Buchanan were promoted to first lieutenants. On February 5 Lieutenant Montgomery resigned, and on February 22 Captain Henry Richbourg resigned and was replaced by Lieutenant James Hawthorne.

On March 2 Sumter court-martialed Henry Rogers for "being out of quarters at Eleven o'clock and being concealed in Colonel Pinckney's house." But spring brought relief from monotony, resignations, and courts-martial. With weather suitable for campaigning, General Howe decided to remove the enemy base in Florida.

Howe ordered Colonel Sumter to equip his regiment for the campaign. On April 10 Sumter issued each man one hundred rounds of ammunition and six spare flints. Nine days later a detachment of fifty marched off with the First Regiment under Colonel Charles C. Pinckney. Soon afterward Sumter followed. At inspection on May 9 he noted that his riflemen were ragged and tired. But on May 13 they marched into Fort Howe in "good health and spirits."

Fort Howe was small and ill-suited to serve as a base for an army. General Howe soon moved down the Altamaha and encamped in an old field above Reid's Bluff. Here conditions were bad, some eight to twelve soldiers crowding into each tent and ten or fifteen cooking in each kettle. Food was wretched. "Some corn meal and salt beef is arrived and has been served to the men," observed Grimké in his *Journal,* "but the former is so extremely sour that the soldiers prefer rice to it, although that article is not of the best kind."

To add honey to their diet, Sumter's frontiersmen began finding and cutting bee-trees. After a few days, however, the riflemen dashed into camp with a harrowing tale. They had found Seeds, their gunsmith, scalped. They had seen a war party of sixteen Indians. Sumter ordered Captain Taylor to pursue the marauders. But Taylor could not find their trail "because of tracks which our men made when out honey hunting."

As the food became worse and the riflemen sickened with dysentery, they began deserting. Sumter ordered Lieutenant Henry Hampton to bring back the deserters. After a chase of more than two hundred miles, on June 7 Hampton returned with his prisoners. He also brought news of the approach of Colonel Williamson and the South Carolina militia. But before Williamson arrived with fresh food and medicine, half of the Carolina Continentals had dropped out from malaria and dysentery. Colonel Sumter came down with the ague and was hospitalized at Sunbury. The command of the riflemen then passed to Lieutenant Colonel Henderson.

In spite of heat, flies, mosquitoes, and rotten food Howe moved on. His troops reached Old Town on the Satilla on June 14, and he sent Henderson on a sweep to St. Mary's River. Captain Edmund Hyrne and Lieutenant Hampton swam the river, but they could find no trace of the enemy. On June 28 Howe reached Fort Tonyn, only to find that Colonel Thomas Browne and his Tories had fired it and rejoined General Prevost.

Governor Houston now brought in the Georgia militia, but he refused to put them under Howe's command. On July 8 Colonel Williamson arrived, but he also refused to put his militia under Howe. The campaign then turned into a vindictive squabble between state and Continental troops, and Prevost leisurely withdrew to Saint Augustine.

Finally ignoring the contentious militiamen, Howe prepared to advance. As he moved, he sent Captains Hyrne and Taylor to scout the enemy. Soon they returned with a report that the British had felled trees in the roads and burned the bridges. A council of officers then voted that the expedition had achieved its objective in driving the British from Georgia.

General Howe immediately ordered the Carolinians home. In late August, Colonel Henderson led the depleted Sixth Regiment back into Charleston. Soon afterward the riflemen were incorporated in the First Brigade under General Moultrie. But the regiment never recovered from the inglorious campaign through Georgia.

Having already returned to his plantation on the Santee, Colonel Sumter did not rejoin his regiment. He was ill, slowly recuperating from malaria. He was disgusted, having suffered in the late campaign from the delays, the stultifying disputes between military and state officials, and the latent antipathy of the militia for the Continentals.

Moreover, Sumter felt completely frustrated. A man of action, with hopes of distinguishing himself in battle, in four campaigns he had stood by with his riflemen while the infantry and artillery had done the fighting and won the glory. In the last two years he had marched his men hundreds and hundreds of miles, and yet they had never fired their rifles in action. Now that the Cherokees no longer menaced the frontier and the British had been driven from the coast, he was finding it increasingly difficult to fill the vacancies in his regiment with men from the Up Country.

With a record less than distinguished, but with the respect and confidence of the men who had served under him, on September 19, 1778, Thomas Sumter resigned his commission as colonel of the Sixth Regiment of the South Carolina Continental Line.

Chapter 4 GENERAL OF VOLUNTEERS

SQUIRE Sumter quietly returned to his planting, speculating, and politicking. The most popular man along the Santee, he canvassed Camden District, and in November he was again elected to the General Assembly. During the session he was in Charleston on public business, but without scruples in mixing the two he also attended to his private affairs. He persuaded the Assembly to authorize a road from Manigault's Ferry to his mills on Jack's Creek. As the charters of both Manigault's and Nelson's ferries were to expire in 1779, he obtained a charter and established Sumter's Ferry. And to develop his vast properties, immediately after the adjournment of the Assembly he borrowed £29,753 from Meyer Moses.

While Sumter lingered on the Santee, American arms were in the doldrums. Following the battle of Monmouth, Washington had moved on to New Brunswick and then to Morristown. After the arrival of the French fleet under Count d'Estaing, he kept the British penned down around New York. Unable to mount an offensive, Clinton contented himself with recruiting Tories, augmenting Lord Rawdon's Volunteers of Ireland and Lord Cathcart's British Legion. Much of the skirmishing around New York was done by Tarleton and the Green Horse of the legion.

Believing the time appropriate, Parliament made overtures for peace, but the Continental Congress rejected the offer. The British then determined to conquer the Colonies. Upon instructions from the War Office, Sir Henry Clinton resumed the offensive in the South.

In a strategic double movement Sir Henry ordered General Prevost to march northward through Georgia and co-operate in an amphibious attack upon Savannah. Before Prevost could arrive, the British fleet sailed into Savannah River and Colonel Archibald Campbell debarked his troops. On September 29, 1778, with a powerful force, which included Major Archibald McArthur's battalion of the 71st Regiment, Lieutenant Colonel George Turnbull's New York Volunteers, Lieutenant Colonel John Hamilton's North Carolina provincials, and Colonel Alexander Innes's South Carolina provincials, Colonel Campbell drove General Howe from Savannah.

In the spring of 1779 Sumter planted a large crop and increased his herds and flocks, hoping to sell provisions to the troops in Charleston. Free of the hardships and ill health of campaigning, he was happy with his family, troubled only by Mary's poor health, her indisposition usually growing worse during the hot, malarial summers. He paid little attention to American efforts to free Georgia, even when General Benjamin Lincoln, who had relieved Howe, moved against Augusta while sending Moultrie and the Carolinians against Savannah.

General Prevost drove Moultrie back into Charleston. After besieging the city for two days, on May 13 Prevost began a slow retreat ahead of Lincoln's returning Continentals. At the Stono he turned and mauled his pursuers. In the violent fighting Colonel Henderson and the Sixth Regiment stood out among the Continentals.

During the following autumn the Americans again tried to recapture Savannah. On October 9, 1779, General Lincoln and Admiral d'Estaing, who had brought a French battle squadron up from the West Indies, opened a combined land and sea attack. The turning point of the costly blunder came when Lieutenant Colonel Francis Marion and the Second Regiment began retreating after having planted their regimental flag on Spring Hill redoubt.

As a countermove to the American threat against Georgia, Sir Henry Clinton began assembling troops and ships for a great amphibious operation. After embarking fifteen thousand men, the dragoon horses, and several batteries of artillery, Sir Henry went aboard the *Romulus,* and on December 26, 1779, Admiral Mariott Arbuthnot sailed from New York. By February, after a tempestuous voyage, his ships began dropping anchor off Tybee Island, a sandy tongue in the mouth of Savannah River.

From Tybee the British Army began moving up the coast, invading and hopping from sea islands to mainland. Lieutenant Colonel Tarleton and the British Legion debarked at Beaufort. Handsome, powerful, active, and witty, Ban Tarleton was a favorite of Sir Henry's. His British Legion, composed of four troops of dragoons recruited among the Tories around Philadelphia and four companies of infantry recruited around New York, was the most distinguished combat team in the British Army. Since all of his dragoon horses had perished in the terrible voyage, Tarleton scoured the islands around Beaufort with ruthless energy and seized every horse, thoroughbred or marsh tacky, to remount his legion. He then took the van of General Patterson's corps marching from Savannah.

As the British forces converged upon Charleston, General Lincoln ordered all units of the American Army into its ramparts. With astonishing incapacity, he allowed Governor Rutledge and the politicians to influence his strategy. Infatuated by Moultrie's defense of the capital against Sir Henry Clinton in 1776 and General Prevost in 1779, the Carolinians argued that their defenses were impregnable. And so, instead of withdrawing, retreating across the Santee, and defying Sir Henry, General Lincoln decided to hold the city and await reinforcements.

The Carolina militia were not fully mobilized, and to rouse them for the defense of their capital Governor Rutledge decided to ride into the Up Country. With a small party, including three members of the Council, on April 9 he slipped across the Cooper and headed toward the Santee. At Lenud's Ferry he met Colonel Abraham Buford and the Third Regiment of Virginia Continentals.

To disencumber his army, Lincoln ordered all military personnel unfit for duty to leave the city. In consequence, Colonel Francis Marion, suffering from an ankle broken in jumping from a window to escape a drinking party, bade farewell to the Second Regiment, crossed the Cooper, and disappeared in the swamps along the Santee.

Soon afterward, while the Americans watched with mesmerized fascination, British commanders began moving into position around Charleston. Admiral Arbuthnot sailed his warships into the harbor. Clinton forced a passage across the Ashley, extended his line to the Cooper, and sealed off Charleston Neck. Lord Cornwallis passed the Cooper, swung around toward Haddrell's Point, and completed the encirclement.

While the British infantry was moving up, Colonel Tarleton and his green-coated dragoons guarded approaches to the city. After a rapid night march, on April 14, 1870, he surprised Colonel William Washington and his Continental dragoons at Moncks Corner. In vicious fighting he drove Washington and his men into Cooper River swamp. After capturing Washington's powerful Virginia-bred horses, Tarleton began sweeping the country along the Santee. Flushed from his hiding place by Tarleton's Green Horse, Francis Marion collected a few veterans, crossed the Santee, and rode off to meet the Continental Army marching southward under Baron de Kalb.

In the meantime, after escaping from Moncks Corner, Colonel Washington crossed the Santee at Murry's Ferry and made his way to Sumter's plantation. He bought food and fodder. After haggling, Washington paid Sumter £100 for a splendid English mare. He then commandeered sixteen horses to help remount his dragoons. But on May 5 Tarleton struck Colonel Anthony White's command of the remounted dragoons at Lenud's, drowning some already in the boats and shooting others who tried to swim the river. Again he seized their horses to mount his green dragoons.

After the British encirclement, Buford realized that his regiment could not fight its way into Charleston. He abandoned his camp at Lenud's. When the Virginians began retreating, Governor Rutledge accompanied them. Rutledge paused at Sumter's, tried to persuade him to take the field again, and then entrusted him with a bag of state funds. In the High Hills they met General Richard Caswell, who also turned back with his North Carolina militia. At Camden the forces separated. Rutledge stopped at Clermont, the home of Colonel Henry Rugeley, twelve miles above the village. Caswell marched toward the Peedee. And Buford continued retreating toward Salisbury.

From his plantation beside the Santee road Thomas Sumter watched the mounting evidence of disaster. He saw Buford retreating, accompanied by Governor Rutledge. He saw Colonel Washington's footsore horsemen. He saw the bedraggled survivors of White's dragoons. Proud and independent, he remained aloof. Except for receiving funds from Rutledge, he volunteered neither service nor advice to his beleaguered countrymen. But fearful of the rolling wave of conquest, he moved Mary and Tom to their summer cottage in the High Hills of Santee.

During the spring Sir Henry Clinton continued his siege of Charleston, moving up slowly in conventional tactics and capturing the outer fortifications. He continued his relentless pressure until Lincoln capitulated on May 12, surrendering the city and its garrison of five thousand Continentals. Sir Henry quickly unfolded his strategy to recover the Province. He ordered a two-pronged drive into the interior, one force to bolster the Tories in the back country and the other to seize the central river basins of South Carolina.

The smaller expedition moved to Dorchester. From there Colonel Thomas Brown and his Tories marched off to Augusta and Colonel Nisbet Balfour and the British light infantry continued on to Ninety-Six. Captain Patrick Ferguson of the 71st Regiment, commissioned a major of provincials and carrying orders to recruit, train, and command the Loyalists in the Up Country, soon followed Balfour.

On May 18 Lord Cornwallis moved toward Lenud's with the main expedition. He sent Tarleton and his Green Horse first across the Santee, with orders to sweep around Georgetown. After crossing with the army, Cornwallis began moving up the Santee road. From Nelson's Ferry he sent Tarleton in search of Buford and Rutledge. On the morning of May 27 Ban Tarleton, his captured Virginia horses carrying a dragoon and an infantryman, left at a gallop. Along the Santee he raced, slashing and burning, while terrified Whigs raced ahead to warn their families and friends.

About ten o'clock next morning young Tom Sumter was riding his pony through the warm High Hills. Suddenly a frightened neighbor galloped past, yelling something about Tarleton and his legion. Tom raced home to warn his father. As Thomas Sumter listened, he neither flinched nor paled. He knew what he must do. Calling Soldier Tom, his powerful African-born body servant, he bade him saddle their horses. After putting on the old uniform he had worn as colonel of the Sixth Regiment, he kissed Tom and Mary farewell. "He left us on the 28th of May, 1780," Thomas Sumter, Jr., wrote his son Francis in after years, "only a few hours before Tarleton's legion passed us in pursuit of Buford."

Tarleton sent Captain Charles Campbell to bring in Sumter. Finding the squire gone, Campbell's dragoons plundered his home. They demanded the key to the smokehouse, but Nancy Davis, housekeeper for the Sumters, tossed it into the grass. Breaking in, they ransacked pantry, larder, and granary. With rude chivalry they picked up the chair in which Mary Sumter was sitting and lifted her into the yard. A demon then hurled a torch into the cottage. As the helpless matron watched the soaring flames, a pitying dragoon slipped a ham under her chair.

After firing Sumter's home, Tarleton and his men swept on through the High Hills. He bivouacked at Camden. While his men scoured the village, Whig riders spread alarm. Veterans and patriots fled into the swamps. Colonel Rugeley, courting both the British and the rebels, woke Governor Rutledge and his party and sent them galloping toward North Carolina. Before daybreak Tarleton's myrmidons swarmed past Rugeley's Mills. On they swept, stopping for neither food nor water, hoping to overtake Buford and his Continentals. About three o'clock on the afternoon of May 29, 1780, they caught up with the Virginians just below the settlements in the Waxhaws.

"Resistance being vain, to prevent effusion of human blood," Tarleton wrote in summoning Buford to surrender, "I make offers which can never be repeated."

Buford returned a defiant answer:

Wacsaws, May 29, 1780

Sir, I reject your proposals, and shall defend myself to the last extremity.

I have the honour to be, etc.
Abr. Buford, Col.

Lieut. Col. Tarleton
Commanding British Legion

After the exchange of letters, Tarleton's advance drove in Buford's rear, and both commanders began preparing for battle.

As he formed his line, Tarleton heard Buford shouting to his men to hold their fire until the dragoons were within ten paces. Realizing Buford's mistake, Tarleton charged. Before the Virginians could fire and reload, the green-coated dragoons were among them, their great sabers swinging in death. The Virginians grounded their muskets, but before Ensign Cruit could lower his flag in surrender, Tarleton sabered him. In the confusion, some of Buford's men tried to reload their guns, and Tarleton's dragoons continued swinging their sabers until the battle turned into a massacre.

"My Lord," Tarleton immediately wrote Cornwallis, "I am extremely fatigued with overtaking the Enemy & beating them—I summoned the Corps—they refused my terms—I have cut 170 Off'rs and Men to pieces."

Colonel Sumter galloped northward from the High Hills. As he rode along the Wateree-Catawba toward Charlotte, he had no plans to rouse the Up Country. He had no hope of recovering South Carolina from the victorious British. He was simply inflamed against the invaders who had driven him from his home and family. He would join any resistance movement. With body and soul he had adopted the cry of "liberty or death!"

In the Waxhaws and the New Acquisition, Sumter began to meet friends, including veterans of the Sixth Regiment which had been disbanded at the direction of the Continental Congress. They had lost neither their love of freedom nor their will to fight. They needed only a leader, but what could he do? Clinton had captured Lincoln's army. South Carolina lay prostrate, her capital in possession of the enemy, her governor fled, her militia without a commander, and her Continentals in prison camps. Then came reports of Tarleton's butchery in the Waxhaws. The Up Country began ringing with the cry of "Tarleton's Quarter."

Sumter now began forming a plan. He would recruit a band of veterans and volunteer militia, turn guerrilla, and lurk in the swamp along Catawba River, bursting out to devastate the homes and scorch the land of the Tories and to kill Britons at the fords and ferries until even Lord Cornwallis should cry for quarter!

Encouraged by what he had heard and seen, Colonel Sumter rode on to American headquarters in Salisbury. There the authorities paid sympathetic attention to his plan. They approved assembling the militia and forming guerrilla bands to harry the advance of the British. On June 1 they issued Sumter nineteen treasury certificates, each for $1,000. With these he turned back toward the Catawba and issued a call to the men in the New Acqisition and the Waxhaws.

After Tarleton's defeat of Buford, Lord Cornwallis thought that he had completed his campaign for South Carolina. His task was now merely to hold and pacify the conquered province. He established a camp and depot for the army at Camden. Leaving Patterson in Charleston, Brown at Augusta, and Balfour at Ninety-Six, he began deploying his regiments in other strategic centers. He sent Major James Wemyss and the 63rd Regiment to Georgetown. He sent Major Archibald McArthur and the first battalion of the 71st Regiment to Cheraw. He sent Lieutenant Colonel George Turnbull and his New York Volunteers to Rocky Mount. And he sent Lord Rawdon and his Volunteers of Ireland to keep peace in the Waxhaws.

The movements of the British regiments emboldened the Loyalists. In spite of the orders of Lord Cornwallis for them not to assemble, they began gathering in bands, threatening the Whigs with cattle rustling, horse stealing, and house burning. As protection and a counterthreat, Colonels William Hill, William Bratton, and Edward Lacey began assembling the Whigs eastward of the Catawba.

Bratton and Lacey camped beside the lands of the Catawba Indians. Soon afterward a regiment of Loyalists encamped at Brierley's Ferry on Broad River. Captain Richard Winn, who lived on Little River below Winnsboro, rode into the New Acquisition and secured a hundred militiamen from Colonel Lacey. With these he marched through Mobley's settlement on Little River, attacked the Tories at Gibson's Meeting House, and sent those at Brierley's fleeing into the Dutch Fork.

The assemblage of Carolinians brought instant reprisal. From Rocky Mount, Colonel Turnbull sent Captain Christian Huck and his dragoons to destroy Hill's Iron Works. They put the torch to everything: "All his fine Iron Works, Mills, dwelling House &

buildings of every kind, even his Negro Houses, reduced to ashes, and his wife and children in a little Log-House," as Governor Rutledge informed the South Carolina delegates in the Continental Congress. Huck, a small, profane, and violent Philadelphia lawyer who commanded a troop of Tarleton's Green Horse, then encamped at White's Mill on upper Fishing Creek. He immediately posted handbills calling upon the inhabitants to renew their allegiance to the King. When the Scotch-Irish refused to pledge their loyalty, he turned upon them with sword and torch.

On Sunday morning, June 11, he set out to seize the Reverend John Simpson, Presbyterian minister to the congregations on upper and lower Fishing Creek. As he approached the church, his marksmen shot down harmless young William Strong as he trudged along carrying his *Bible*. Hearing the shots, Simpson's wife rushed her children from the manse and hid in the orchard. From there they watched Huck burn their home. Learning that Preacher Simpson had deserted his pulpit and joined the militia gathering around Colonel James Williams, Captain Christian Huck exclaimed, "God Almighty has turned rebel. But if there are twenty Gods on their side, the rebels shall be conquered."

Huck's violence brought only stronger resistance. More Whigs joined the militia. "About this time I was informed that Colonel Sumter was in Salisbury with a few men waiting for reinforcements," said Colonel Hill in his *Memoirs*. "I then wrote to him, informing him of our situation & that there was a probability of our making a handsome stand—and that we were about to form a junction with General Rutherford in North Carolina."

Sumter had already left Salisbury. With a band of staunch refugees he had encamped at Tuckasegee Ford on the Catawba. Here he was joined by some veterans from his old Sixth Regiment and two hundred Catawba Indians. With these followers Sumter moved down river and united with other Carolinians at King Hagler's Branch in the lands of the Indians.

As the Whigs rallied to their militia leaders, a body of Loyalists, stirred up by Colonel James Moore, assembled at Ramsour's Mill on the Little Catawba. To disperse them General Rutherford began collecting the scattered bands of Carolinians. Before marching to join Rutherford, the officers and men at Hagler's decided to select a commander in chief. Since South Carolina had no chief executive, legislature, or judiciary to guide them, they met in a simple democratic convention.

Admiring militiamen quickly nominated Colonels Hill and Bratton. Colonel Winn, who was president of the convention, then observed that Colonel Sumter, an old, experienced officer was in camp. "Surely," said Winn, "he is the most proper person to take command."

The militiamen knew Sumter through service with him or by reputation. "If we choose you as our leader," they asked, "will you direct our operations?"

"I am under the same promise with you," Sumter replied. "Our interests and fates are and must be identical. With me as with you it is liberty or death."

With backwoods informality the members of the convention cast their ballots and on June 15, 1780, elected Thomas Sumter their leader. "It was then moved and seconded that Colonel Thomas Sumter should be appointed a Brigadier General," said Colonel Winn in his *Notes,* "and that the President be directed to make out a commission to that effect and sign the same in due form."

The members of the convention then agreed to continue in a body and to serve under Sumter's command until the end of the war. They further agreed to furnish their own food, clothing, arms, and horses. Solemnly they declared that "they would support the laws, both civil and military, by every means in their power," said Colonel Winn; and that "they would oppose the British and Tories by force of arms, which arms was never to be laid down until the British troops was drove from the State of South Carolina and the independence of the United States acknowledged."

This expression of principles, reminiscent of practices in the militia, was without legal precedent. But the men at Hagler's considered it binding. And, as Robert Wilson, elected lieutenant during the convention, afterward wrote: "This was the first organization of the militia after the fall of Charleston."

In the organization, General Sumter appointed Colonel Winn his aide. Having served beside Sumter in the Snow Campaign, during the defense of Fort Moultrie, and in the abortive campaign of 1777 in Georgia, Winn admired his chief. Six feet tall, athletic and handsome, the colonel was sanguine and jocular, a proper foil to the aloof, taciturn general.

While General Sumter was organizing his militia, Lord Cornwallis began preparing for the invasion of North Carolina. He sent Tarleton to Charleston to equip the British Legion for the campaign. He recalled Lord Rawdon to Camden and then left for Charleston to restore Royal government in South Carolina. Upon the withdrawal of Rawdon's Volunteers of Ireland from the Waxhaws, Rutherford ordered the Carolina militia to march against the Tories at Ramsour's. But while they were marching, on June 20, 1780, local Whigs attacked and dispersed the Loyalists. General Sumter and his men were near enough to hear the roar of the guns, but they were too late for the battle. Believing that the Tories should pay for the war, he applied to both civil and military authorities for permission to gather enough plunder from the defeated Loyalists to equip his corps. After receiving authority to seize and impress, giving a receipt in the name of North Carolina, Sumter rounded up a few horses and wagons and bivouacked under the oaks around the spring on Hagler's Hill, which because of the scarcity of provisions his men derisively nicknamed Poor Hill. Moving farther down east of the Catawba in search of pasturage for his horses, he established a camp on Clem's Branch of Sugar Creek, some fourteen miles below Charlotte.

Whigs soon came trooping into the camp on Clem's Branch. With officers and men whom he had known during the Snow Campaign, the expedition against the Cherokees, and in the Continentals, including about eighty veterans of the Sixth Regiment, General Sumter began forming his brigade. His men gathered by sections and districts and elected their officers. And then in his loose manner of discipline, instead of close-order drill and routine calisthenics, he began toughening and training them in individual prowess by competitive sports, emphasizing running, jumping, swimming, and wrestling. In two weeks he was satisfied. With five hundred men well organized and officered, on July 4 he emerged from hiding and boldly camped at Old Nation Ford on the Catawba.

Sumter's encampment at Old Nation brought out other leaders.

Colonel James Williams, who lived at Mount Pleasant plantation on Little River, about fifteen miles from Ninety-Six, came in with a small party. On July 5 Williams wrote his wife of the "South Carolina militia commanded by Colonel Sumter, to the amount of five hundred, now in camp at this place, and in expectation of crossing the river today." Approaching Colonel Hill, with whom he had served in the General Assembly, Williams asked to join the

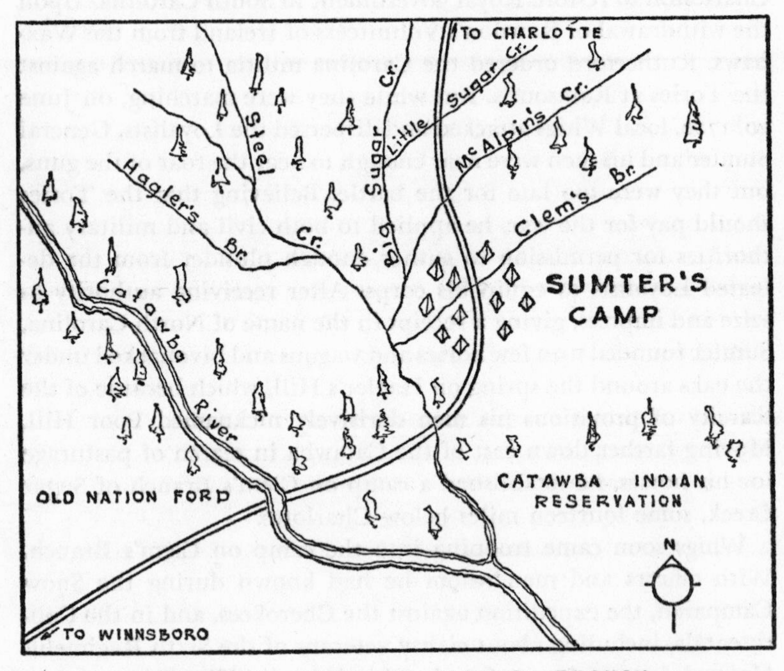

SUMTER'S CAMP ON CLEM'S BRANCH

expedition. As Sumter needed a commissary officer, he assigned Major Miles and twenty-five men, four wagons, and some horses to Williams and set him gathering supplies.

Upon his return to Charleston, Lord Cornwallis issued a proclamation inviting the rebels to renew their allegiance. Believing their cause now lost, Colonel Andrew Pickens, Colonel Isaac Hayne, and Brigadier General Andrew Williamson laid down their arms. "The surrender of General Williamson at Ninety-Six and the reduction of Hill's Iron Works by the dragoons and militia under Turnbull," Lord Cornwallis informed Clinton June 30, "has put an end to all resistance in South Carolina."

Cornwallis was mistaken. Sumter's encampment at Old Nation spread dismay among the Loyalists. His brigade offered a serious threat to the British posts at Rocky Mount and Hanging Rock. To meet this emergency, on July 7 Lord Rawdon sent Colonel Rugeley the names of the American officers, empowering him to offer five hundred guineas to the traitor who would lead General Sumter into a British ambush. Because Colonel Lacey's father was an ardent Tory, Rawdon suggested that Rugeley first approach Lacey.

When treachery failed, Rawdon ordered Colonel Turnbull into action. Turnbull immediately wrote Captain Huck, still encamped at White's Mill: "You are hereby ordered, with the cavalry under your command, to proceed to the frontier of the province, collecting all the royal militia with you on your march, and with said force to push the rebels as far as you may deem convenient."

With his detachment of dragoons, mounted infantry, and militia, on July 11, 1780, Captain Huck marched around the head of Fishing Creek and raided the plantation of Captain John McClure. He caught young James McClure and Edward Martin, his brother-in-law, melting down pewter dishes and molding bullets. He ordered them hanged at sunrise. When Mrs. McClure pleaded for her boys, Huck slapped her with the flat of his sword.

Unobserved, Mary McClure slipped from the house, saddled a horse, and galloped in search of her father. She found him in Sumter's camp, and that evening Colonel Bratton, with Captain McClure and about a hundred and fifty volunteers, set out to rescue the McClures. As they marched, Colonels Lacey and Winn joined them. Soon they had collected five hundred men.

Upon reaching his home Colonel Bratton learned that after visiting the McClures, Captain Huck had stopped at his plantation and demanded that Mrs. Bratton prepare dinner for him and his troops.

"Where is your husband?" Huck asked.

"In Sumter's army," she replied. A trooper slashed at her throat with a reap hook. He missed.

Bratton learned that soon after dinner Huck had marched about a quarter of a mile and bivouacked on the plantation of James Williamson. Several nimble-footed scouts soon reported that the enemy had pitched their tents on both sides of the road between the rail fence around the barn and the picket fence around Williamson's house. There the troops were lying in great insecurity, without pickets or patrols and with only a sentinel posted in the road at each end of their camp.

Colonels Bratton and Lacey divided their men and waited. Then swiftly, in the deep night, each swung his column through the fields, approaching the camp from opposite ends of the road. At daybreak they struck, the militia opening with buckshot at seventy-five yards.

The surprised British sprang to arms, formed, and charged with fixed bayonets. The Americans fired a second volley. Again the Britons charged, but they were hemmed in by the fences. Huck dashed from Williamson's house, sprang on his horse, and waved his sword for a third charge. At that moment a sharpshooter named Carroll toppled him from his saddle, blood spurting from a gaping hole in his throat.

"Captain Huck, encouraged by meeting no opposition, encamped in an unguarded manner, and was fatally surprised and routed," Lord Cornwallis soberly reported to Clinton on July 15. "The Captain was killed, and only twelve of the Legion, and as many of the militia, escaped."

At the time his volunteer militia defeated Huck, General Sumter was in North Carolina desperately seeking money, arms, and men. As a former rifleman, he set off to visit the Gillespie brothers, famed rifle makers who lived near the Blue Ridge. These armorers were hard-riding, fox-hunting Presbyterians whose major passion was cockfighting. They owned a blue game hen whose chicks were famed throughout the Carolina mountains. None had ever flinched, none had ever shown a white feather, and Old Tuck had never lost a fight.

Reaching the Gillespie forge, Sumter found the fires drawn and the brothers crouched around a cockpit. As Sumter bargained for rifles, they marveled at his courage in leading what undoubtedly was a forlorn struggle. They swore that he was a chick of the blue hen. Dressed in his blue coat, with scarlet facings and golden epaulettes, and wearing a hat with a cock's feather, he looked like Old Tuck. Thomas Sumter was a gamecock! Soon the Carolinas were ringing with the nickname of Gamecock.

Chapter 5 GAMECOCK OF THE CAROLINAS

THOMAS Sumter now commanded the only corps of Whigs still organized and fighting in South Carolina. With instinctive knowledge of handling troops, he developed crude systems of intelligence and logistic support. Long familiar with the roads and rivers of eastern Carolina, he kept informed of the condition of every ford, bridge, or ferry. Through his spies he learned the position, number, and commanding officer of every British detachment. And he knew the mettle of his Scotch-Irish troops, for in shallow graves at Williamson's lay proof that these immigrants would fight to protect their fields, cabins, and barns.

"Having been well informed that you are Marching to the relief of this Country," on July 17, 1780, Sumter wrote Baron de Kalb, who was moving slowly through North Carolina with the Continental Army originally sent to relieve Charleston, "I think it my duty to give you the earliest intelligence of the situation and force of the enemy, with such other things as appear the most interesting from the best accounts."

Sumter then gave the location of each British post and the number of troops in its garrison, estimating the total to be 3,482. Within fifteen days Lord Cornwallis could concentrate these detachments in Camden and call out ten thousand Loyalist militia. "To obviate this, your Excellency will I hope pardon me for the freedom I take in giving my opinion," he wrote, launching into strategy that soon became an obsession. "The method I should propose to prevent this junction and accumulation of Force, would be, to detach a body of light troops to take post on the south side of Santee River at Nelsons and Manigaults ferries. This will effectually cut off their retreat to Town, and thereby prevent them from forcing the Militia to retreat with them, or from their gathering together the Tories, and also from stripping the country of all its resources."

De Kalb received Sumter's outline of strategy on July 21. He already knew of the uprising under the Gamecock, for the army now had a few staunch Carolina refugees. Colonel Marion commanded a band of men and boys, ragged, unarmed, and poorly mounted. Major Peter Horry was serving as a supernumerary aide, and Major Thomas Pinckney was marching with the Continentals. The baron was dawdling along, however, waiting for Major General Horatio Gates, the hero who had defeated Burgoyne at Saratoga, to overtake and assume command of the army. He refused to take action before Gates's coming, merely endorsing Sumter's report: "I will lay the letter before General Gates at his arrival."

The Southern campaign was now moving rapidly toward its climax. Sumter continued ranging the Up Country agitating, rallying, and organizing the Whigs. Cornwallis tarried in the Low Country, deploying the British, sustaining the Tories, and reorganizing the Royal government. And on July 25 General Gates caught up with De Kalb at Wilcox's Mill on Deep River. Unmindful of General Charles Lee's sarcastic advice that he should not swap his Northern laurels for Southern willows, Gates began driving his ailing, hungry, and poorly trained soldiers toward Camden.

Eager to try his gaffs upon Turnbull's New York Volunteers before the arrival of the Continentals, on July 28 the Gamecock moved down the Catawba and bivouacked at Land's Ford. During the fighting at Williamson's Colonel Winn had saved the life of a Tory, and in gratitude the man had joined the Whigs. Sent to spy out Turnbull's camp, he returned with information that the New York Volunteers were encamped around a large frame house situated on a high hill in the boulder-strewn triangle below the confluence of Rocky Creek and the Catawba.

During a conference with his officers Sumter decided to attack the post at Rocky Mount. As Major William R. Davie, an ardent young patriot just out of Princeton, with a troop of North Carolina dragoons and a few mounted riflemen, lay encamped near the Waxhaws he asked the major to create a diversion by moving against the post at Hanging Rock. While Davie was making a brilliant feint, the Gamecock crossed Fishing Creek, quietly forded Rocky Creek, and on Sunday, July 30, 1780, attempted to surprise Turnbull. He failed, however, for his horsemen ran into and scattered a band of Tories, some of whom ran squawking into the bastion.

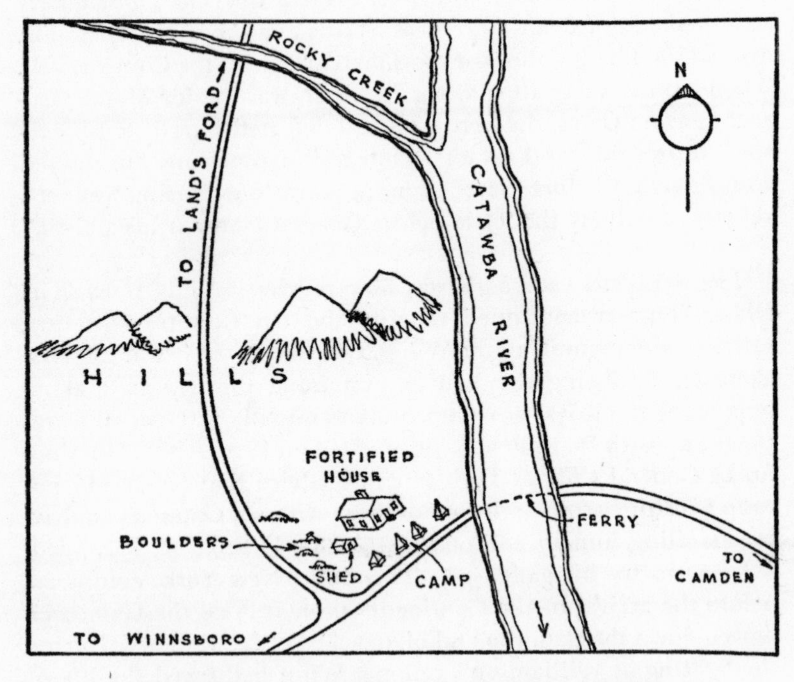

TURNBULL'S CAMP AT ROCKY MOUNT

After reconnoitering Rocky Mount, the Gamecock asked his aide to summon Turnbull. Colonel Winn prepared a formal demand for surrender:

30 July, 1780

Sir:

I am directed by Gen'l Sumter to demand a surrender of Rocky Mount. Therefore you will surrender this place with the men, etc., under your command, which will be considered as prisoners of war.

R. Winn

Sumter dispatched an officer under a white flag to deliver his ultimatum. But George Turnbull, a Loyalist from Connecticut and one of the ablest field commanders under Cornwallis, did not frighten. He asked that hostilities cease for an hour while he studied the proposal. At the expiration of the truce, he sent a defiant reply:

> Sir:
> I have considered your summons and return for answer, that duty and inclination induce me to defend this place to the last extremity.
>
> Turnbull, Colo. Command't
>
> 30 July, 1780

Upon receiving Turnbull's defiance, Sumter opened his attack. "This was made under the impression that the Enemy was in a large framed house: the walls of which were only thin clap boards, and we supposed that our balls would have the desired effect by shooting through the wall," said Colonel Hill in his *Memoirs,* "but so it was, that from the time we received this information until the time the attack was made the Enemy had wrought day and night and had placed small logs about a foot from the inside of the wall and rammed the cavity with clay, and under this delusion we made the attack; but soon found that we could injure them noway, but by shooting in their portholes."

After desultory firing, sniping, and skirmishing for about an hour, the Gamecock became impatient and ordered a frontal attack. His men charged across the yard and began firing only ten paces from the house. But after Colonel Andrew Neal, son of Colonel Neal of the Ring Fight, and seven privates had been slain by Turnbull's sharpshooters, Sumter pulled the survivors back to the shelter of a line of boulders.

As they lay in safety, Sumter called a council of his officers. And "it was discovered that there was a large rock, and between this rock and the fort, stood a small house which might be fired by throwing fire brands over the rock, and that this house would communicate the fire to the house the Enemy was in and as we had the command of the water they could not possibly extinguish the flames," said Colonel Hill. "From this ledge of Rocks where the army lay, to the rock near the house was about 100 yards free of any obstruction; and it is well known that when any object is going from or coming to a marksman, the marksman had near as good a chance as if the object was stationary; it was then proposed by the General and other officers for two men to endeavor to fire that small house, but the undertaking appeared so hazardous that no two men of the army could be found to undertake it."

Colonel Hill and Sergeant Jim Johnson finally volunteered. Then with ingenious woodcraft their comrades encased them in "rich lightwood split and bound with cords to cover the most vital parts of our bodies, as well as a large bundle of the same wood to carry in our arms," said Hill; "being thus equipped we run the 100 yards to the rock."

Standing behind the boulder, the two men began the assault, Hill peering around the edge and watching for a sally and Johnson lighting and tossing brands upon the smaller house. But before they could set the house on fire, the British burst out with gleaming bayonets and chased them back to their comrades behind the ledge.

Keen and unflinching, Sumter ordered a second attempt. While the riflemen spattered the passageway with lead to prevent another sally, Hill and Johnson, again encased in lightwood armor, raced to their boulder. "We then had an opportunity of making a large fire behind the rock, and throwing fire brands on the roof of the little house," said Hill, "and we staid until the roof was in flames, and the heat of it had caused the wall of the great house to smoke."

The two valiant incendiaries again raced back to the ledge. "And here I beg leave to remark that Providence so protected us both, that neither of us lost a drop of blood, altho locks of hair was cut from our heads and our garments riddled with balls," said Hill. "Scarcely had we time to look back from behind the rock where our men lay, in hopes to see the fire progressing, but to our great mortification, when the great house was beginning to flame, as heavy a storm of rain fell, as hath fallen from that time to the present, and which extinguished the flames," concluded Hill. "We were then forced to retreat under as great mortification, as ever any number of men endured."

After retreating six miles Sumter formed a bivouac, for the

thunderstorm had caused such a flood that he could not ford Rocky Creek. By then the Tories whom he had flushed at daybreak had ridden to summon aid from the post at Hanging Rock. During the night some three hundred British infantrymen marched in, and next morning Turnbull made a show of pursuit. Unconcerned, since he had come to fight, the Gamecock sent Colonel Winn back to protect his rear and marched unmolested to his old camp at Land's Ford.

"On Sunday morning 23rd ultimo with about five hundred Men I attacked Rocky Mount," General Sumter, so busy that he glanced at the calendar and misdated his battle, wrote Major Pinckney, who had been appointed aide to General Gates. "The action continued upwards of Eight hours, was often in thirty feet of their works, but they were so constructed that I could by no means force them. I made an attempt to fire them in the evening, and should have succeeded if the afternoon had not proved so excessively wet. My led being exhausted I withdrew."

Just as Sumter had foreseen and warned De Kalb, as soon as the Tory spies reported Gates's rapid advance, Lord Cornwallis began concentrating his forces around Camden. He ordered Wemyss to move up to the High Hills. He advised Rawdon to call in the troops under Turnbull. And he sent Tarleton and some convalescent dragoons back to the concentration.

On August 1 Tarleton and his dragoons jogged out of Charleston. After floundering through the swamps, on August 6 he crossed the flooded Santee at Lenud's. Dashing across Williamsburg, he burst into Kingstree in an attempt to capture the leading Whigs. But upon learning that Major John James had five hundred militiamen under arms at Indiantown, he galloped off along Black River, stopping only long enough on Pudding Swamp to put the torch to the home of Captain Henry Mouzon.

Tarleton's raid infuriated the Scotch-Irish. From Indiantown Major James sent an officer up the Peedee to find Gates and ask for an experienced commander. Veterans of the Second Regiment, mindful of the defense of Fort Moultrie and the attack upon Spring Hill redoubt, suggested that Gates send Colonel Francis Marion.

While Cornwallis was mustering his forces to meet the army under Gates, General Sumter waited at Land's Ford, impatient, grim, and daring. He was not discouraged by the repulse at Rocky Mount. "This active partisan was thoroughly sensible that the minds of men are influenced by enterprise, and that to keep undisciplined people together, it is necessary to employ them," wrote Tarleton admiringly in his *Campaigns*. "For this purpose he again surveyed the state of the British posted upon the frontier."

Learning that the infantry reinforcement was still at Rocky Mount, the Gamecock decided to strike the weakened post at Hanging Rock. After holding a council of officers, which included those of Colonel Robert Irvin and Major Davie, on the evening of August 5 he began fording the swollen Catawba. The swirling red waters bore horses and riders downstream, and after a perilous crossing the militia assembled on the eastern bank, wet, battered, and discouraged, some having lost their arms and others their horses. Undaunted by loss or suffering, Sumter took the lead and by morning had covered the sixteen miles of ruts and mud to Hanging Rock.

On the heights above Hanging Rock Creek lay some fourteen hundred men, commanded by Major John Carden of the Prince of Wales' American Regiment, their camp extending for half a mile along the stream. On their left, separated from the others by a narrow wood covered with thick undergrowth, lay Colonel Samuel Bryan's corps of North Carolina Loyalists. In the center, their front protected by low earthworks thrown up in an open field and their green regimental flag rippling above them, lay two companies of infantry from the British Legion, commanded by Captains Kenneth McCulloch and John Rousselet. And on their right, camped in and around some farmhouses, lay scattered units of infantry, cavalry, and artillery, all under the immediate command of Colonel Robinson.

About six o'clock on August 6, 1780, after the enemy had finished breakfast and scattered to their routine duties, the Gamecock divided his troops into three contingents, commanded by Colonels Irvin, Lacey, and Hill. Colonel Winn and Major Davie commanded the reserves. Assigning an enemy camp to each contingent, Sumter ordered his commanders to begin moving into position.

Against the advice of cavalryman Davie, he allowed his militia to ride up the hill, dismount, and then begin the attack.

Colonel Irvin swung far to the right before turning upon the camp of Colonel Bryan. Concealed by rocks and trees, his Mecklenburg riflemen poured a murdering fire into the surprised and milling Tories. As rifles crackled and balls whistled, the Loyalists broke

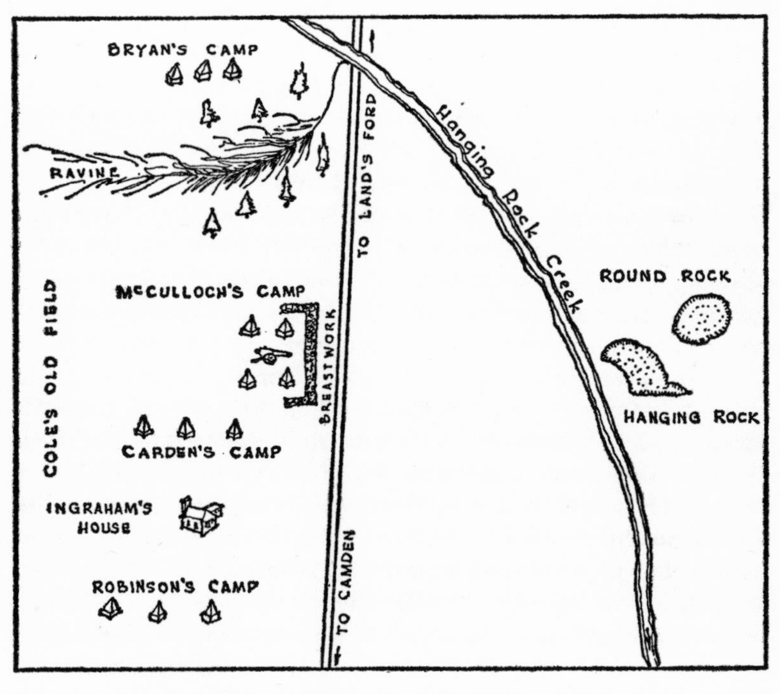

BRITISH CAMP AT HANGING ROCK

and fled into the center of the camp, spreading confusion and terror as they ran. Charging after them, Winn's and Davie's men completely routed Bryan's corps.

Without pausing, the Carolinians struck the camp of the British Legion. But the legionnaires, hardened combat veterans, formed in a countercharge, their bayonets shining cold and deadly. Back and forth the combatants rushed, man to man and gun to gun, until the field was littered with the dead and dying. After Carolina riflemen had struck down Captain McCulloch and sixty of his men, the legion infantry faltered and then began retreating. But checked by the shouts and flashing sword of Captain Rousselet, they formed a second time and charged back into the carnage.

At the height of the fighting, the Americans bore McCulloch, the humane senior captain of the legion infantry, from the field. As he lay bleeding and gasping, he called for water. Pityingly Major Joseph McJunkin, whose forefathers had also come from the Highlands, lifted the head of the dying Scot and gave him a drink from his canteen. Moments later McJunkin plunged back into the fighting.

As the Carolinians were blunting Rousselet's charge, a company of British regulars, moving unnoticed through a wooded swamp, struck and turned their right flank. After bolstering the legionnaires, they continued their advance, firing and charging by platoons. But the riflemen under Hill and Lacey, dodging behind rocks and trees and brushpiles, began an enfilading fire that completely destroyed the attacking column.

During the fighting the Gamecock was magnificent. Recklessly sitting his foaming charger, his long hair flying and his golden epaulettes a shining target for enemy sharpshooters, or galloping from division to division, shouting commands or encouragement or praise, he was Old Tuck. Like the gamest slasher cock he neither shrank nor cowered when a rifle ball ripped into his thigh. Scorning a cry of pain before his men, he continued to ride, cheering, animating, and directing the fighting.

Replenishing his failing supply of ammunition by stripping the dead, Sumter quickly threw his entire force upon the British Legion. In savage fighting the Gamecock drove them into the camp of Colonel Robinson. There the British troops became massed, "and they fell so fast by their unseen enemy that their officers were obliged to push them forward by their sabers," said Colonel Hill in his *Memoirs*. "The loss of the British in the action was great in killed and wounded. The Prince of Wales Regiment was almost annihilated." With only nine survivors in his regiment, Major Carden lost his nerve and resigned the command to Captain Rousselet.

Then the unexpected happened. As Captains Stewart and Mc-

Donald, with forty mounted infantry of the British Legion were riding from Rocky Mount to the concentration at Camden, they heard sounds of battle. Swinging east and galloping along the road toward Salisbury, they soon reached Hanging Rock. Veterans skilled in stratagems, they extended their horsemen in a long line and galloped into the hottest of the fighting. But as the Carolinians began falling back, Major Davie charged the British horsemen with his dragoons and drove them into the woods. During the respite Captain Rousselet wheeled his defeated troops into a hollow square.

"The utmost exertions were made by Colonel Sumter and the other officers to carry the men on to attack the British square," said Davie in his account of the battle. But the men failed to rally. Thirsty, and hungry, and tired, after three hours of fighting, they had had enough. For the next hour, while the British watched, they ransacked the camp, looting and eating and drinking. Finding several puncheons of rum, the young cockerels soon began crowing. And after learning from prisoners that Turnbull, his troops marching at double time, was only four miles away, Sumter called, "Boys, it is not good to pursue a victory too far!"

As the Americans began forming to withdraw, the British buglers sounded a fanfare and the men in the square gave three cheers for King George.

"Boys, can't you answer them?" shouted Sumter.

The Carolinians gave three rousing cheers for George Washington. They then marched off, with Major Davie and his dragoons protecting their rear. "As the troops were loaded with plunder, and encumbered with their wounded friends, and many of them intoxicated," Davie confessed, "this retreat was not performed in the best military style."

Sumter's attack upon the post at Hanging Rock was brilliant, his strategy sound, his tactics faultless. His volunteers fought like veterans, and the battle, as William James wrote in his unpublished life of Sumter, "in proportion to numbers engaged was certainly the most bloody fought during the revolutionary war."

The Gamecock halted his withdrawal at Davie's camp in the Waxhaws. After dark, he called in Soldier Tom, the bodyguard whose presence reminded him of Mary and young Thomas in the

High Hills. Swearing him to secrecy, he asked the faithful servant to dress his wounded thigh. After spending two days recuperating, attending the sick and wounded, and reorganizing the effectives, on August 9 he began a long battle report. Feeling a slight in not receiving an answer from De Kalb, instead of writing directly to General Gates, he addressed his report to Major Pinckney, an old friend who could be trusted to show it to the general.

Sumter gave the details of the action at Rocky Mount and then stated his reasons for deciding to cross the Catawba and attack Hanging Rock. "I accordingly began to pass the River on Saturday evening," he wrote. "The Rapidity of the current was so Great I was not only thereby much Delayed but met with considerable Loss, however proceeded on, but by these delays was obliged to alter my mode of attack, and instead of Making it at Day break, Concealed myself untill Six o'clock, allowing them to Scatter, and then Go on with precipitation, as I knowed their number, much more considerable than my own. In this manner I proceeded and Should have Succeeded according to my wishes if they had not been Reinforced that Night with three hundred men from Rocky Mount, and a troop of Dragoons from Camden. These Circumstances I was acquainted with before the Enemy was alarmed, but I had Six hundred brave men upon whom I could Depend, therefore resolved to proceed.The enemy had three Large encampments, their lines so extensive that it was imposable to attack the whole at once. In consequence of which I proceeded against the Most Considerable of the Tory encampment and that of the British which lay in the Center, all upon advantageous heights. In about half an hour I had possession of Col. Bryant's Camp, the action still very hot in the British, who were well posted and with the advantage of a field piece and open Ground all Round them. They had detached a column to Support Bryant, who through a swamp found means to turn my Right flank. The action was Renewed upon that Quarter. At length every man of them was either killed or taken. The British Camp was then attacked with Greater Violence. They sustained it with Great Bravery for Near an hour, at length gave way Leaving me in full possession of their Camp also. They Rallied again in Col. Robinson's encampment, and notwithstanding their opposition was but feeble, and I in possession of Two-thirds of that Camp also, for More than half an hour, yet was obliged to leave them from Several causes: the action having Continued without intermission for three hours, Men fainting with heat and Droughth, numbers Kild and Wounded. But the true Cause of my not Totally defeating them was the want of led."

The Gamecock soberly estimated the enemy's loss at two hundred and fifty killed and wounded. His troops had taken seventy prisoners. His own loss was smaller: twenty killed, forty wounded, and ten missing. Captain John McClure had been mortally wounded, but Colonels Hill and Winn were recovering. Of his own inflamed and swollen thigh he said nothing, but he concluded: "Although I have wrote much, it is with much pain I have wrote at all."

Chapter 6 DEBACLE AT FISHING CREEK

"BOTH British and Tories are panic struck," Sumter wrote Pinckney, in summarizing the effect of his triumph at Hanging Rock; "and I am well convinced that fifteen hundred men can go through any part of the state with ease. This will not be the case ten or fifteen days hence, especially if they have time to gather the Militia."

Strategist Sumter again suggested using the rivers to baffle the enemy. "I doubt numbers will join them," he wrote, "to prevent which I take the liberty to say, that was there about fifteen hundred Men to Take post at the High Hills or at Nielson's ferry it would inevitably Ruin their Army, as they could by no Means effect a Retreat without going far to the Westward, and perhaps not without going through Georgia."

After finishing his report, Sumter called in Captain Kemble, a brave but ragged survivor of Hanging Rock, and instructed him to ride northward in search of the Continental Army. Should it be possible, after delivering the letter to Major Pinckney, he wished Kemble to give a personal report to General Gates, emphasizing the staunchness of the embattled Whigs along the Catawba and the strategy of deploying troops along the Santee.

After dispatching Kemble, the Gamecock turned to problems of his own command. During the return from Hanging Rock, Colonel James Williams, his commissary officer, had joined the corps with his men and wagons. While they were encamped in the Waxhaws, with the Gamecock *hors de combat,* Williams asked to be allowed some troops with whom to scourge the Tories below the border of the Carolinas. With Sumter's permission, he called for volunteers, hoping to recruit enough to drive Balfour and Ferguson from the district around Ninety-Six.

Enlisting the aid of McJunkin, Colonel Stein, and Colonel Thomas Brandon, a burly rough-and-tumble fighter from the Irish settlement along Fair Forest, he crossed the Catawba. To supply his detachment he carried off the horses, wagons, and provisions already collected for Sumter's troops. His action broke the regulations of the convention. As Sumter equipped, fed, and supported his army with material captured from the British and food confiscated from the Tories, Williams' embezzlement was anathema. The Gamecock sent trusted Colonel Lacey with a small guard to bring back the public property.

Colonel Lacey overtook Williams on the eve of his tour of the border. He demanded the return of the public goods. Williams demurred. Too adroit to start a row involving his guard and Brandon's Irishmen, Lacey asked Williams to walk out of camp for a private conference. He then presented a pistol to Williams' breast and informed him "that if he made any noise to call for assistance he was a dead man." After Lacey had expostulated with him on the baseness of his conduct, said Colonel Hill in his *Memoirs,* "Williams gave his word of honor that he would take back all the public property and as many of the men as he could persuade to go back."

But Williams was rash, tough, and fearless. Back in camp and surrounded by his own loyal followers, he refused to honor an oath taken under threat of death. Instead, with Sumter's troops and supplies he marched rapidly along the border and joined Colonel Charles McDowell and his North Carolina militia at Cherokee Ford on Broad River.

Soured by the absconding of Williams, the Gamecock roused his battered troops and crept up to Land's Ford. Threatened by a shortage of food, he began preparing to squeeze the Tories in the Dutch Fork. Just before he marched, however, Captain Kemble galloped in and reported that Gates was at hand. On the night of August 7 the Continentals had camped on Little Black Creek only forty miles north of Camden. Kemble's report changed all plans. Instead of riding to flog the Tories, Sumter stood by to co-operate with the American Army.

At the approach of Gates, Lord Rawdon also changed his strategy. He began calling in the detachments and pleading for Cornwallis to return to Camden. But as General Patterson, commandant of Charleston, had fallen ill of malaria, Lord Cornwallis lingered in the capital. To meet the threat he began redeployment of his troops. He ordered Balfour to send his light infantry from Ninety-Six to Camden and to come quickly to relieve Patterson. He sent Colonel Cruger and his battalion of DeLancey's New Jersey Volunteers to replace Balfour. And he also sent Colonel Alexander Innes, with Major Thomas Fraser and his South Carolina provincials, to support Cruger.

During the hurried shuffling of forces the Whig colonels at Cherokee Ford learned that Colonel Daniel Clary and a large party of Tories had encamped at Musgrove's plantation on the Enoree. They knew that Ferguson was at Colonel Winn's plantation below Winnsboro. Knowing of the withdrawal of Balfour and the weakened condition of the garrison at Ninety-Six, only twenty-four miles from Musgrove's, but not knowing of the arrival of Cruger and Innes, Colonels Williams, Clarke, and Shelby decided to strike Colonel Clary. About an hour before sunset on August 17, with Brandon in the lead because he was in familiar country, the Whigs rode from Broad River. Through the hot summer night they jogged and cantered and galloped, never stopping in their forty-mile journey. Just before dawn on August 18, 1780, they halted in sight of Musgrove's Ford.

Retiring quickly and bivouacking on Cedar Shoals Creek, the Whigs sent out a patrol. These tired horsemen soon clattered back from a bloody skirmish with a Tory patrol. At their heels galloped a countryman. He reported that on the previous afternoon Colonel Innes and a powerful force had reinforced Clary at Musgrove's Mill.

Realizing that Colonel Innes, reputed a fighter, would be upon them before they could escape on their jaded horses, the Carolinians began throwing up a breastwork of logs, stumps, limbs, brush, and loose earth. After Williams, Clarke, and Shelby had posted their men behind this work, Captain Shadrack Inman volunteered to ride to the mill, provoke the enemy, and then lure them past the ambuscade.

Inman struck the British camp, and Innes began pursuing him. Back they went, Inman's horsemen careering and firing, and Innes' infantry pressing relentlessly after them. At a point about two hundred yards from the breastwork, Inman feinted toward their advancing center. Innes drove him back with the bayonet. Whigs in the ambush opened with buckshot at seventy paces. Before they could reload, however, Innes drove Shelby's men from their protection. As Clarke began wheeling his Georgians to their support, a Watauga rifleman knocked over Innes.

"I've killed their commander!" he shouted. "I've killed Innes!"

Upon the wounding of Innes the British started retreating, with Americans in hot pursuit. As the Whigs began taking prisoners, two stalwarts grabbed the bridle of Colonel Clary's horse. Bold and quick-witted, he escaped after shouting angrily, "Damn you, don't you know your own officers?"

The Whigs captured two hundred prisoners. Seeing intrepid Captain Inman fall to a retreating marksman, the colonels halted the chase. Fearful of getting caught between Cruger and Ferguson, they immediately mounted, every three horsemen taking a prisoner whom they shifted from crupper to crupper as their trotting steeds began to show fatigue. For sixty miles they retreated, stopping only to rest their horses and eat green peaches and raw field corn. Even in their flight they passed the van of Ferguson's corps by less than five miles. They finally encamped safely near Gilbert Town. From lack of sleep, exposure to the sun, and the effects of peaches and corn, the men became ill, their blackened faces and eyes so swollen that they could scarcely see or recognize each other.

After camping near Gilbert Town for several days, the colonels decided to separate. Clarke hastened along the mountain ridges toward Georgia. Shelby headed back toward the Watauga to recruit more troops. And Williams, left in charge of the prisoners captured at Musgrove's Mill, began marching them toward Hillsboro. At the capital he claimed all credit for the victory. As a reward, on September 8 Governor Abner Nash authorized him to raise a hundred horsemen in North Carolina. Soon afterward Governor Rutledge promoted Williams to the rank of brigadier general of militia.

As Gates continued driving his weary troops down the road to Camden, Lord Rawdon became disturbed. Finally he marched out and camped on the high ground west of Little Lynches Creek. On August 10 Gates reached Little Lynches. Swinging abruptly to the right and fording the creek, he outflanked Rawdon and marched on to Rugeley's Mills. When Sumter learned that the American Army was at Rugeley's, only twelve miles from Camden, he began moving down the Catawba. From Land's Ford on August 12 he wrote Major Pinckney, sending the latest intelligence and strongly urging upon Gates the strategy of controlling Santee ferries from the High Hills. "Should his Excellency Gen'l Gates think proper to send a party over Pinetree Creek or at the High Hills or at Nelson's Ferry," he wrote, "it would totally ruin them."

The Gamecock was exuberant. Attracted by his reputation for fighting, fresh regiments were coming in. Colonel Charles Myddelton had brought in his men from the lower Congaree. Colonel Thomas Taylor, a former Virginian, had come in with the militia from around Congarees. And Colonel Henry Hampton was on the march with his riflemen from Broad River.

There were others. From North Carolina came his nephew Captain John Sumter, whose father Colonel William Sumter, had moved from Preddy's to Burke County. And from the Barbary coast came Yusef ben Ali and one who called himself John Scott. The Gamecock welcomed the corsairs, making a scout of Ben Ali and a bugler of Scott.

As Gates lay at Camp Clermont, he became intrigued by Sumter's strategy. He ordered the Gamecock to move down the Catawba-Wateree, seizing fords and closing ferries. On August 15 he sent Colonel Thomas Woolford, with a hundred Maryland Continentals, three hundred North Carolina militiamen, and two brass three-pounders, to join the foray down the Wateree. And to complete the strategic pincers, he sent Colonel Francis Marion to Williamsburg with orders to take command of Major James's militia and start a boat-burning foray up the Santee.

Sweeping down the Catawba, the Gamecock found that the enemy had abandoned Rocky Mount and Hanging Rock. He sent Colonel Taylor rushing down the Wateree. Taylor surprised and captured Fort Carey, a small redoubt guarding Wateree Ferry behind Camden. He also captured thirty prisoners and thirty-six wagons loaded with corn, rum, and other provisions. That afternoon he captured fifty of the British light infantry marching from

Ninety-Six, as well as six wagons loaded with their baggage, a drove of three hundred cattle, and a flock of sheep.

That evening the Gamecock sent a memorandum to Gates. "Have just time to inform you that Early this morning I took possession of all the passways over the Wateree River, from Elkins foard to Mr. Whitaker's ferry, five miles below Camden," he wrote. After reporting Taylor's capture of Fort Carey, he concluded, "I intend to keep possession of it if I can until I am honored with your Excellencies further commands."

But Sumter loved plunder. When the British began crossing the river below the fort during the night, he forgot his promise and moved his men and booty to safety ten miles up the Wateree.

Meanwhile, on the evening of August 10, after turning the command in Charleston over to Colonel Balfour, Lord Cornwallis heeded the pleas of Rawdon and turned his horse toward Camden. By riding night and day he reached the village during the night of August 13. Next morning he inspected his troops and listened to intelligence reports. After shifting and strengthening his corps for battle, at ten o'clock on the night of August 15 he marched from Camden. Colonel Webster commanded the van, and Tarleton and his dragoons brought up the rear. Slowly they moved through the darkness, stumbled over Saunders' Creek, and then crawled on toward Rugeley's.

Having decided to surprise the British, on the same morning Gates issued similar orders for his army to march at ten o'clock that night. Arrogant, without knowledge of his own corps or proper intelligence of the enemy, he began pushing toward Camden.

About halfway between Rugeley's and Camden at two-thirty in the morning of August 16, 1780, the advance guards of the two armies collided. Surprised, after desultory skirmishing, both sides drew back while Gates and Cornwallis formulated their plans. At dawn each deployed his troops for the coming battle.

Cornwallis sent Webster with the 23rd and 33rd regiments to his right, their line extending from the main highway to a gum swamp. To his left he sent Lord Rawdon with the Volunteers of Ireland, the infantry of the British Legion, and Hamilton's North Carolinians, their line extending from the highway to a swamp. Behind each wing he posted a contingent of the 71st Regiment. And in column along the road he stationed Tarleton and his Green Horse.

Gates posted his troops well. Opposite Rawdon on his right he put his veteran Continentals, the Marylanders under General Gist, and the Delawares under Baron de Kalb. In the center he stationed General Caswell and the North Carolina militia. On his left he placed the Virginia militia under General Stevens. Satisfied with his battle line, he ordered the Virginians to open the attack.

As the American skirmishers moved forward, Cornwallis ordered Webster to give them the bayonet. The red-coated British charged, their bayonets gleaming sinister in the hazy morning light. Unable to take cold steel, the Virginians threw down their guns and fled. Wheeling his veterans upon the North Carolinians, Webster drove them from the field. He then began rolling up the flank of the Continentals struggling valiantly with Rawdon's troops. Old Baron de Kalb, unhorsed and fighting afoot, received eleven wounds. The Maryland and Delaware regiments fought gallantly until "a part of the British cavalry, under Major Hanger, was ordered to charge their flank, while Lieutenant Colonel Tarleton, with the remainder of his regiment, completed their confusion," said Tarleton in his *Campaigns*.

The rout then turned into slaughter. All day in the terrible August heat Tarleton and his horsemen pursued the fleeing Americans. Satiated with blood and death, the green demons finally halted at Hanging Rock, twenty-two miles from the field of battle.

Horatio Gates galloped past his scampering troops and fled toward Charlotte. Meeting Major Davie, he shouted for the dragoons to fall back as Tarleton would soon be upon them. "My men are accustomed to Tarleton and do not fear him," yelled Davie. But seeing the completeness of the debacle, he sent Captain Nathaniel Martin and two dragoons across the Wateree to warn Sumter and appoint a rendezvous below Charlotte.

Sumter was already creeping up the river road. At daybreak he had heard the roar of guns, but he was still ignorant of the outcome of the battle. After listening to Captain Martin, he began forcing his march, but his progress was slow. The weather was torrid, his men were nearly exhausted and their horses ridden

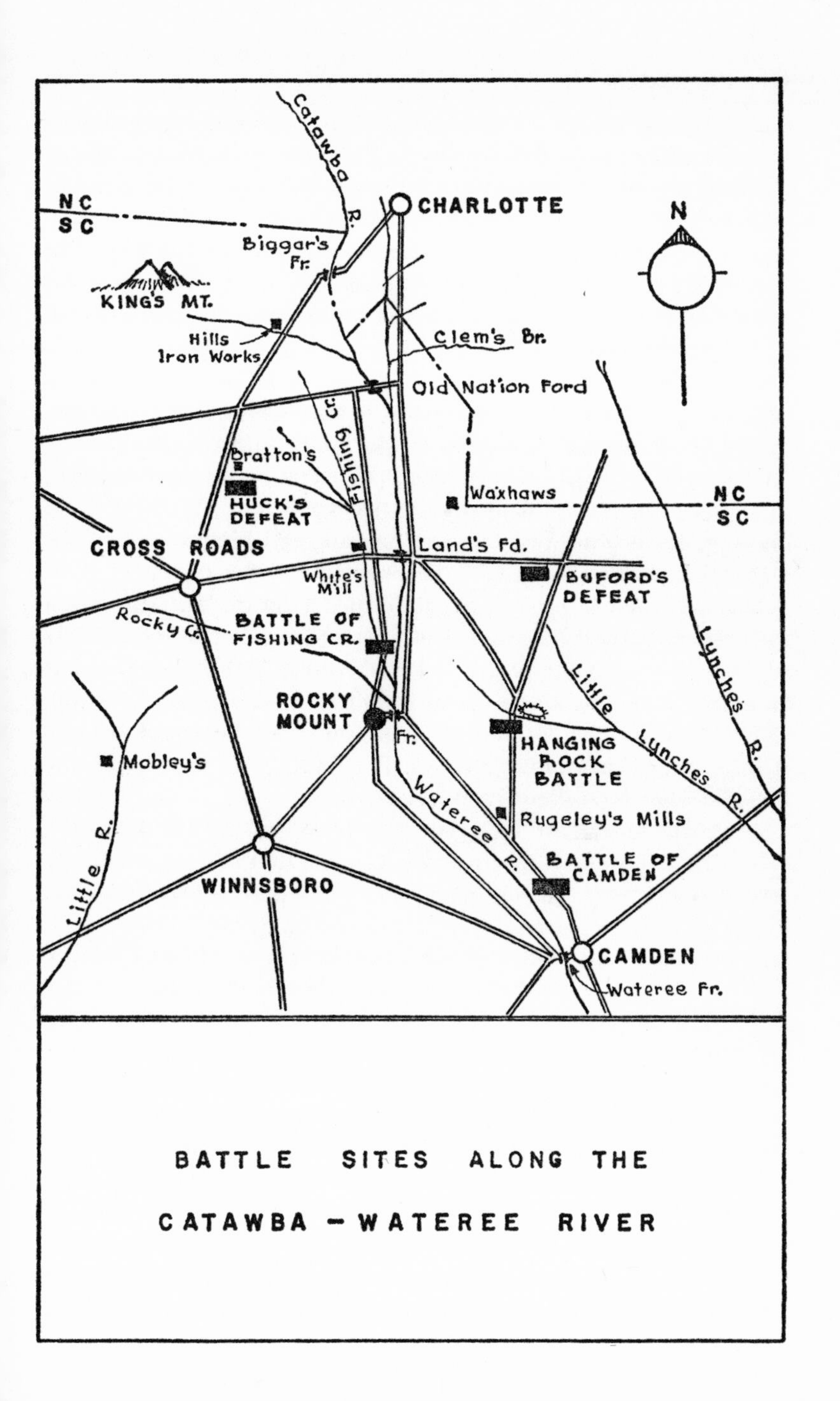

BATTLE SITES ALONG THE CATAWBA – WATEREE RIVER

down, and the corps was encumbered by prisoners, wagons, and straying cattle.

Lord Cornwallis was moving with contrasting swiftness. Immediately after the battle he marched on and encamped at Rugeley's. There he awaited impatiently the return of Tarleton, for the Tories had reported that Sumter was moving slowly up the Wateree with the only surviving combat troops in South Carolina. Could he but crush the Gamecock, he would bring his campaign to a glorious end.

Even though harried by thoughts of pursuit, Sumter would not forfeit his plunder. All day, all night, and again all next day he marched, his troops growing more exhausted and disorganized. Finally reaching his old camp at Rocky Mount, he went into bivouac. Incautious and unafraid, he allowed his troops to light campfires, cook and eat, and then sleep until dawn.

Early on the morning after the battle, Banastre Tarleton, with three hundred and fifty men and a three-pounder, set off rapidly up the east side of the Wateree. By afternoon he had learned that Sumter was moving along the road on the opposite side. Reaching the ferry at Rocky Mount, through the dusk he could see the twinkling fires in Sumter's camp. Forbidding his men to kindle fires, he went into silent bivouac.

At dawn on August 18, 1780, Sumter moved up the Catawba, slowly, cumbersomely, incautiously. Certain that he was beyond the reach of Cornwallis, he neglected to send out patrols. After crossing Fishing Creek at Cow Ford, he posted a couple of vedettes and marched on to the camp he had used after his repulse at Rocky Mount. Beside the Catawba he halted, went into bivouac, stacked arms, and gave his men camp liberty.

The Gamecock entrusted the security of his camp to Major Robert Crawford, officer of the day. Exhausted from herding his undisciplined troops and from lack of sleep, he tossed his hat with the cock's feather on the ground, laid aside his blue coat with the red facing and gold epaulettes, and pulled off his boots. Then he stretched out on a blanket in the shade of a wagon.

Before dawn Tarleton roused his legion. After scouts reported that Sumter had decamped, he put his infantry and cannon aboard the ferryboats, swam his horses across the Wateree, and set off on the fresh trail. All morning he followed the Gamecock, the road winding and broken and the heat near tropical. At noon he reached Fishing Creek.

After selecting a hundred dragoons and sixty infantrymen from his tired legion, with his horses carrying double, Tarleton crossed the creek and pushed rapidly forward. Captain Charles Campbell, who had burned Sumter's house in the High Hills, galloped ahead with his squadron. Sweeping around a bend, they ran into Sumter's vedettes. The riflemen fired, killing a dragoon. Before they could reload, Campbell's men cut them to pieces.

Sensing their prey, Tarleton and his legion galloped along the high ridge between Fishing Creek and Catawba River. Suddenly Campbell stopped. Along the river bank below him lay Sumter's camp, completely insecure and disorganized, some of the militia cooking and eating, some sleeping in the shade, and some swimming in the river. Some were robbing peaches from the orchard of a Tory named Reaves. That morning they had captured several puncheons of rum, and some were drinking and others already drunk. Major Crawford was pouring himself a drink.

"The decision and the preparation for the attack was momentary. The cavalry and infantry were formed into one line, and giving a general shout, advanced to the charge," said Tarleton in his *Campaigns*. "Universal consternation immediately ensued throughout the camp; some opposition was, however, made from behind the waggons, in front of the militia."

Sumter had heard the firing of his vedettes, but after being assured by Colonel Myddelton, who had ridden patrol, that it was only butchers killing beeves, he rolled over and fell asleep. Suddenly he awoke, with Captain John Steele shaking him. Sleepily he peered from under the wagon. Was he dreaming? Fighting, confusion, and terror were spreading throughout his camp.

The Gamecock saw the Green Horse between his men and their arms, their great sabers whirling and flashing. He saw gigantic Colonel Woolford and his officers trying to cut their way to their guns, only to fall under the enemy's vicious sabers. He saw Colonel Lacey and his men fighting heroically around the wagons. He saw a Whig rifleman topple Captain Campbell. He saw the rest of his troops running, diving, swimming, fleeing in all directions.

Springing up, Sumter cut the halter of a wagon horse and vaulted upon his bare back. Shouting orders and encouragement, he tried to rally his men. The militiamen were too frightened to heed. When he saw Colonel Lacey running toward the swamp, he realized that he had lost the fight. Urging his clumsy charger into a gallop, he followed Lacey. Soon thinking himself out of range of the muskets, he looked back. At that moment his horse lumbered beneath an oak, and he crashed head-on into a limb. Tumbling insensible to the ground, he lay a long time as if dead.

Regaining consciousness, Sumter found his horse. After wandering all night, he reached the home of John Barnett. "Do, Mrs. Barnett, let me have something to eat," he asked hungrily, "if only a piece of Johnny-cake and a cup of milk."

As the Gamecock began eating his first meal in twenty-four hours, he turned to Susannah Barnett. "Do, Miss Sukey, fix my hair." As the young woman ran her fingers through his matted locks, he added: "Never mind combing it, it is so tangled."

Susannah tied his brown curls into a club, and soon afterwards he joined the stream of fugitives passing Barnett's. Next morning Thomas Sumter rode into the camp of Major Davie, a brigadier general without servant, soldier, or vestige of a brigade.

"Colonel Sumter, who had taken off part of his clothes on account of the heat of the weather, in that situation, amidst the general confusion, made his escape," Tarleton said in his *Campaigns*. The Green Dragoon was confident that had the Gamecock been in uniform he would have been killed or captured. He reported that, besides eight hundred horses captured, "one hundred and fifty of his officers and soldiers were killed and wounded; ten continental officers and one hundred men, many militia officers, and upwards of two hundred privates, were made prisoners; two three pounders, two ammunition wagons, one thousand stand of arms, forty-four carriages, loaded with baggage, rum, and other stores, fell into the possession of the British."

But many of Sumter's men escaped. Colonel Myddelton got away. Major Crawford, fortified with rum, swam the Catawba under fire, crawled out on the farther bank, and waved disdainfully at the enemy sharpshooters. Colonel Lacey outran his pursuers and headed for Rocky Creek. On Tarleton's march to Camden, seeing their captors loaded with spoils and prisoners, Colonels Taylor and Hampton broke from the line, rolled down a hill, and vanished. The survivors quickly reassembled at Davie's camp. Despite his losses, a week after the debacle the Gamecock had reorganized his corps and was again patroling the fords of the Catawba.

On the retreat from Fort Carey, Sumter had entrusted his portmanteau containing his papers and the cash and certificates left by Governor Rutledge to Soldier Tom. During the melee at Fishing Creek, Tom hid the bag in some bushes in a cove of the Catawba. In one of the sweeps downriver he recovered the bag. On August 26 General Sumter bought forty-two-hundred dollars' worth of linen cloth for saddle blankets from William McGibbony of Mecklenburg. Soon afterward, the clothing committee appointed by Gates issued him seven yards of duffel, two and one-half yards of blue cloth, and one and three-quarters yards of scarlet, so that he might replace his torn trousers and the coat left under the wagon at Fishing Creek.

Sumter's escape and quick reorganization of the Carolina militia astounded Lord Cornwallis. "The severity of the Rebel government has so terrified and totally subdued the minds of the people, that it is very difficult to rouse them to any exertions," he wrote Sir Henry Clinton on August 29. "The taking that violent and cruel incendiary General Rutherford has been a lucky circumstance, but the indefatigable Sumter is again in the field, and is beating up for recruits with the greatest assiduity."

Although suffering castigation and remorse for his own defeat, Gates was no less impressed. "Colonel Sumter since his surprise and defeat up the west side of the Wateree, has reinstated and increased his corps to upwards of 1,000 men," he wrote General Washington on August 30. "I have ordered him to continue to harass the enemy upon that side."

Chapter 7 GAMECOCK AND SWAMP FOX

WHILE the Gamecock was collecting and inspiring his troops, Lord Cornwallis began moving toward North Carolina. After disposing of his prisoners and providing quarters and attendants for his troops ill with malaria, on September 8, 1780, he marched the infantry along the road toward Charlotte. He sent Tarleton and the British Legion up the west side of the Wateree, with orders to cross at Blair's Ford, but during the march the Green Dragoon suffered a violent attack of yellow fever. His troops carried him to White's Mill on upper Fishing Creek. For two weeks he lay near death.

"Tarleton's illness is of the greatest inconvenience to me at present, as I not only lose his Services," Cornwallis wrote Balfour on September 21 in an oblique compliment to Sumter's guerrillas lurking along the Catawba, "but the whole Corps must remain quite useless in order to protect him."

Deciding that he could no longer delay his invasion of North Carolina, on September 22 Cornwallis detached Major McArthur and the 71st Regiment and left them to guard Tarleton. Then with Major George Hanger in command of the Green Horse, he resumed his march toward Charlotte. "Tarleton is vastly better!" he wrote Balfour. "His illness has been truly unfortunate," he confided in another reference to Sumter's men; "it has prevented our demolishing the militia while it was assembling."

As soon as Tarleton had recovered consciousness, McArthur's Highlanders strung a hammock across the uprights in a wagon, tumbled the dragoon into it, and set out on the Steel Creek road for Charlotte. "My spies bring me accounts this morning that the enemy have evacuated their camp at White's Mill and it is supposed they have crossed the river at Island Ford," Sumter informed General Jethro Sumner on September 23. "Perhaps they mean to be troublesome to you. They have been collecting guides for different purposes and have offered twenty guineas to any one who will conduct them privately to my camp."

With a new price of twenty guineas upon his head, Sumter turned his great energies into rousing the Up Country. He visited Colonel Elijah Clarke and his Georgians encamped at Island Ford on the Catawba. He called upon Colonel Pickens to forget his new allegiance and to embody the Whig militia around Ninety-Six. But while the Gamecock was hovering on the flank of the British, watching, writing, and planning, James Williams came to Island Ford.

The newly commissioned brigadier general "had his commission publicly read and required all the officers and men under his immediate command," said Colonel Hill in his *Memoirs,* "but much to his well deserved mortification they all to a man knowing his recent conduct in deserting his post and embezzling the public property as before mentioned refused to have anything to do with him or his commission and if he had not immediately left the camp he would have been stoned out of it."

During the confusion occasioned by Williams, Lord Cornwallis sent Lord Rawdon to surprise the Americans. As Rawdon, with his Volunteers of Ireland and the dragoons of the British Legion approached, Sumter's militia were assembling in convention. "Your author as chairman of the Convention called it together in order to deliberate on some plan respecting General Sumter's commission as it was protested by Williams," continued Hill in his *Memoirs,* "but before any progress was made in the business the firing commenced across the River between our guard and Rawdon's men. This soon broke up the convention and the army marched up the River and encamped that night in an uncommon thick wood, where we supposed we were safe from the horse of the enemy."

Hill resumed the convention. The militia voted to send a delegation to inform Governor Rutledge that they were determined to serve only under General Sumter. An adroit politician, Sumter made sure that the delegates were officers most loyal to him. He then agreed to turn the command over to Colonels Hill and Lacey until Rutledge settled the question of rank between him and Williams. On September 30 he appropriated $7,679 for the expenses of Colonels Richard Winn, Henry Hampton, and John Thomas "at the request of the people upon their being appointed by them to wait on Gov. Rutledge, and Gen. Gates at Hillsborough." Zealous and not entirely satisfied that the delegation would present his claims properly, the Gamecock followed them to Hillsboro for a personal interview with the governor.

Upon the arrival of Sumter and his colonels at Hillsboro on October 4, Governor Rutledge, also an astute politician, paid careful attention to their claims. He quickly realized his mistake in commissioning Williams, and on October 6, 1780, rectified it by giving Sumter the command in South Carolina. "Herewith you will receive a commission as brigadier general," he wrote the Gamecock. "You will be pleased to embody, as soon as possible, all the militia of South Carolina whom you can collect and hold them in readiness to co-operate with the Continental forces receiving orders for that purpose. In the meantime you will employ the men whom you assemble, in such manner as may render the most effectual service to that State. This must in a great measure depend upon the circumstances and your own judgement." But knowing Sumter's boldness, the governor added a caution: "Your own prudence will restrain you from entering on too hazardous Enterprises."

Colonel Francis Marion obeyed Gates's orders to ride to Kingstree and take command of the militia in Williamsburg. On August 17 he began a boat-burning ascent of the Santee. Although privately informed of the debacle at Camden, the little Huguenot kept the news from his men and continued to ride and burn. On the evening of August 24, 1780, he lay in bivouac at Nelson's Ferry.

After nightfall a deserting ensign of the Loyalist militia sneaked into Marion's camp. He reported that Captain Jonathan Roberts in command of an escort of thirty-eight men from the Prince of Wales and Loyalist regiments, who were marching a batch of prisoners of war to Charleston, had camped in great insecurity around Sumter's house on Great Savannah.

Before daylight Marion was in the saddle. After sending Colonel Hugh Horry and sixteen mounted infantrymen to seize the ford across Horse Creek, to cut off any reinforcements from Major

James Wemyss and the 63rd Regiment encamped in the High Hills, he swung across the fields toward the back of Sumter's house. In his haste Horry stumbled into a sentinel, changed his plans, and charged down the lane in front of the house. Marion then closed in upon the rear. His troops found the enemy asleep, their muskets stacked in the front yard. After a scuffle, they released one hundred and fifty Continentals of the Maryland Line.

Marion turned quickly back toward Kingstree. During his retreat several of his prisoners escaped, and all except three of the Marylanders forsook him. As he raced across Williamsburg, the militia also deserted. With fifty men he crossed Port's Ferry and pitched camp on the eastern bank of the Peedee.

Cornwallis ordered Wemyss to carry sword and torch into Williamsburg. "I should advise your sweeping the country entirely from Kingstree Bridge to Pedee, and returning by the Cheraws," he wrote on August 28. "I would have you disarm in the most rigid manner, all Persons who cannot be depended on and punish the concealment of Arms and ammunition with a total demolition of the plantation."

In consistency with British policy of fighting Americans with Americans, Cornwallis ordered the Loyalist militia to co-operate with Major Wemyss. In response Major Micajah Ganey called out the Tories between Peedee and Little Peedee rivers. On September 4, 1780, he marched to surprise Marion. But having learned of Ganey's plans, Marion also marched before day. At Blue Savannah on Little Peedee he ambushed and routed Ganey.

Having learned from Major James that Wemyss had invaded Williamsburg, Marion recrossed the Peedee and moved up to Indiantown. But the militia failed to come to his call. After finding his daring band hopelessly outnumbered by the Loyalists, provincial troops, and the 63rd Regiment under Wemyss, he began retreating toward Great White Marsh, an impassable morass at the head of Waccamaw River in eastern North Carolina.

Major Wemyss followed Marion to the Peedee. Upon the escape of his enemy he then began using the torch. "A sedition shop!" he cried as he fired the Indiantown Presbyterian Church. He burned the home and demolished the plantation of Major James. Then bayoneting sheep, shooting cattle, firing gristmills, and scorching plantations, he laid waste a swath fifteen miles wide on the seventy-mile route from Kingstree to Cheraw.

After the Gamecock had surrendered his brigade to the convention of officers, Colonels Hill and Lacey assumed command and moved up the Catawba to Tuckasegee Ford. From Colonel William Davidson they learned that Colonel Patrick Ferguson was marching a thousand well-trained Loyalists from Gilbert Town to Charlotte and that Shelby and Clarke were collecting the militia of the Carolinas and Georgia in hope of preventing his joining the British Army. They set off toward the rendezvous at Cowpens. As they were marching, General Williams overtook the corps, read his commission, and again tried to take charge. Hill informed him "that there is not an officer or man in the whole army who will submit to your command."

Next morning Williams again tried to take over Sumter's troops. Colonel Hill offered a compromise, but Williams spurned it, intimating "that by virtue of his commission he would command the whole." His declaration angered the militia. "He was told to absent himself and not attempt to march with us or the North Carolinians, as the consequences would be serious," Hill said in his *Memoirs*. Nevertheless Williams trailed along behind Sumter's brigade.

At Cowpens, a small eminence about six miles from Broad River, the militia held another convention. Because Colonel William Campbell and his Virginians from the Holston Valley had come the longest distance, they elected him commander in chief. Williams tried but failed to divert the assemblage from Ferguson to the Tories around Ninety-Six. Then Campbell selected about nine hundred who were well mounted and set out at dark, his horsemen plunging through the drizzling rain and stumbling over broken roads. Crossing Broad River at Cherokee Ford, they struggled onward and on the afternoon of October 7, 1780, found Colonel Ferguson encamped on the summit of King's Mountain.

After concealing their horses, Campbell and Shelby began leading their men up the road on the eastern end of the mountain. Colonel Lacey commanded Sumter's troops, for Colonel Hill, still suffering from the wound received at Hanging Rock, had been placed in command of the reserves. From his station at the foot, Hill condemned Ferguson's decision to defend the crown: "the sides of the mountain being very Rocky and steep as well as a great number of fallen and standing trees so that the Americans could attack his camp on all quarters."

Upon Campbell's order, the militiamen began closing in: firing, reloading, darting from tree to tree and log to log, and firing again. Onward they surged, and as Colonel Hill said, "there was very little military subordination as all that was required or expected was that every Officer and man should ascend the mountain so as to surround the enemy on all quarters which was promptly executed."

Major Ferguson and his Loyal infantry fought with great valor. Ferguson was a distinguished marksman, the inventor of a breech-loading rifle that he had demonstrated before King George. But he had trained his men in standard British tactics. When the rifle-men of Campbell and Shelby closed in, he "trusted much to the bayonet."

Ferguson's tactics were fatal. "In the commencement of the action he ordered a charge upon the Americans, and the ground was so rough as before mentioned that they were not able to overtake the Americans," said Hill. "In this manner four different charges were made and with the same success. By this time the Americans were within shot of the whole of their camp chiefly under cover of rocks and trees."

With his Tories surrounded by Whigs fighting Indian fashion, Patrick Ferguson decided to cut his way down King's Mountain. Brandishing his sword in his left hand, his right arm having been shattered at Brandywine, he shouted an order. At that moment he fell, pierced by seven balls. With compassion James Williams rushed to his aid, but a sheet of fire blazed around the Carolina brigadier. "On the top of the mountain, in the thickest of the fight, I saw Colonel Williams fall," said Major Thomas Young in his *Memoirs;* "and a braver or a better man never died upon the field of battle."

Upon the death of Ferguson, Captain Abraham DePeyster raised a white flag. But, as Hill said, "a number of men not knowing the intention of their signal continued to fire and it was some time before the officers could get them to cease firing."

The American militia killed or captured every member of Ferguson's command except a small party away on a forage. So complete was their victory that at Charlotte, only twenty-eight miles away, Lord Cornwallis, almost helpless with malaria, remained unaware of the catastrophe that had overwhelmed his reinforcement. On October 9 he begged Colonel Tarleton to lead his dragoons to locate Ferguson, but Tarleton refused, pleading weakness from the attack of yellow fever. Next day Cornwallis ordered him "to reinforce Ferguson wherever he could find him," Tarleton said in his *Campaigns*. "Accordingly Tarleton marched to Smith's Ford, below the forks of the Catawba, where he received certain information of the melancholy fate of Major Ferguson."

The destruction of Ferguson's corps completely deranged the British invasion of North Carolina. Assailed by swarms of militia inspired by the indefatigable Sumter, his supply line threatened by Marion, and his forces too weak and scattered to fight Gates, Lord Cornwallis decided to return to South Carolina. On October 14 he evacuated Charlotte and began retreating toward the Waxhaws. Upon reaching the Catawba, he gave way to an attack of malaria.

Lord Rawdon assumed command of the British Army. Troubled by his exposed position, he dispatched Tarleton and his dragoons to find a suitable spot for a winter camp. They galloped through the country between the Catawba and Broad rivers and finally selected Winnsboro. Rawdon followed, and after floundering through the swamps and creeks, their wagons saved by the vigorous efforts of the Tories, on October 29, 1780, the British Army marched into the village. Cornwallis and his officers seized the mansions of the Whigs, and his troops pitched tents on the rolling grounds of Mount Zion Academy.

While returning from Hillsboro, General Sumter met Major George Tate at Salisbury. From Tate he learned of the defeat of Ferguson. He became jubilant. With imagination kindled and hopes buoyant, he clapped spurs to his horse and galloped through the red hills below Charlotte. He found his brigade encamped on Bullock's Creek, a few miles below King's Mountain. During the

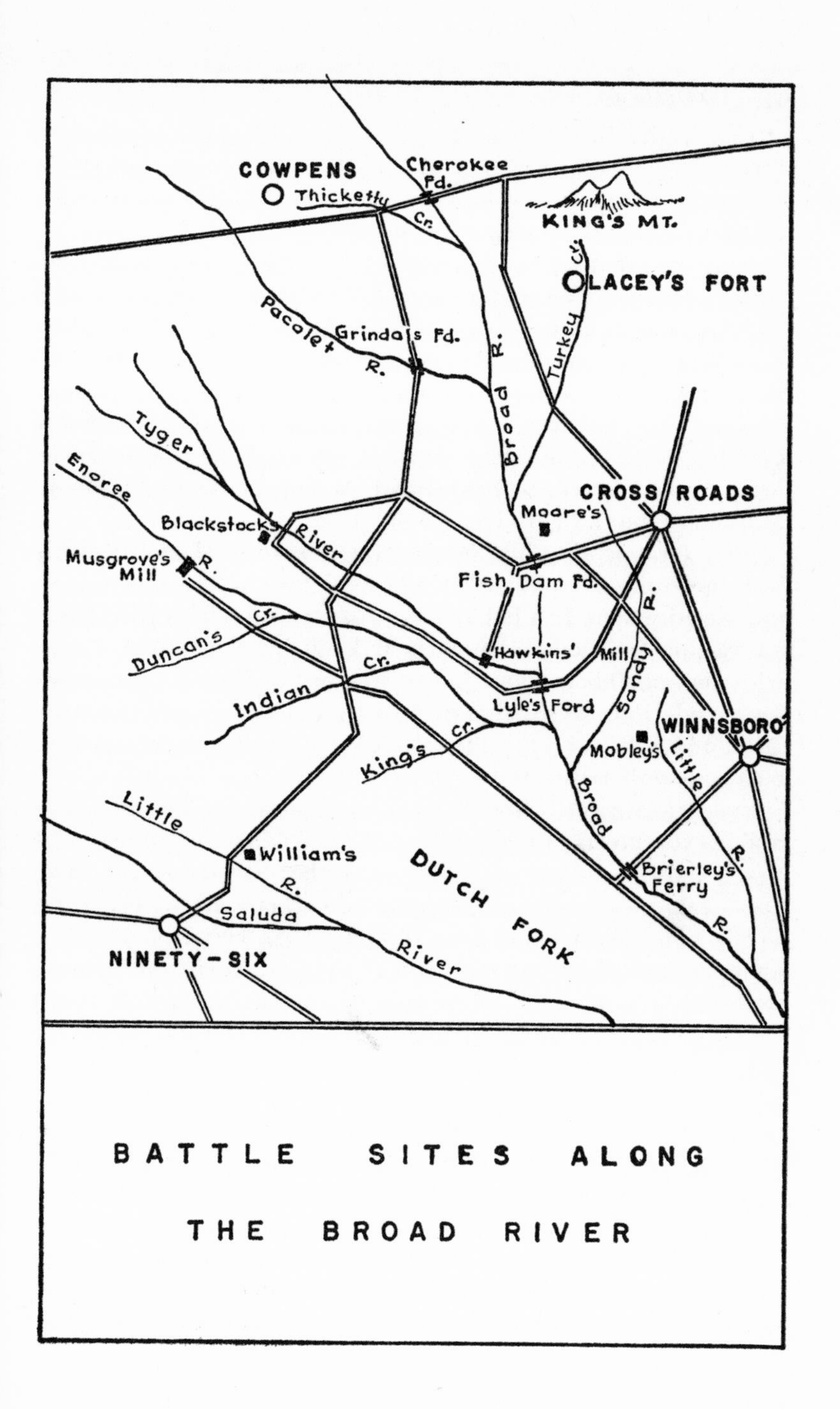

BATTLE SITES ALONG THE BROAD RIVER

retreat of the British from Charlotte, he disbanded his troops. But as soon as Cornwallis halted at Winnsboro, he recalled his men and encamped at Hill's Iron Works in the New Acquisition.

Sumter's brigade now became the advance corps in the American Army, for as soon as General Gates had learned of the victory at King's Mountain, he began deploying his troops for a campaign in South Carolina. In accordance with strategy he had discussed with Sumter in Hillsboro, he sent General William Smallwood to New Providence, General Daniel Morgan to Hanging Rock, and Colonel Davie to the Waxhaws, with orders to converge upon Camden. He asked Sumter to use his militia to create a diversion between the Catawba and the Broad. And on October 11 he wrote Marion, asking him "to create some little diversion below."

After disappearing into White Marsh, Francis Marion and his band lay quiet. He was gathering intelligence and waiting for an opportunity to make a bold stroke. His men were busy patrolling, scrounging for food and fodder, and nursing their comrades ill with malaria. Then Major James, who had returned to Williamsburg, rode into camp with stirring news. Colonel John Coming Ball and his Tories lay at Shepherd's Ferry on Black Mingo Creek, a crossing only twelve miles below Indiantown.

Emerging stealthily from White Marsh, on September 27 Marion and his volunteers cantered along the Waccamaw and bivouacked under the live oaks at Kingston. Next day, September 28, 1780, they swam their horses across Little Peedee, crossed the Peedee at Port's, and passed Lynches at Witherspoon's Ferry. After a fast gallop, at midnight they fell upon the Tories. In violent fighting, with muskets roaring and buckshot whistling around a tavern called the Red House, they drove Ball from his camp on Black Mingo.

Marion immediately recrossed the Peedee, dashed through the sand hills, and joined a concentration of Whigs at Amis' Mill on Drowning Creek. The leaders were assembling their militia to drive Major Wemyss from Cheraw. Before they could strike, however, Cornwallis ordered Wemyss to march to Camden.

Learning that Major Ganey had gathered the Tories drubbed at Blue Savannah and reinforced those under Colonel Benjamin Cassells at Georgetown, Marion decided to visit the little seaport.

"On Sunday the 8th instant, I set off from McGuines sixty-five miles from Georgetown," he reported to Gates on October 15, "and got in the town by twelve o'clock the next day."

Upon the approach of Marion's advance guard on October 9, 1780, Ganey and his Tories charged out to meet them. As the squadrons galloped past each other, redheaded Sergeant McDonald, a Scot from Cross Creek and one of Marion's staunchest fighters, slew Lieutenant Evans with his sword. When the furious swordsman turned upon the other Tories, Ganey wheeled back and fled. For two miles the Scotsman pursued him, straining and slashing, while their horses heaved and snorted. As they turned Richmond Corner, McDonald stood in his stirrups and lunged with his musket, the polished bayonet plunging into the back and bursting through the breast of Ganey.

"They were the most active persons against us," Marion said in reporting the fight with Evans and Ganey, "and the head of all the Tories on the lower part of Peedee."

Marion followed the retreating Tories. "I found Colonel Cassell in a redoubt, which enclosed the jail, a brick building," he reported to Gates. "After reconnoitering it around, I found it too strong to storm with such men as I had."

Upon returning to Amis', Marion received Gates's letter requesting him to create "some little diversion." Back he rode into Williamsburg, and soon his scouts reported that Colonel Benjamin Tynes, a former member of Thomson's rangers and now commandant of the Loyalist militia in the High Hills, had called out his regiment and encamped on Tearcoat Swamp, a small stream in the forks between the Pocotaligo and Black rivers. Moving swiftly up Black River, on October 25 Marion found the Tories assembled on an old muster ground on the Tearcoat. Charging into their camp in the late evening while the farm boys were chatting, singing, and playing, he sent them squandering into the Tearcoat.

After running down and capturing Colonel Tynes, Marion's horsemen galloped up to Camden, sending a shiver through Turnbull's New York Volunteers. Quickly returning to the High Hills, they encamped at Singleton's Mill, thus cutting the British supply line between Nelson's and Camden. Colonel Balfour rushed fifty soldiers to Moncks Corner. "But," he wrote Cornwallis, "the numbers and spirits of the Rebell partys so far outbalances that of our militia, that a post in the High Hills of Santee, or at Kingstree Bridge, is now absolutely necessary, otherwise communication is at an end betwixt the Army and this Town."

As soon as the British Army had reached Winnsboro, Colonel Turnbull wrote Tarleton, begging him to bring his dragoons and drive Marion from the supply route. In shuffling his troops to honor Turnbull's plea, Lord Cornwallis ordered Major Wemyss, who had mounted his 63rd infantry on horses stolen from Whigs in his wandering from Kingstree to Camden, to move up to Winnsboro. In his letter Major John Money, aide to Cornwallis, wrote: "This damned Georgetown business has totally altered the arrangements intended for you."

In accordance with Gates's strategy the American forces began converging upon Camden. Sumter moved down from Hill's Iron Works and encamped at Stallings' plantation on Fishing Creek. "It has been agreed that I shall march as near to Winnsboro as can be done with safety," he confided to Colonel Winn. "This will draw Tarleton and a large body of infantry after us. This will weaken Lord Cornwallis so much that General Smallwood, with the Continental troops and what North Carolinians can be collected, is to fall on Cornwallis."

Upon learning that Tarleton had ridden toward the High Hills, thereby shortening the reach of Cornwallis, Sumter began creeping nearer Winnsboro. After sweeping along Sandy River and quieting the Tories in Mobley's settlement, he boldly encamped at Moore's Mill, only thirty miles from the British army.

Upon the departure of Tarleton and his Green Horse, Cornwallis assigned Major Wemyss the task of scouting. With his mounted infantry and a squadron of Tarleton's horse, Wemyss began patrolling the roads between the Broad and the Catawba. On November 7 he raced into Winnsboro with exciting news. General Sumter had encamped at Moore's.

After listening to Wemyss' plea, Cornwallis agreed to his trying his spurs against the Gamecock. Late on the following afternoon the major headed up the road east of Broad River, followed by the dragoons under Lieutenant Moore Hovenden and mounted infantry under Lieutenant John Stark. Beside him rode a guide named Sealy, a notorious Tory that day paroled by Sumter. Just before marching, Wemyss had called in Sealy and five dragoons and with barbaric candor assigned them the job of finding and slaying the Gamecock.

But Sumter had left Moore's. After paroling Sealy, who had aroused suspicion by pretending conversion to Whig principles, the Gamecock moved five miles down Broad River. After dark he

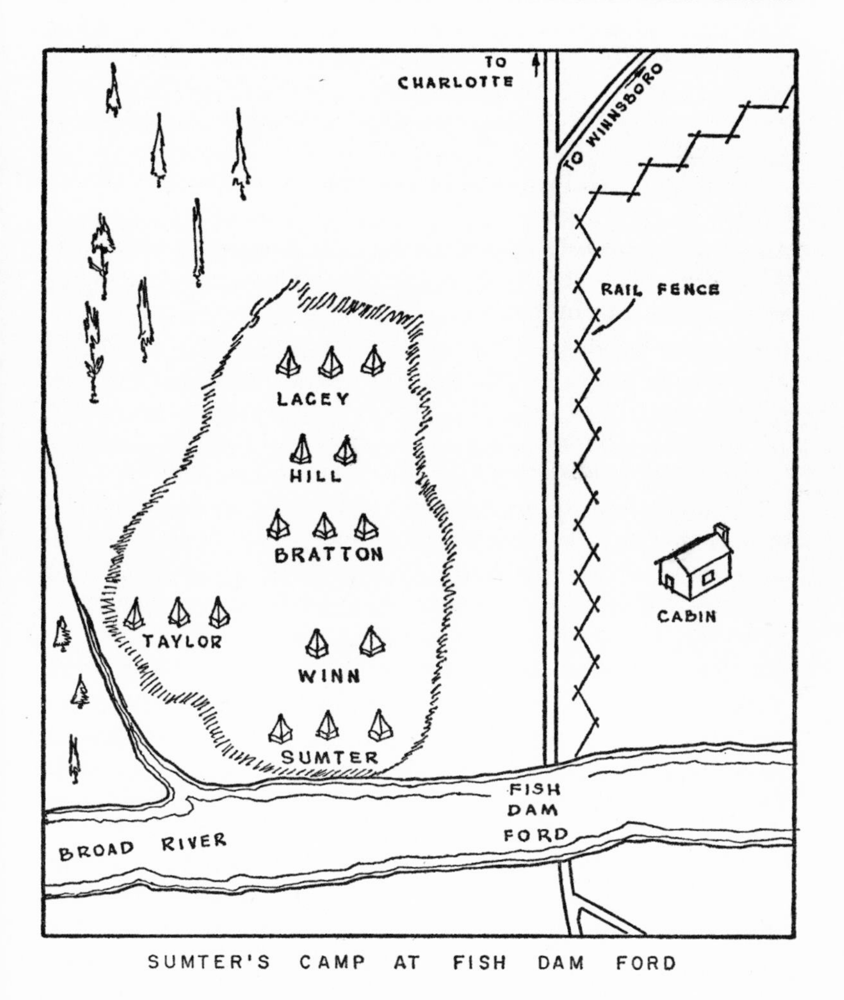

SUMTER'S CAMP AT FISH DAM FORD

bivouacked at Fish Dam Ford, a place where Indians or early settlers had built an ingenious weir of stones to trap fish swimming up the shallow stream. "The General takes post immediately at the ford," said Colonel Winn in his *Notes;* "Colonel Winn to his left directly on the bank of the river; Colonel Taylor on a square to the left of Colonel Winn; and Lacey, Bratton, and Hill in front about three or four hundred yards."

Riding briskly along at the head of his troops, about one o'clock on the morning of November 9, 1780, Wemyss stumbled into this encampment. "Wemyss forgot that he is an infantry officer and rode into battle," Cornwallis chuckled sardonically. But the major paid for his mistake. Of the first five shots from Sumter's vedettes, one struck him in the arm and another in the leg. When Wemyss fell from his horse, Lieutenant Stark, to whom the major had confided neither his orders nor his plans, led a cavalry charge down the ridges. As his riders passed in front of the sentinels' campfires, their silhouettes made splendid targets, and Sumter's marksmen began toppling them from their saddles.

Sealy and his dragoons "strained down to make prisoner of the General, which they nearly effected owing to the orderly sergeant not giving notice of the alarm in time," said Colonel Winn. "Before he could put on his clothes, they were up with him. By jumping a fence and running through a briar patch he saved himself." Hatless, barefoot, and without coat or trousers, he crawled under an overhanging ledge above Broad River.

There he lay shivering in the November frost, listening to the running, shouting, and firing of his men. After the tumult had died, he eased out and found his horse. "When General Sumter and myself met at Nixson's," said Colonel Winn, "he informed me when he was cut off, being in his shirt sleeves, he verily believed he would have perished from cold had he not got a horse, getting on him bareback and hugging his neck."

At daybreak Sumter began assembling his troops. Before crossing Broad River, however, he prepared a battle report for General Smallwood. "I have just time to inform you that I was attacked about three o'clock this morning by a party of dragoons and mounted infantry, about two hundred in number, with a large party of Tories, under the command of Major Wemyss," he wrote.

"The attack was as precipitate and violent as can be conceived. They first charged on horseback and were repulsed. The infantry immediately dismounted, formed and charged with bayonet. The cavalry at the same time charged on the right of Major Wemyss division. The horse was again beat back in disorder. The infantry succeeded better, and made the division under Colonel Taylor give way, but not until the whole division had fired, and several of the men been bayonetted upon the spot, and, for want of the means of defending themselves, gave way. At the same instant, so warm a fire was poured down upon the enemy from Colonel Lacey's and Hawthorn's divisions, that they broke and moved off some distance, where they mounted and sent off some of their wounded, who were soon after followed by the whole.

"I have twenty-five prisoners, among which is Major Wemyss, wounded, one surgeon and Sergt. Major, & seven killed. A parcel of excellent horses and arms were taken. My loss was four killed; ten wounded. Officers and men generally behaved with a great deal of bravery, reserving their fire until the Enemy were within ten steps of them. There was a party, who had a person acquainted with me, who brought them on through every opposition, and enquired for me upon the alarm posts, and it was with the greatest difficulty that I escaped being cut to pieces before the pickets got in."

Before retreating to Winnsboro, Stark gathered his wounded, removed them to a cabin, lighted a fire, and left them under a flag. Next morning, while examining the papers of Major Wemyss, Sumter found a list of the houses burned in the foray between Kingstree and Cheraw. Knowing that should his militia read this incrimination, it would become the death warrant for Wemyss, the Gamecock, just barely escaped from assassination, generously tossed the paper into the flames.

When Tarleton reached Singleton's Mill, he found only dead campfires. Hoping to lure Marion's horsemen into an attack, he began sending small detachments of his dragoons through the High Hills. Learning that Colonel Marion was encamped on Jack's Creek, on November 7 he ambuscaded his corps around the home of Mary Richardson, widow of the late General Richard Richardson. Attracted by the light of the campfires, Marion began moving up. But Widow Richardson slipped fearlessly through Tarleton's lines, found her son Richard, and sent him to warn the Carolinians. Wheeling back, they rode Richbourg's Mill Dam across Jack's Creek. As they went into bivouac, Marion exclaimed, "Now we are safe!"

During the night a Tory prisoner escaped and before daylight on November 8, 1780, the guards led him to Tarleton. He reported the location of Marion's bivouac, and immediately the dragoon roused his men for a chase. When he reached Richbourg's, however, he found that the Carolinians had already fled toward Kingstree. All morning the horsemen raced. Up Jack's Creek and down Pocotaligo River Marion galloped. Colonel Tarleton followed through field and wood and swamp, and after covering twenty-four miles in seven hours, stopped at Ox Swamp. Glancing from his tired horses to the roadless bog, Tarleton shouted to his green-coated dragoons, "Come, my boys! Let's go back and pick a fight with the Gamecock. As for this damned old fox, the devil couldn't catch him!"

Upon reaching Nelson's Ferry, Tarleton began suppressing rebellion with the torch. On November 9 and 10 he burned thirty houses. Before crossing Jack's Creek, he fired Sumter's Mills. He then rode on to punish Widow Richardson. In his cruelty he even dug up old General Richardson who had lain in the family grave yard for six weeks that he might "look upon the face of such a brave man."

On November 11 Tarleton again camped at Singleton's Mill. There he issued a proclamation calling upon the inhabitants of the High Hills to make their submission. Before the commandant of the hated British Legion could receive any submission, however, a courier handed him a letter. "Major Wemyss attacked Sumter at Fish Dam at one o'clock this morning, contrary to his plan, which was to wait until day light; the consequences is that Wemyss is wounded and left, and about twenty men," Cornwallis informed him. "I am under the greatest anxiety for Ninety-Six, and trust you will lose no time in returning to me."

Disgruntled over the escape of the Swamp Fox, the Green Dragoon turned back to pick his fight with the Gamecock. As he galloped toward Winnsboro, he met courier after courier. "Sumter is at Hawkins Mill on Tyger River with what he calls a thousand men, bragging much of his Victory; our friends are all in the utmost Terror and running down to the Congaree as fast as possible." Cornwallis wrote on November 13. "I rather think the Legion had better march up the Wateree as you will then threaten Lacey, Smallwood & Sumter."

Cornwallis then sent a note to Major McArthur, guarding Brierley's Ferry with the 71st Regiment: "Tarleton is advanced to Camden and I hope we shall soon put a stop to Mr. Sumter's bragging."

Chapter 8 VICTORY AT BLACKSTOCK'S

AFTER crossing Broad River at Fish Dam Ford, General Sumter marched to Hawkins' Mill on the Tyger and a junction with some Georgians under Colonels John Twiggs, Elijah Clarke, and Benjamin Few. With ten colonels and a thousand men in his corps, on November 13 he encamped at Nixon's plantation on the Enoree. As he prepared to move against renegade Colonel Moses Kirkland and the Loyalists who had fortified the home of General Williams on Little River, he began sending out raiding parties. He sent Major Samuel Hammond to frighten the Tories around Faust's in the lower Dutch Fork. He ordered Colonel Taylor to raid Summer's Mills. And he dispatched one hundred and fifty horsemen to Brierley's to spy out the camp of Major McArthur.

In the meantime the Green Dragoon and his legion were racing toward Broad River to pick his fight with the Gamecock. Early on the morning of November 18 he reached McArthur's camp. As his troops were dirty and his horses tired, he sent them down to the river's edge to freshen up. At that moment Sumter's horsemen galloped up to the opposite bank. Without dismounting, they discharged their rifles, knocking over a horse and a soldier of the 63rd Regiment. Quickly unlimbering his three-pounder, Tarleton sent the attackers scurrying back to Nixon's.

Concealing the green coats of the British Legion and flaunting the red of McArthur's Highlanders, so that Sumter's scouts would not discover his return from the Santee, Tarleton began preparing for a campaign. He sent his infantry across Broad River in ferryboats with instructions to seize the opposite bank. After dark he led his dragoons across a ford three miles below Brierley's. At ten o'clock that night he encamped several miles inside the Dutch Fork.

On November 19 Colonel Tarleton sent parties of scouts across the Enoree and toward the Saluda. Late that evening they returned with intelligence that Sumter was moving to attack the post at Williams'. At daybreak Tarleton marched up the Enoree and camped near the mouth of Indian Creek. But during the night a malcontent of the 63rd Regiment deserted, stole a horse, and galloped off to warn the Americans. Before day on November 20, 1780, Sumter knew that Tarleton, with the British Legion, McArthur's 71st Regiment, the mounted infantry of the 63rd, and a detachment of Royal artillerists, was moving along the Enoree. He realized that his enemy was trying to cut him off from the fords and then drive him against Cruger's troops at Ninety-Six.

The Gamecock was ready to stand and fight. But could his militia face a charge of the powerful British dragoons? He called in his colonels. They voted to take position behind some strong natural defense. Colonel Thomas Brandon, campaigning in familiar country, knew that the strongest position they could reach was the plantation of Captain William Blackstock, with its woods, fences, and buildings situated among the steep hills above the Tyger. Heartened by their counsel, before daylight Sumter wheeled around and began retiring. At the Enoree he posted a detachment under Captain Patrick Carr to watch for Tarleton. He also left the Tory prisoners with Carr. Then, after fording the river, he began forcing his march toward Blackstock's.

Tarleton also marched before daylight. Striking Sumter's trail in the late morning, he, too, began forcing his march. As the van of his dragoons approached the Enoree, Captain Carr and his militiamen fled, leaving the prisoners. Before the Tories could identify themselves, the dragoons were upon them, their long sabers flashing and slaying. "The advance guard of the British dragoons charged this body," said Tarleton in his *Campaigns* trying to conceal his mistake, "and defeated them with considerable slaughter."

All day the Green Dragoon chased the Gamecock. About three o'clock he realized that Sumter would pass the Tyger before dark. To prevent this he ordered his infantry and artillery to slow down to a normal pace and he set out afresh with his cavalry.

After retreating through the hills between the Enoree and the Tyger, his troops pausing neither for food nor water, about four o'clock Sumter reached Blackstock's. There he turned and faced his pursuer. After stacking arms, the backwoodsmen began building fires of twigs and dead branches. Calmly they skewered their meat and began baking wads of dough on the ends of long green sticks. While they were eating, Mrs. Mary Dillard, who had seen the British line of march from her home six miles below Blackstock's, galloped into camp and told Sumter that Tarleton was rushing up without infantry or artillery.

A few minutes later Colonel Taylor came racing in, his wagons loaded with flour from Summer's Mills. As they burst through Sumter's rear guard under Major McJunkin, Tarleton's van charged them, their sabers flashing and whistling. When the enemy turned and made a stand on the hill opposite Blackstock's, the Gamecock realized that Tarleton was waiting for his infantry and artillery. Basing his conjecture upon Mrs. Dillard's report, he shrewdly guessed that the reinforcements could not arrive before night. He now faced a difficult choice. He could hold his defensive position until dark and then ford the Tyger and disband his brigade, or he could pick a fight with the Green Dragoon.

As Sumter faced his enemy, he was in a position of great tactical advantage. On his right lay a long, steep hill crowned with several eminences and thickly wooded with oak, pine, and hickory. On his left, as Colonel William Hill afterward reported in his *Memoirs,* for "about a quarter of a mile there was a very large and strong fence not made with common rails but with small trees notched one on the other." On a hill at the end of this lane stood Blackstock's house. Adjacent to it were a barn and three smaller houses, all solidly built from hewn oak logs. Below the house lay a field of about fifty acres sloping gently down to a spring branch. Behind him the hill sloped steeply away to the swiftly flowing Tyger. And in front the road wound back to the hill on which Tarleton was rapidly mustering the British.

Sumter established his command post west of the spot where the road crossed Blackstock's hill. He then stretched a cordon of sharpshooters across the mouth of the lane. He stationed Colonel Henry Hampton and his Broad River riflemen in the barns around Blackstock's house. Along the lane and across the upper end of the field he strung the Georgians under Colonel Twiggs.

Below the wooded eminences on his right he spread the troops under Colonels Taylor, Bratton, McCall, Hill, and Lacey, with orders for Lacey's men to creep as close as possible to the British. And behind him on the slope above Tyger River, Sumter placed his reserves and a small rear guard under Colonel Winn.

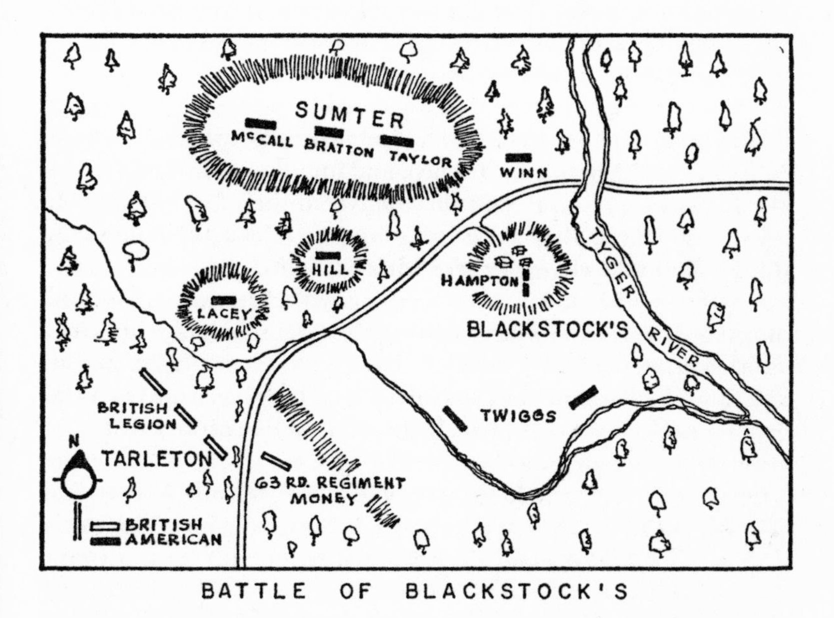

BATTLE OF BLACKSTOCK'S

As the Blackstock family watched Sumter's maneuvers, they remained indoors, frightened but resolute. Captain Blackstock was away in Colonel Roebuck's regiment, but spunky as her husband was brave, Mrs. Mary Blackstock threw a shawl around her shoulders and went to call upon Sumter. "General," she exclaimed tartly, "I won't have any fighting around my house."

But Mary Blackstock was too late. While Sumter was disposing his troops, Tarleton was making his countermoves. As fearless as the Briton was, he did not wish to pit two hundred and seventy British troops against a thousand American militiamen. He wished to pin them against the river and harass them until the arrival of his cannon and the kilted Highlanders of the 71st Regiment. So he ordered Major John Money to dismount the infantry of the

63rd, cross to the right of the road, and take a position at the lower end of Blackstock's field. To the left of the road, their flank against the wooded hill and their front poised for a charge down hill, Tarleton formed the dragoons of the legion.

Sumter was excited as he watched the British. Always thinking in large numbers, grand strategy, and massive tactics, the Gamecock was at the peak of his career. He was eager to fight, and like a blooded cock, he ruffled his hackles, spread his wings, and flashed his shining gaffs. Impetuously he ordered Colonel Few and Major McJunkin with four hundred infantrymen to maneuver down the sloping field, across the branch, and uphill against Money. His troops obeyed promptly, but they delivered their fire at too great a distance. While they were struggling to reload their muskets, Money's infantry charged them with bayonets.

American militiamen were familiar with firearms. They had known men to recover after being accidentally shot while hunting. But they were afraid of cold steel. They could not stand before the saber and the bayonet. Twigg's men began backing away from the eighty men under Money. Slowly they fell back uphill and into the woods behind Blackstock's.

But in his eagerness Major Money led the 63rd into disaster. He charged too near Blackstock's house, and at two hundred yards Hampton's riflemen opened on the red coats with golden epaulettes. Lieutenant Cope tumbled into the grass. A few seconds later Lieutenant Gibson fell. As the 63rd neared the woods, Money slumped to the ground.

While his infantry were battling on the eastern end of Blackstock's field, Sumter galloped headlong over to Colonel Lacey and ordered him to flank Tarleton's left and attack the idle dragoons. So intent were the British in watching the fighting across the valley that Lacey stole unperceived to within seventy-five yards of them. At his command, his troops opened with buckshot. Twenty dragoons tumbled from their saddles. But, as Tarleton said in his *Campaigns:* "Lieutenant Skinner bravely repulsed the detachment which threatened the flank."

Realizing that his infantry teetered on the verge of disaster, Colonel Tarleton ordered his dragoons to go to their support. As the Green Horse charged, huzzaing and swinging their long sabers,

Tarleton wheeled toward the prostrate form of Major Money. Springing from his horse as the bullets of sharpshooters whistled around him, he lifted his comrade into his saddle, crawled up behind, and bore him to safety.

"The Americans," said Colonel Hill in his *Memoirs,* "having the advantage of the before mentioned fence together with the thick wood just by the fence that before they got through the lane in their front both men and horses fell so fast that the way was nearly stopped up—a retreat was then ordered which was a pleasing sight for the Americans to behold—so many falling either by wounds or stumbling over the dead horses or men."

After witnessing Lacey's attack, Sumter and his escorts turned back toward the command post. Rashly he spurred his charger forward to get a better look at the retreating enemy. But through the drizzle a platoon of the 63rd with muskets still loaded descried an American officer with golden epaulettes. Instantly their guns swung into aim. Sumter turned sideways in his saddle, throwing his right shoulder between his heart and their fire. Five buckshot ripped into his chest. Another plunged under his right shoulder, chipped a splinter from his backbone, and came to rest in his left shoulder. "Captain Gabriel Brown was killed on my left hand and General Sumter was on my right," Captain David Hopkins wrote his sons. "It happened from one platoon of the enemy on their retreat."

The Gamecock only gritted his teeth and rode through the gathering dusk. When he reached his command post, his aides helped him dismount. Captain Robert McKelvey heard something sprinkling on the dry November leaves. Glancing quickly at the erect, powerful general, he saw a stream of blood trickling down his coat and spattering on the ground.

"General, you are wounded!" he cried.

"I am wounded," Sumter replied grimly. "Say nothing about it."

As his disabled right arm dangled limp from his pierced shoulder, Sumter asked Colonel Hampton to thrust his sword back into the scabbard and call a man to lead off his horse.

"Say nothing about it," the Gamecock again cautioned McKelvey and Hampton. He knew that the morale of the militiamen depended largely on that of their leaders. In the climactic moment of his glorious victory over Banastre Tarleton, Thomas Sumter did not wish rumor to spoil his triumph. But as he stood unflinching at his post, his strength ebbing rapidly, he realized that he had become too weak to direct his troops. Calmly he told Hampton, "Request Colonel Twiggs to take the command."

The chick of the blue hen had passed the zenith of his fighting. His aides carried him to a bed in Blackstock's house. Soon he was scarcely able to speak. He lay quietly for a while and then, unwilling to admit pain to his subordinates, he called Soldier Tom.

"Tom," he whispered, "I'm badly wounded. Get the doctor."

Summoned from aiding the wounded on the field, Dr. Brownfield realized that the Gamecock was bleeding to death. Quickly turning him over on his stomach and bidding him grasp the bedposts, Brownfield ripped off the bloody coat and slashed into Sumter's shoulder. Without anesthetic he began probing for the ball, while his patient writhed, his great muscles quivering and knotting. After removing the buckshot and staunching the blood, Brownfield put a field dressing upon the wound.

Sumter was now barely conscious, and his aides decided to move him to safety. With ingenuity they made a crude litter by stretching an uncured bull hide over two poles and lashing these between two horses. Into this they laid the helpless Gamecock.

Colonel Lacey and a bodyguard of a hundred of his stoutest troops took charge of the prostrate general. They lighted a flare and crept slowly down Blackstock's hill and forded the Tyger. Through the darkness and chill November rain they escorted him safely to Adam Goudelock's house at Grindal Shoals on Pacolet River. There a doctor gave him a sedative and dressed his shoulder. After crossing Broad River, Lacey and his men halted and threw up a small redoubt on the north side of Turkey Creek, while an escort of five men hurried the Gamecock on to his old camp on Steel Creek in the New Acquisition.

As soon as Colonel Twiggs took command, he began consolidating the victory. He ordered the militia to pursue the retreating 63rd. When the British dragoons wheeled back from Blackstock's lane, Major James Jackson and his Georgians dashed after them and captured thirty riderless horses. Twiggs then sent out parties to rescue the wounded. Making no distinction between Americans and Britons, his men brought all they could find to the shelter of the houses. "It is but doing bare justice to General Sumter to declare that the strictest humanity took place upon the present occasion," observed Lieutenant Roderick Mackenzie in his *Strictures* on Tarleton's *Campaigns*. "They were supplied with every comfort in his power."

After the dead and wounded had been counted, Colonel Myddelton prepared a battle report. "About 4 o'clock, P.M., the videttes in front apprised us of the enemy's approach by the discharge of their pieces," he wrote. "In a few minutes they appeared within 400 yards of our camp, dismounted their infantry, and formed in a field. The General detached two parties to skirmish with them, while he founded his line upon an eminence and posted some men behind the houses and fences at the foot of it. The parties detached kept up a loose fire, and the enemy retired to a wood, under the cover of which they made their disposition of cavalry and infantry for an attack, and immediately advanced to the charge. The conflict was warm, and the enemy were repulsed; they rallied, made a second charge, and were repulsed again; they made a third, and our people in front were obliged to yield to the impression, but the fire from the eminence gave them such an effectual check, that they quitted the field in great disorder, and retired with the utmost precipitation. We pursued, but the approach of night prevented our taking any advantage of their plight. They left 92 dead, and 100 wounded upon the field. Our loss is but trifling, only three killed and four wounded—among the latter is General Sumter."

When the British troops had returned to their original positions, Colonel Tarleton began retreating. He led his troops into bivouac on a hill about two miles from the field of battle. Despite his own gallant behavior, for the first time in his meteoric career the Green Dragoon had been defeated. Determined to wipe out his humiliation, he spent the evening getting ready for a second pitting with the Gamecock.

But Tarleton was disappointed. After rain and darkness settled over the field, Twiggs ordered Colonel Winn to light campfires and keep them burning during the night. He then dismissed the other colonels. Silently they led their men down hill and forded the Tyger. Safely across, they disbanded their regiments and allowed their men to go home from the war. Sumter's powerful corps disintegrated. Many of his militiamen did not return to the field again during the Revolution.

"Sumter is defeated, his corps dispersed, & himself dangerously wounded," Tarleton said in his report to Cornwallis. "But my Lord I have lost men—50 killed & wounded & Officers which are losses to the public Service—Poor Money is wounded but not dangerously—Gibson and Cope killed—Also numerous Legion wounded & every officer I have my own included killed or wounded —The Rebels were commanded by Sumter—Clarke Lacey Brannon were also present—1000 in all & were attacked by 190 Cav'y & 90 Inf'y on most unapproachable ground."

Realizing that Cornwallis would demand his reasons for fighting Sumter on unapproachable ground, Tarleton wrote a postscript. "The Enemy attacked the 63d & forced me to action before the cannon, Legion and light Inf'y could be brought up."

Master of the field, with the dead, wounded, and prisoners in his possession, Tarleton asked Major McArthur to bring his wagons and a surgeon to Blackstock's. Cornwallis immediately sent Dr. John Stewart. Upon their arrival Tarleton crossed the Tyger and began pursuit of the Americans. For two days he trailed them. At the head of the Tyger he turned back, and from there wrote a second report to Cornwallis, giving a detailed account of his repulse. "It was difficult for me to maneuvre for want of intelligence and I had to pass the Ennoree three miles before I could strike at Sumter—You will see my Lord by my letter of yesterday that I could only bring up 80 of 63rd and 190 cavalry—I did not mean to attack Sumter, only to harass and lie close to him till I could bring up the rest of the Corps, as he could never pass the Tyger if I had attacked.

"The 63rd were attacked by the Enemy which brought on the affair."

The British commanders feared Thomas Sumter. They tried every means to kill him. Lord Rawdon offered Colonel Lacey five hundred guineas to betray him. Another offered twenty guineas to anyone leading him to Sumter's camp at Island Ford. Major

Wemyss commissioned Sealy and his confederates to murder him in his tent at Fish Dam Ford.

Tarleton now attempted to finish off the helpless man. "Three young men who were of Ferguson's Corps have promised to fix Sumter immediately," he wrote openly to Cornwallis. "I have promised them for the deed 50 guineas each in case he falls into our hands."

"I have no doubt but your victory will be attended with as good consequences to our affairs as it is with honour and credit to yourself," Cornwallis replied in tacitly approving the plan to assassinate the Gamecock. "I shall be very glad to hear that Sumter is in a position to give us no further trouble; he certainly has been our greatest plague in this country."

"I hope tomorrow to complete the destruction of our enemies in this district," Tarleton replied on November 25. "Sumter is now reported dead."

Chapter 9 WOUNDS BEYOND HEALING

THOMAS Sumter was already recovering. Snug in bed at Colonel Samuel Watson's home on Sugar Creek, with Soldier Tom waiting on him and the militia of the New Acquisition standing guard, the Gamecock had passed the crisis. His powerful body animated by an indomitable spirit, he had overcome his loss of blood and had emerged from his ordeal with mind clear and active. Although still feverish and wracked by pain, he was eager to renew his campaign. From his bed he had already begun directing the Carolina militia. His scouts had intercepted Tarleton's letter to McArthur, and he had ordered a detachment to ambush the Highlanders and seize their wagons.

Upon learning that General Gates had returned to Charlotte, Sumter dictated to an aide on November 25, the day of Tarleton's report of his death: "I am exceedingly happy to find that you have moved forward with the Continental Army, as Tarleton's Legion, 71, 63 and some light companies were sent to destroy my command near seventy miles distant from Lord Cornwallis. He must, therefore, be in a weak situation and easily taken, the advantage of an opportunity which you no doubt sir, would wish to avail yourself of."

In spite of his ebullience, the Gamecock was wretched and after hinting that Gates should immediately throw the reorganized American Army against Cornwallis, he admitted his own impotence. "My hurry, and distress I am with my wound will I hope sufficiently apologize for my being so laconic," he said. "I am without medicine or necessaries of any kind, and feel the want of them much."

Upon receiving Sumter's letter, Gates ordered Dr. William Read of the Continental Hospital at Salisbury to rush to the Gamecock. On November 29 Governor Rutledge, freshly arrived in Charlotte, called for an escort of cavalry, climbed into his saddle, and galloped off to the camp in the New Acquisition. Sumter welcomed the visit of the governor, but he refused to enter the hospital at Salisbury. Weak but filled with fire and enterprise, he pleaded for an immediate strike against Cornwallis.

After the conference, Rutledge turned back to Charlotte exceedingly depressed. He admired the indomitable courage of the Gamecock, but he was moved to tears on seeing him and his ragged guerrillas. He sickened at the ruins of Hill's Iron Works.

Sumter was more cheerful than Rutledge. "I feel myself something relieved from the fever this morning, but my shoulder is still painful," he wrote Gates on December 1. "I have this moment received from undoubted authority, that Earl Cornwallis still lies at Winnsborough with less than five hundred and much exposed."

Still feverish, as well as excited by the opportunity of striking Cornwallis, Sumter unwisely returned to command. At the request of the governor, he ordered a wagon convoy dispatched to bring supplies from Newbern. Moved by his own terrible suffering, he advanced Captain Richard Hampton sixty thousand dollars in certificates to purchase medical supplies. He ordered his militia to collect and store ammunition at Hill's Iron Works. With or without Continentals, as soon as he could ride he would attack Cornwallis.

His men rode into camp with some captured Tories. Better than any of his contemporaries, except perhaps Francis Marion, Sumter understood the hopes and fears of the Loyalists. He knew that they were less interested in political theory than in the practical effects of theft, arson, and murder. He knew that most of them were men of conscience. Before sending the prisoners on to Gates, he walked among them, talking, pleading, forgiving, and inviting them to join his troops. He then wrote the general laconically, "I thought proper to reduce the Number of Tory prisoners by liberating and taking into the Service such as were judged to be good men."

While the Gamecock slowly recuperated at Watson's, accumulating supplies and recruiting his brigade, two movements of great importance were under way. Congress had sent a new commanding general to the South, and Lord Cornwallis had ordered reinforcements from Virginia. Both the American general and the British troops were moving rapidly toward South Carolina.

As early as November 11 Smallwood had informed Sumter that the Continental Congress was recalling Gates. The offensive against Winnsboro now collapsed as the Continentals waited for their new commander in chief. On December 2, 1780, Major General Nathanael Greene rode into Charlotte.

With a distinguished reputation throughout the army, Nathanael Greene, stocky, well-built, and powerful, with curly brown hair and ruddy complexion, was a fighting Quaker. Born in Rhode Island, the son of a farmer and blacksmith, he had run a forge at Coventry. Self-educated but widely read, especially in the literature of war, he had early joined the Kentish Guards, an act for which he was expelled from the Society of Friends.

Entering politics, Greene became the military leader in Rhode Island, and soon after the battle of Lexington he was appointed brigadier general. Hard, sober, and conscientious, he quicky molded his troops into the best-disciplined corps in the American Army. After distinguished fighting around New York and at Trenton, Brandywine, and Monmouth, in 1778 he accepted appointment as Commissary General of the American Army.

When the Continental Congress passed a resolution inquiring into the conduct of General Gates at Camden, Congressman John Mathews of South Carolina suggested that Washington appoint General Greene commander of the Southern Department. "You have your wish in the officer appointed to the Southern command," Washington wrote Mathews. "I think I am giving you a general, but what can a general do without men, without arms, without clothing, without shoes, without provisions?"

For two days after reaching Charlotte, Greene rested, conferred with Gates, listened to reports, and consulted Governor Rutledge. Knowing that Sumter had great knowledge and understanding of conditions in South Carolina, the governor wrote him:

Charlotte, Sunday
Dec. 3rd, 1780

To

Brigadier Genl. Sumter,

Dr. Sir:—

Major Genl. Green is arrived. I wish you wd. come to or near this place as fast as your Health and the Weather will permit.

In Haste Yrs.
J. Rutledge

On December 4 General Greene assumed command of the American Army. Because Sumter was too weak to come to Charlotte even though Rutledge had sent his driver with a horse and carriage for him, on December 8 the general and the governor set out to visit the Gamecock. They found him convalescing in the home of John Price, his armorer, who lived in a strong stone house near the Tuckasegee Ford. In a long and animated interview, they discussed strategy, and Sumter pleaded that Greene attack Cornwallis.

From his keen intelligence service the Gamecock knew every move of the British. A spy whom he had sent to Charleston reported that large numbers of British reinforcements were arriving from both Virginia and England. After debarking in Charleston, units of reinforcements were moving toward the front. Two hundred recruits for the 7th Regiment had arrived from England, but Colonel Balfour declared them unfit to march with the regulars. Afraid that Marion's relentless guerrillas might cut the dawdling recruits to pieces in Santee swamp, Lord Rawdon sent Major Robert McLeroth and the 64th Regiment to escort them from Nelson's to Camden. In spite of McLeroth, on December 13 Marion and seven hundred horsemen chased them from Halfway Swamp to Singleton's Mill.

Greene returned to headquarters and threw Sumter's strategy before a council of war. "I proposed to Generals Smallwood and Morgan the attack upon Lord Cornwallis," he informed Sumter on December 12. They were against it as being impracticable. They realized that the army was destitute of provisions and equipment and woefully deficient in training and coordination. They feared that it was not in shape to attack even a small force of British regulars. "I am not altogether of this opinion," Greene assured the

Gamecock, "and therefore wish you to keep up a communication of intelligence, and of any changes of their disposition that may take place."

Although the Gamecock had seen the chance to attack Cornwallis dissipated by inertia during the change of command, he was still eager and sanguine. "General Greene complains greatly for provisions and forage," he wrote the governor on December 14, placing his logistic and intelligence systems at the disposal of the commander; "if he thought proper to send over a party of horse or foot or both, they might be very well supplyed at my Camp and would be of very great service in supporting the foragers, and unless some movements are made speedily or parties sent over, I shall be obliged to order the Troops away, they are but few in number and is exceedingly exposed. There is a stir among the Enemy which indicates a speedy movement."

Aware that as soon as the reinforcements should reach Winnsboro, Lord Cornwallis would open his winter campaign, General Greene began formulating his own plans. Seizing an idea that Sumter had vigorously proposed during their conference, he made it a basic part of his own strategy. "Governor Rutledge shew me a couple of notes which you sent him, wherein you express a desire to have a detachment made from this Army on the other side of the Catawba," he wrote the Gamecock on December 15. "The measure you wish I have been preparing for ever since I was with you."

Greene selected General Morgan to carry out Sumter's plans. The famed rifleman now commanded a brigade formed from the surviving Delaware Continentals, Lieutenant Colonel John Eager Howard's Maryland Continentals, and Lieutenant Colonel William Washington's Continental dragoons.

"With these troops you will proceed to the west side of the Catawba river, where you will be joined by a body of volunteer militia, under the command of Brig. Gen. Davidson, of this state, and by the militia lately under the command of General Sumter," Greene said in his orders to Morgan on December 16. "For the present, I give you the entire command in that quarter, and do

New York Public Library

Brigadier General Thomas Sumter

New York Public Library

Major General Horatio Gates

New York Public Library

Major General William Moultrie

New York Public Library

Colonel Wade Hampton

National Portrait Gallery

Lord Cornwallis

Courtesy of The New-York Historical Society, New York City

Governor John Rutledge

Courtesy of The New-York Historical Society, New York City

Brigadier General Andrew Pickens

Brigadier General Francis Marion

Library of Congress

British Museum

Lord Rawdon

New York Public Library

Brigadier General Daniel Morgan

Colonel William Washington

New York Public Library

Lieutenant Colonel Henry Lee

Courtesy of The New-York Historical Society, New York City

Mrs. H. M. Fagan

Lieutenant Colonel Banastre Tarleton

New York Public Library

Major General Nathanael Greene

hereby require all officers and soldiers engaged in the American cause to be subject to your command."

In placing the Carolina militia under Morgan's command, without first consulting General Sumter, Nathanael Greene blundered. Shuffling the volunteer soldiers around in callous routine, as if they were Continentals, deeply offended their proud, sensitive leader. Governor Rutledge immediately recognized Greene's blunder. He dashed off a note advising Sumter that Morgan would stop at Price's on his way beyond the Catawba. In confirming the assignment he wrote tactfully, "I wish he may have what he wants from the South Carolina militia."

As the major development of his strategy, Greene decided to move the American Army to a camp beyond Peedee River. Here he would lie safely behind an unfordable stream. He would be in a territory rich in provisions. He could refresh, recruit, and train his troops. He could quickly reinforce Morgan's troops and cooperate with Marion's guerrillas. And he would be in a pivot from which, should Cornwallis march northward, he could throw his army ahead of the British. Or he could swing to the south and cut all British lines of communication with their base of supplies in Charleston.

Sent ahead of the army, Colonel Thaddeus Kosciusko, the chief engineer, laid out a camp on Hicks' Creek across the Peedee from Cheraw, and in spite of rain, ice, and mud, on December 20 Greene evacuated Charlotte. Brigadier General Isaac Huger marched the army toward Haley's Ferry on the Peedee, and General Morgan headed for the country beyond Catawba River.

"I think Morgan's March to the Westward will afford an opportunity for obtaining a good supply of Necessaries from Hampton's Store," the governor wrote Sumter on Christmas Day. "I hope you will not omit that blow."

The British were puzzled by Greene's actions, and Lord Cornwallis ordered his Tory spies and scouts to report every movement of the Americans. By December 26 his intelligence had become so disquieting that Cornwallis twice wrote Tarleton encamped at Brierley's. "A man came this morning from Charlotte town; his fidelity however, very doubtful," he said in his first letter; "he says, that Greene marched on Wednesday last toward the Cheraws, to join General Caswall, and that Morgan, with his infantry and one hundred and twenty-four of Washington's light horse, crossed Biggar's Ferry, on Thursday and Friday last, to join Lacey." That evening he confirmed the report: "Morgan and Washington have passed Broad river."

Usually imperturbable, Lord Cornwallis now became thoroughly aroused. He was further disturbed when General Robert Cunningham reported from Fort Williams: "From the best authority am convinced the Rebels are embodying at Ramsour's Mill, in all probability intend moving their operations towards this Quarter." Morgan's passing Broad River indicated a concentration against Ninety-Six.

"If it would not be inconvenient, his Lordship would wish to see you tomorrow," Lieutenant Henry Haldane, aide to Cornwallis since the death of Major Money, wrote Tarleton on December 27. Next morning Tarleton rode over to Winnsboro. During his conference with Cornwallis, it was decided that he should cross Broad River and oppose Morgan's advance. Their decision was too late. Operating in front of Morgan, Colonel Washington decided to frighten the Tories. In a feint he sent Colonel Joseph Hayes and forty dragoons toward Fort Williams. McArthur disgustedly informed Cornwallis: "General Cunningham & his people quitted the fort on Saturday night & mounted for 96."

Fearful of increased American activity, Cornwallis sent Haldane galloping toward Broad River on the night of January 1, 1781, with orders for Tarleton to reinforce Cruger at Ninety-Six. "Lt. Col. Tarleton proposes moving immediately," Haldane informed McArthur at daybreak, "and will join your battalion at the ferry."

But the alarm was needless. Morgan had not moved toward Ninety-Six. Suffering from hemorrhoids and sciatica aggravated by the chill, rainy weather, the Old Wagoner could scarcely sit his horse. He was dissatisfied and wished to rejoin Greene. "My situation is far from being agreeable to my wishes or expectations," he wrote on January 4, requesting permission to end his encampment near Colonel Henderson's plantation on Pacolet River. "Forage and provisions are not to be had. Here we cannot subsist, so that we have but one alternative, either to retreat or move into Georgia."

"It is my wish also that you should hold your ground if possible," replied Greene, "for I foresee the disagreeable consequences that will result from a retreat. If moving as far as Ninety-Six, or anywhere in the neighborhood of it, will contribute to the obtaining more ample supplies, you have my consent. Col. Tarleton is said to be on his way to pay you a visit. I doubt not but he will have a decent reception and a proper dismission."

Events now began racing toward their climax. Tarleton was already in search of Morgan. At Winnsboro, Lord Cornwallis had reorganized his army and was awaiting only the arrival of Major General Alexander Leslie and his corps of twenty-three hundred men before invading North Carolina. Nor were the Americans idle. Scouts from the legion of Lieutenant Colonel Henry Lee had arrived at Camp Hicks. Greene and Rutledge decided to send the Virginians down the Peedee to join the Swamp Fox on Snow's Island. And to give Francis Marion, still a lieutenant colonel in the Continentals, requisite authority, on January 1, 1781, the governor sent him a commission as brigadier general of militia.

During these exciting days the Gamecock sat at Price's and fretted. His wound was so badly inflamed that he could scarcely move his arms. He could not mount a horse, and yet he longed to be at the head of his troops.

"I am impatient to hear of your perfect recovery and of seeing you again at the head of the Militia," Greene wrote him encouragingly on January 8. "General Morgan has gone over to the West side of the Catawba agreeable to what I wrote you before I left Charlotte. But I expect he will have but few men from your Brigade until you are in a condition to appear at the head of them. Your influence in bringing them out is not only necessary, but the means you have of obtaining intelligence is not less important. I lament exceedingly your wounds confining you so much longer than I was flattered with, from appearances at the time I was with you; and I esteem it no less unfortunate for the public than myself. If Genl. Morgan don't meet with any misfortune until you are ready to join him I shall be happy, as your knowledge of the Country and the people will afford him great security against a surprise."

Affable, but with an unfortunate penchant for lecturing subordinates, Greene attempted to put the role of the militia in perspective. "When I was with you, your soul was full of enterprise," he wrote. "The salvation of this country don't depend upon little strokes; nor should the great business of establishing a permanent army be neglected to pursue them. Partisan strokes in war are like the garnish of a table, they give splendor to the Army and reputation to the Officers, but they afford no substantial national security. They are most necessary and should not be neglected, but should not be pursued to the prejudice of more important concerns. You may strike a hundred strokes, and reap little benefit from them unless you have a good Army to take advantage of your success. The enemy will never relinquish their plan, nor the people be firm in our favour until they behold a better barrier in the field than a Volunteer Militia who are one day out and the next at home." He continued: "There is no mortal more fond of enterprize than myself, but this is not the basis on which the fate of this country depends. It is not a war of posts but a contest for States."

Greene then turned to the civil war devastating South Carolina. "Plunder and depredation prevails so in every quarter I am not a little apprehensive all this country will be laid waste," he exclaimed. "Most people appear to be in pursuit of private gain or personal glory. I persuade myself though you may set a just value upon reputation your soul is filled with a more noble ambition."

Quaker Greene was honest, but his letter enraged the Gamecock. Because of Greene's reflection upon the volunteer militia, the wounded brigadier took umbrage, violent and personal. Although he could scarcely raise his sword arm, he also began rankling over Morgan's commanding his brigade.

Unaware of Sumter's prejudice, Morgan sent Captain John Chitty to ask Colonel Hill to assemble his regiment and gather some provisions. His action raised a complex question of law, military regulations, and courtesy. The Articles of Association did not give the Continental Congress authority over state troops. As a Continental, according to the military laws of South Carolina, General Morgan had no authority over Hill.

Under the South Carolina constitution the governor was the commander in chief of the militia, and at Camp Hicks, Governor

Rutledge was in the state. Rutledge had unquestioned authority, but as the senior brigadier general of the militia Sumter believed that so long as he was able to relay the governor's orders they should be transmitted through him. Upon being bypassed, he grew imperious. He sent word to the colonels in his brigade to obey no order unless it came through him. Colonel Hill, one of Sumter's most loyal friends, refused to call out his regiment.

Morgan reported the incident to Greene. Disheartened, the Old Wagoner requested that "I may be recalled with my detachment, and that Gen. Davidson and Colonel Pickens may be left with the militia of North and South Carolina and Georgia."

"I am surprised that General Sumter should give such an order," Greene replied. "I wish you to take no notice of the matter," he counseled Morgan, sketching a pattern of behavior toward the wounded Gamecock. "Write to him frequently, and consult him freely. He is a man of great pride and considerable merit, and should not be neglected."

With a guarded insinuation Greene concluded, "I am persuaded he will see the impropriety of the matter and correct it in future, unless personal glory is more the object than public good."

One of the bravest and most capable of the Continental officers, Daniel Morgan had once been so humiliated that he had resigned his commission. Ill, aching, and sympathetic with the suffering Gamecock, he generously replied, "With regard to Gen. Sumter, I think I know the man so well that I shall take no notice of what he has done, but follow your advice in every particular."

Greene realized that Sumter was suffering, so he wrote an exceedingly long, tactful letter, cautiously bringing in that Morgan had mentioned "some embarrassment which has arisen from an order of yours to Colonel Hill not to obey any orders from him unless it came through you."

After alluding to the chain of command, he continued, "Genl. Morgan is an exceeding good officer and understands his duty perfectly well, and I know he has the highest respect for your character, and therefore am persuaded if there has been any interference different from the general principles, which would govern military affairs, it must have happened through inadvertence or from a persuasion that you did not mean to exercise command during the time of your indisposition."

Hoping to smooth the ruffled feathers of the Gamecock, Greene concluded amicably, "If anything in his conduct has had the appearance of indelicacy or neglect, I hope you will not suffer it to bias your conduct from that line which has given you weight and influence among your Countrymen. It is the mark of a great mind to rise superior to little injuries and our object should be the good of our Country and not personal glory."

While the American generals wrangled, Lord Cornwallis started toward North Carolina. After writing out his plans for the campaign, Colonel Tarleton, with his British Legion, Major Timothy Newmarsh's 7th and McArthur's 71st Regiment, and scattering units of light infantry, artillery, and dragoons, began moving slowly through the Dutch Fork. With him marched the recruits of Newmarsh's Royal Fusiliers whom Marion had frightened so badly at Singleton's. They had been assigned garrison duty at Ninety-Six, but Tarleton now asked permission to keep them during his drive against Morgan.

Cornwallis granted Tarleton's request. "I shall march on Monday & direct my course for Bullock Creek," he confided. "Leslie will march on Tuesday by the river road for the same place."

After balks and delays, on January 8 the British Army evacuated Winnsboro. Slowly the troops slogged toward the border, the roads slick and miry from torrential rains. "I have not heard from Tarleton since Tuesday," Cornwallis wrote General Leslie on January 12. "I believe he is as much embarrassed with the waters as you are."

"The rains have put a total stop to Leslie," Cornwallis then complained to Rawdon. "I do not think it right to advance too far."

"Leslie is at last got out of the swamp & reached this day the neighborhood of Rocky Mount," Cornwallis informed Tarleton on January 14. "I have not heard of Morgan's moving, but conclude he will now cross Broad River."

General Morgan was still on the Pacolet, but after Tarleton had crossed the Enoree at Musgrove's Mill and headed toward the Tyger, he began to worry. "The enemy's great superiority in numbers, and our distance from the main army, will enable Lord Cornwallis to detail a superior force against me," he complained to Greene on January 15. "My force is inadequate to the attempts you have hinted at." And then the Old Wagoner concluded his report. "Colonel Tarleton has crossed the Tyger," he said. "It is more than probable we are his object."

Morgan immediately retreated from the Pacolet. That night he camped at Burr's Mill on Little Thicketty Creek. The following day he retreated on to Cowpens. Here he bivouacked to await the coming of Colonel Andrew Pickens and three hundred Carolina riflemen, veterans who had been with Sumter at Blackstock's.

Colonel Tarleton swiftly followed. About sunrise on January 17, 1781, he reached Cowpens. Eager to fight and confident of victory, he began arranging his line of troops. With conventional tactics, he placed his dragoons on each flank and his artillery between the infantry of the British Legion and the 7th Regiment. He formed his reserve of McArthur's Highlanders.

Surprised but not flustered, Morgan arranged his line to suit his troops. Near the foot of the long, sloping hill he posted a detachment of sharpshooters with orders to fire and fall back. Behind these skirmishers he placed Pickens and the Carolina militia, with orders to fire and then file quickly to the left. Across the wooded brow of Cowpens he stationed Colonel Howard and the Continentals. And behind the knoll he hid the cavalry of Colonel Washington.

At Tarleton's signal the colorful British line began advancing. The American sharpshooters fired and fell back. Pickens' militia fired until the advancing enemy began using the bayonet. Then they filed off in good style. Misunderstanding an order, the Continentals, too, began retreating. Sensing victory, Tarleton ordered a charge. Up hill raced his infantry, their bayonets flashing, their ranks breaking, and their line turning into a yelling, struggling mob.

Seeing the disorder, Morgan shouted to Howard, "Face about! Give them one fire and the day is ours." At Howard's command, the veteran Continentals wheeled around and delivered a withering broadside from the hip. The British line staggered. The recruits of the 7th threw themselves upon the ground and bellowed "Quarter!"

Before Tarleton realized what was happening and could bring his dragoons into battle, Howard's Continentals had charged through the hole left by the recruits, swarmed into the rear of the British, and begun rolling up the flanks. Fifteen minutes later, his entire infantry killed or captured, Banastre Tarleton and his dragoons were fleeing from Cowpens.

The whole country began ringing with praise of Morgan. "I have the particular pleasure to congratulate you on the entire defeat of the enemy under Lt. Col. Tarleton," Greene exultantly wrote Francis Marion on January 23. "Major Giles this moment arrived brings the glorious intelligence."

Thomas Sumter, in his refuge at Price's only fifty miles from Cowpens, heard the glorious news. But he did not join the chorus. He sent no congratulations. "I find such excessive difficulty in writing that I can't possibly be as particular as necessary," he said in a routine letter to Greene on January 25. "I am still but poorly."

The Gamecock was deeply hurt. He felt that Morgan had used his strategy and some of his troops to bring down Tarleton. Ten days after the battle he wrote Morgan, but he was laconic:

Catawba River, 28th January, 1781

Dear Sir:

I have every reason to believe that the enemy are not more than 1,600 strong. I have had them repeatedly counted, and could ascertain their number to a man, if I knew what had escaped the defeat of Col. Tarleton—upon which happy event I most heartily congratulate you.

I am, &c.
Thomas Sumter

Sumter now decided to felicitate Greene. "You express a desire of seeing me again in the field," he wrote from Price's on January 29. "I am happy to know that the service for which you most Immediately wanted me, is no longer needfull, & Genl. Morgan has fortunately relieved you from your apprehensions for his safety, by defeating Coll. Tarleton, a circumstance of great consequence, upon which I must beg leave, most heartily to congratulate you."

But as he wrote, his gorge rose from Greene's insinuations about personal glory. The Gamecock was no glory fighter. "When I had the Honour of a conference with you if I discovered any injudicious thirst for enterprise, private gain, or personal Glory," he asserted manfully, "I am sorry for it, and shall be doubly Mortified to find that my endeavours, together with the Good people of South Carolina, have not tended the least Degree to promote the Publick Good; I lament that private Gain is the primary Object with too many, and as much lament that the desire of Fame is not more sought after, as to the Former the world I think will acquit me, but the latter reason & Conscience convinces I have not been arrogant & designing but allways meant to conduct & demean myself, so as to tend most to the Publick Good, & the satisfaction of my superior officers."

He confessed embarrassment from Morgan's command and orders, "as I have been concerned but little in either trust," but he pledged himself to "act upon such principles with Gen. Morgan, as is most likely to tend to the publick Good."

Then like a dutiful soldier, Thomas Sumter ended his apology: "I still find myself but poorly, but have hopes of being able to ride tolerably in a few days, when I shall be happy to receive your Commands."

Chapter 10 RESCUE OF MARY

"I HAVE the pleasure to hear by General Morgan that you are almost well enough to take the field," Greene wrote from Sherald's Ford on the Catawba on January 20. "Nothing will afford me greater satisfaction than to see you at the Head of the Militia again; and I can assure you I shall take a pleasure in giving you every opportunity to exercise that talent of enterprise which has already rendered you the terror of your enemies and the idol of your friends."

Hoping that the Gamecock, who lay only twenty miles away, would come for a personal reconciliation, Greene concluded, "If you are well enough to ride up to Beatty's Ford, I shall be glad to see you there. I wish to consult you upon a particular plan of operation."

The unexpected appearance of the American general on the Catawba reflected a complete change of strategy. As soon as Greene heard that Morgan had sent the prisoners taken at Cowpens to Virginia and was slowly retreating northward ahead of Cornwallis, he turned over the army at Camp Hicks to General Huger, called for a horse and escort of dragoons, and galloped off to join the Old Wagoner. He found Morgan rallying the North Carolina militia and trying to hold the fords along the Catawba.

As Greene had promised, on January 31 he rode down to Beatty's Ford. He was disappointed, however, for Sumter did not come, and there was no time to arrange another rendezvous. Returning scouts reported that the British at Ramsour's Mills were burning their baggage and surplus stores. Realizing that Cornwallis was turning his entire army into light troops and that pursuit was imminent, Greene headed toward Guilford, ready to assume command should rheumatism overwhelm General Morgan.

At Cowan's Ford, six miles below Beatty's, on February 1 Cornwallis forced a passage across the Catawba after his battalion of

Guards had killed General Davidson. Morgan immediately began retreating, his rear often in sight of the advance guard of the British. Gradually his troops pulled ahead. On February 4 he reached Trading Ford on the swollen Yadkin River, seven miles ahead of the enemy at Salisbury. His rear guard crossed just before the arrival of Tarleton and his dragoons.

At Trading Ford, General Greene answered Sumter's letter of January 29 and 31. "When I had the pleasure of an interview, I discovered nothing mercenary or illiberal in your disposition," Greene replied without rancor on February 3. "On the contrary I was charmed with the spirit of enterprise which I flattered myself would be no less beneficial to your Country than honorable to yourself. I still entertain the same sentiments; and I can assure you I shall be equally happy in an opportunity to do justice to your merit as to Genl. Morgan. In what respect General Morgan's command embarrassed you I am at a loss to imagine; but I dare say I could explain it to your perfect satisfaction in a few minutes, could I have the happiness to see you. I consider you both valuable men, as well as brave and good Officers; and I hope the merit of one don't in the least detract from the other. It is true I wish to see you again in the field; and *I have ever considered it a great misfortune* that you were wounded on my first coming to the command."

Greene then turned to strategy. He had ordered General Marion to cross the Santee. He had instructed Pickens, promoted to brigadier general for his part in defeating Tarleton, to recruit around Ninety-Six. "It is my ardent wish you should embody your Militia as soon as your health will permit," Greene concluded. "This force may be usefully employed against the enemy in South Carolina; and whether it is employed there or with the Continental Army when collected, you will have the command of the whole."

By commission from Governor Rutledge and assignment from General Greene, Thomas Sumter was now commander in chief of the South Carolina militia. With the brigades of Marion and Pickens under his command he had force enough for a vigorous campaign. The idea was tonic for mind and body. From a dejected convalescent sitting around Price's, he quickly changed into a fighting cock, defiant and eager for a pitting.

The Gamecock loved to think in terms of strategy. Sometimes his plans became grandiose and failed, but he never made the opposite mistake of too little and too late. From his spies he knew the conditions in the line of British posts beginning at Georgetown, extending through the Santee basin, and ending at Augusta. Although Greene had warned him against the attempt, Sumter believed that he could recover Carolina by destroying these posts.

The Gamecock believed that a surprise attack could carry Fort Granby. A rapid foray down the Congaree could surprise and capture Belleville. A further sweep down the Santee could topple Fort Watson. A junction with Marion's brigade could give the Carolinians such overwhelming superiority that they could drive the enemy back into Charleston. With one powerful effort they could end the war.

As General Sumter began planning his prospective campaign, estimating his need of men, horses, and ammunition, he received a letter from Secretary Thomson of the Continental Congress. Urged by a memorandum from Greene, on January 13, 1781, the Congress had voted its thanks to Sumter for his victories at Hanging Rock, Fish Dam Ford, and Blackstock's.

Proud and confident, Sumter issued a call for the colonels of his brigade to assemble their militia and meet him at the old camp ground in the Waxhaws. As the more ardent came straggling in, even though his shoulder was almost rigid and his wound still draining, he walked undaunted among his followers, greeting, haranguing, and inspiring them. Lord Cornwallis, he said, had marched into North Carolina to dig a grave for himself and the British Army.

For once the Gamecock had miscalculated his resources. After Cornwallis had marched out of South Carolina, the troops whom he had left to hold the state were quiet and the country was enjoying relative peace. With schools and churches closed, with roads broken and bridges destroyed, and with trade and commerce dead, Carolina was desolate. The people had to survive by their own efforts, and the men welcomed this respite in which to do their plowing and planting. Instead of the thousand men who had turned out before Blackstock's only two hundred and eighty came to the Waxhaws.

Still weak and too impatient to wait for more, on February 16 Sumter cantered off toward the Congaree. In high spirits his horsemen covered the ninety miles, and before daylight on February 19, 1781, they crossed the river and swept down upon Fort Granby. But some irresponsible Whig had revealed their coming to the Tories, and they failed to surprise Major Andrew Maxwell.

Thrown back in his initial attack, Sumter laid conventional siege to Granby. He cut the road and river traffic. He ordered his men to advance behind rolling tobacco hogsheads and to build a screen of logs in front of the ramparts. With a countryman's skill in using fence rails he erected a tower from which his riflemen could fire into the fort.

The Gamecock then called for the help of the Swamp Fox. "Hurry of busines obliges me to be laconick," he wrote Marion on February 20. "I arrived at this place yesterday morning about four o'clock. Shortly after, attacked the fort, with which I have been ever since engaged. Everything hitherto favourable, and have no doubt but I shall succeed, if not interrupted by Lord Rawdon, who, I know, will strip his post as bare of men as possible to spare, to obviate which, as far as may be in your power, it is my wish that you would be pleased to move in such a direction as to attract his attention, and thereby prevent his designs. Timely assistance in this way portends much good to this State."

Not wishing to offend the sensitive little Huguenot by a display of his authority, Sumter ended his letter with cordiality: "I shall be happy to receive an account of the state of things to the East and Northward. If you can, with propriety, advance Southwardly so as to co-operate, or correspond with me, it might have the best of consequences."

In a postscript he wrote: "I am extremely short of ammunition: if you are well supplied, should be much obliged to you to send some into the neighborhood of Buckingham's ferry." As Buchanan's Ferry, miscalled Buckingham's, crossed the Santee opposite the High Hills, Sumter evidently planned to visit Mary and Tom.

Lord Rawdon interrupted Sumter's investment of Fort Granby. Immediately upon learning of the foray, he ordered Lieutenant Colonel Welbore Ellis Doyle and a battalion of the Volunteers of Ireland to support Maxwell. Expecting Sumter to retreat up Broad

River, Doyle seized the fords above Friday's Ferry. He then bore down upon the Carolinians with his veteran infantry.

Sumter fooled him. Quickly raising the siege, he galloped down the road toward Eutaw Springs. Next morning, February 21, 1781, after a dash of thirty-five miles, he surprised and threw a cordon around the post at Belleville. Cutting through Colonel Thomson's plantation, he tightened his grip by seizing the boats on the Congaree.

After skirmishing all afternoon, the Gamecock attempted to storm Belleville. His militiamen gained a foothold on the ramparts around the mansion, but Lieutenant Charles McPherson fought them off. Having no siege guns, the backwoodsmen tried to fire the building by hurling lighted brands against the cypress weather-boarding. McPherson's men threw water on the flames. At dusk Sumter drew off, leaving a detachment to continue the siege. Moving two miles downstream, he went into bivouac at Manigault's plantation.

Learning of the approach of a train of twenty wagons, with an escort of fifty British soldiers, Sumter laid an ambush behind the tangled vines and evergreens on Big Savannah. Waiting with Bratton's men until the enemy marched into an open glade, he ordered an attack. The British quickly formed and returned the fire. After seven rounds, seeing Lacey galloping to join Bratton, they raised a white flag. In spite of the enemy's signal for a parley, Lacey's men discharged their muskets, killing seven and wounding seven others.

Lacey's ignoring a white flag angered the British commanders, and they accused Sumter of brutality. "A few days ago," Colonel John Watson, builder of Fort Watson, wrote Marion, "after Genl. Sumter had taken some waggons on the other side of the Santee, and the escort of them had laid down their arms, a party of his horse who said they had not discharged their pieces came up, fired upon the prisoners and killed seven of them. A few days after we took six of his people. Enquire how they were treated."

In the captured wagons the Carolinians found enough arms, ammunition, and clothing for three regiments. They also found several heavily banded chests used in shipping gold. Elated by the prospect, Sumter loaded the plunder into flatboats, placed Captain John McClure and a militia guard over the ferrymen, and engaged

Robert Livingston to pilot the craft to a rendezvous below Nelson's Ferry. But Livingston was a conniving Tory, and before Captain McClure discovered his treachery, boats and plunder were moored under the threatening guns of Fort Watson.

Apprised of Sumter's raid, Lord Rawdon dispatched Major McElroth, with the 64th Regiment, a squadron of dragoons, and a fieldpiece to the relief of McPherson. These veterans left Camden on the double and by early afternoon were crossing the Congaree at McCord's Ferry. About three o'clock the van marched into view of Belleville. The defenders began singing, shouting, and firing at random. Sumter threw his men into battle formation, and McElroth backed away some four miles. But the Gamecock then acknowledged failure, called off his troops, and began retreating down the Santee.

Sumter's boldness had led him into a perilous situation. Behind him were two regiments of infantry, augmented by Hessians and Tories from Granby and Belleville. Ahead lay the road to Charleston. To extricate his raiders he would have to turn either westward and ride around Ninety-Six, or eastward and cross the flooded Santee.

But Sumter was in familiar country, aware of every line, path, or road. Slowly, with complete self-assurance, he made his choice. Turning abruptly toward the river just below Eutaw Springs, he halted at the high bluff on the plantation of William Flud.

As his men roamed along the bank, they found a cypress dugout, stout and sound, but so small that it could carry only a paddler and three passengers. Immediately Sumter began sending his troops across, three soldiers in the canoe and their horses swimming alongside and astern. As a round trip took half an hour, for two days the Gamecock lay vulnerable, his raiders bivouacked on both sides of the Santee.

Smarting from the loss of his plunder, after the audacious crossing, General Sumter decided to surprise Fort Watson. Without reconnaissance and unaware that Watson's entire regiment, augmented by provincials and militia, lay behind the palisades, he struck at high noon on February 28, 1781. As his men charged through the dog fennel and brambles, the British opened with murderous fire. Man after man tumbled into the broom sedge.

When the survivors began to falter, Sumter called off the attack, retreated about five miles, and bivouacked at Farr's plantation on Great Savannah.

"I passed the river last night at Mrs. Flud's, have been at Colonel Watson's station, and find that he has collected his whole force at that place," he wrote Marion on February 28. "I think it advisable that we form a junction, or at least approach so near as to co-operate upon the shortest notice."

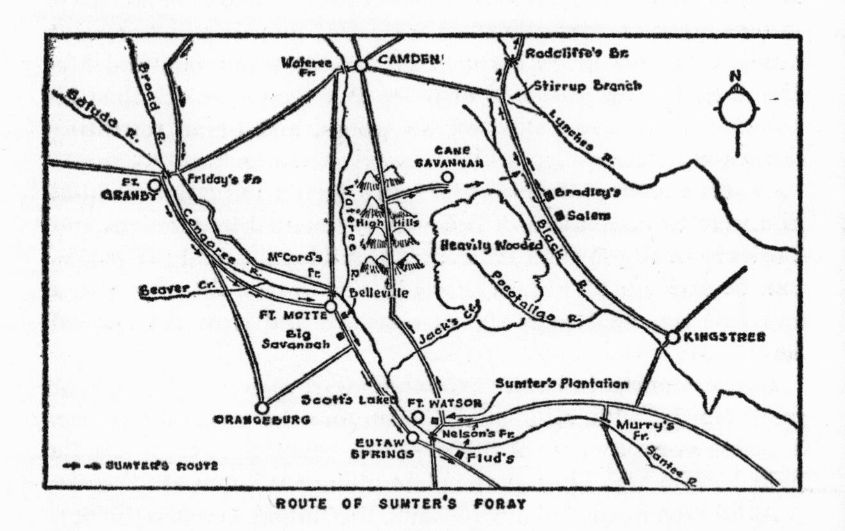

ROUTE OF SUMTER'S FORAY

The respite at Farr's quickly turned into misery. Even after his defeats the Gamecock was sanguine, ready for another fight with Colonel Watson. But his followers were molded from less heroic material. They began complaining, and as their morale sank, he moved to his own plantation on Great Savannah, there bidding the grumblers help themselves to fodder, corn, and fattening shoats. But even as they feasted the militiamen began deserting. The North Carolinians mutinied. And although General Marion immediately answered his letter, the cautious Swamp Fox did not rush to aid the Gamecock.

Although there was little co-operation between the Gamecock and the Swamp Fox, there was no animosity between these Partisans. Whenever Marion's brigade was near Murry's Ferry, General Marion camped on the plantation of Josiah Cantey, brother of Mary Sumter. And during the six months that Mary had lived behind the British lines, Marion had used his spies and couriers to relay letters between Mary and Thomas Sumter.

Instead of Marion's brigade coming, rumors spread that Lord Rawdon was on his way to visit the Gamecock. Frustrated but resolute, at sunset on March 2 Sumter broke camp. Leading his raiders gingerly around Fort Watson and galloping through the High Hills, at dawn he was at Cane Savannah. Alone he rode to the home of Mrs. Clarke to surprise Mary and Tom.

Sumter's greeting was brief. He had come for his wife and son. Time was short, and having neither wagon nor litter and scant material for a makeshift, he hurriedly folded a mattress and strapped it across the back of a horse. Gently he lifted Mary into the improvised saddle and settled her in the arms of a Negro woman astride the animal. Laying his pistols across his pommel, he clutched the reins of Mary's horse, and swung soberly into his saddle. Minutes later, surrounded by two hundred resolute horsemen, the Gamecock headed into the trackless pine barren stretching from the High Hills to Black River.

All that wintry day the Sumter cavalcade plunged across the barren, Thomas stiffly sitting his charger and leading Mary's horse with his aching right hand; Mary leaning against her attendant; and Tom cavorting among the soldiers. Forty miles they rode, scarcely stopping for food or water. Helpless but courageous, Mary kept up with the men, even though her horse careened and stumbled, brambles raked her legs, and swinging branches whipped her face black and blue. After dark they forded Black River and paused for the night, Sumter and his family at the home of James Bradley and his men in a bivouac under the oaks around Salem Presbyterian Church.

Next morning a courier dashed up to Bradley's with a letter from General Marion. Tardily obedient to Sumter's call, the Swamp Fox was moving up Black River and had reached Benbow's Ferry. But with the war only a distant rumble the Williamsburg militia were more interested in planting than in fighting. Few had answered Marion's summons and his brigade was too weak for campaigning.

"Yours of the 2d instant has this moment come to hand," Sumter answered by the courier. "I am very sorry to be so far out of the way of meeting with you at a time when there is the greatest occasion for it. I made no doubt but your route to me would be by the way of King's Tree, or the Ferry, and after receiving yours of the 28th ultimo, informing me what the number of your men were, I found you to be very weak, and the enemy near at hand in force, this determined me to move on to meet with you—to concert measures for our further operations, which is still absolutely necessary. I shall therefore remain at or near this place for that purpose, and beg that you may come this way with all possible speed, if not convenient with all your men to facilitate an interview, please to come with a few."

The senior general ended cordially, "Near this place I mean to remain until I hear from you again." But the Gamecock did not remain long at Bradley's. While he sat waiting for Marion, the British commanders were searching for him. Marching toward the High Hills with his Volunteers of Ireland, Rawdon hoped to crush the raiders against Watson's advancing regiment. But learning that Sumter had paused only to pick up his family, he hurried back to Camden. On the morning of March 6 he dispatched Major Thomas Fraser and his South Carolina provincials into the section between Scape Hoar Creek and Lynches River.

Realizing that the Swamp Fox was not coming to Bradley's, at daybreak on March 6, 1781, Sumter called his men, set Mary again in her mattress saddle, and headed up the road toward the Waxhaws. At Stirrup Branch he met Fraser.

The Gamecock dared not turn back. Even though he should expose his family to battle, he decided to cut his way to Radcliffe's Bridge. Sending the frightened women to safety, he opened the attack, directing the firing and making the woods ring bellowing, "Lie down, Tom! Lie down! Lie down!"

After the first brush with Fraser's men, a militiaman who had not distinguished himself, found Tom in hiding. Hoping to win favor with the general by pretending that he had been protecting the lad, he led Tom to the Gamecock. After listening to his story, Sumter snapped, "We need soldiers, not dry nurses."

In a running fight, which left the road dotted with dead and dying men, Sumter drove Fraser's Loyalists into the swamp along Lynches River. Calling in his horsemen and gathering his family, he then clattered across Radcliffe's Bridge and disappeared on a circuitous route to the New Acquisition.

"Fraser yesterday fell in with Sumter (who was advancing this way) between Scape Hoar and Radcliffe's Bridge," Rawdon informed Watson on March 7. "A smart action ensued, in which the enemy were completely routed, leaving ten dead on the field and about forty wounded. Unfortunately none of our Dragoons had joined Fraser, so that he could not pursue his victory. Sumter fled across Lynches Creek and continued his retreat northward; he had his family with him, so that I think he has entirely abandoned the lower country."

Young Tom Sumter was excited by the roaring guns, but he sickened at the sight of blood and death. Son of an unflinching father and a fearless mother, he crawled upon the horse behind Mary and held her courageously in his arms until they reached the home of John Barnett. As Mrs. Barnett and Susannah bustled around, trying to comfort their battered and exhausted guest, Thomas Sumter relaxed, well pleased that the grim task of bringing his family from behind the enemy lines had ended in triumph.

The Gamecock soon rode on to the Waxhaws. His camp was usually warm and friendly. He now found it cold, his men quiet and sullen. After three weeks of fruitless campaigning, they were angry, declaring that they had been led on a wild-goose chase. They felt ill-used in rescuing Sumter's family. They were bitter over leaving one-fourth of their number on unnamed battlefields. Finally the militia raised such a clamor against their commander in chief "for deceiving them with regard to Lord Rawdon's strength," as Robert Gray asserted in his *Observations,* "that he was obliged at a muster to enter into a long vindication of his conduct."

Chapter 11 FOUNDING THE STATE TROOPS

AFTER quieting the clamor in his brigade, General Sumter released the militia. He knew that they were anxious to return to their spring plowing, and he had no plans for another campaign. Although he had failed to crack the British line, he was not discouraged. Repulses are only the visible side of war. Men willing to die for liberty can surmount temporary failure. Had he possessed a single cannon, in five minutes he could have toppled Granby, Belleville, or Fort Watson.

"I marched on Tuesday the 16th Ultimo from the Catawba with about Two hundred & Eighty men for the Congrees," Sumter wrote Greene. "I proceeded from thence to the enemies posts at Col. Thompson, Nelson's ferry, South Lake etc. was within fifty miles of Charles Town but finding I should get no assistance from Genl. Marion thought proper to return which I have happily Effected, with very inconsiderable loss—as I still labour under the Misfortune of having but little use of my Right hand and Writing Very painful therefore."

Because his shoulder, still swollen and aching, prevented his writing a full account of the expedition, the Gamecock called in Captain Wade Hampton, "a Valuable and Intelligent officer who will wait upon you for that purpose, on whose information you may Rely—and to whom you may communicate with Safety—he is fully acquainted with my late operations and partly with my Designs in future."

With a cold trail before him Captain Hampton set out toward Trading Ford in search of the American Army. There Morgan had escaped across the flooded Yadkin, but when the British dragoons dashed off toward the shallow fords, he realized that Tarleton was maneuvering to get in front of him. The Old Wagoner began driving his troops and by night had reached Guilford Courthouse. But that grueling ride ended his career. So ill from rheumatism that he could no longer sit a horse, Daniel Morgan asked to be relieved of his command. Four days later the hero of Cowpens climbed into a buggy and set off for his home in the Valley of Virginia.

On February 9 General Huger reached Guilford with the army from Camp Hicks. Soon afterward Light Horse Harry Lee marched in with his Legion. But the Virginia cavalier was crestfallen. Even while hurrying to overtake the others, he had murmured against losing an opportunity of campaigning with the Swamp Fox. "The invitation which the posture of affairs on the other side of the Santee," he confided to Greene, "held out to a proper attempt, was so pleasing, that I regret exceedingly my recall from that country."

With the British in Salem threatening to outflank his army, Greene began retreating toward Boyd's Ferry over Dan River, the water barrier to southern Virginia. Before leaving Guilford, however, he sent Francis Marion a memorandum. "General Sumter is desired to call out all the militia of South Carolina and employ them in destroying the enemies' stores and perplexing their affairs in South Carolina," he said. "Please to communicate and concert with him your future operations."

As the Americans retreated, Lord Cornwallis tried to provoke a decisive battle. His army bristling with reinforcements, he chased Greene to the Dan. But the river was flooded, the result of a month of winter rains, and the Americans had drawn all flatboats to the northern bank. And so, after Tarleton had destroyed the fieldwork at Boyd's, Cornwallis turned back to Hillsboro. There he issued a proclamation inviting all loyal subjects to repair to the Royal standard.

The Loyalists throughout North Carolina began assembling. At the muster ground between the Haw and Deep rivers, Colonel John Pile embodied his regiment. On February 21, 1781, Greene sent Light Horse Harry and his green-coated dragoons to disperse these Tories. Mistaking Lee's troopers for Tarleton's Green Horse, Pile allowed himself to be surprised and his men cut to pieces when they returned Lee's salute with "God Save the King!"

Greene recrossed the Dan and followed Lee back into North Carolina. With Lord Cornwallis lying at Alamance, he encamped between Troublesome and Reedy creeks. Realizing that since the failure of the Loyalist uprising Lord Cornwallis wanted to break away toward Wilmington, Greene began two weeks of marching, countermarching, and maneuvering. Finally he halted defiantly at Guilford.

On March 15, 1781, Cornwallis accepted the challenge. After arranging his troops, he began cannonading the center of the American line. He then ordered his infantry to advance. As they moved forward, their bayonets glistening, the American militia broke and fled, leaving the fighting to the Continentals. For two hours the battle raged and roared, victory swinging between the armies. Finally the American right wing gave way, and even though the Continentals retreated in good order, they left Cornwallis master of the field.

His victory was Pyrrhic, for British dead and dying cumbered the ground. Even seemingly invulnerable Ban Tarleton had been twice wounded, eventually losing two fingers from his right hand. His army too weak to fight Greene a second time, on March 18 Lord Cornwallis began retreating toward Wilmington, on his way to dig a grave for the British at Yorktown.

Soon after the battle of Guilford Courthouse, Captain Hampton reached Greene's headquarters. "I received your letter by Capt. Hampton and am happy to hear of your successful skirmishes," Greene wrote Sumter on March 23. "I lament exceedingly that you did not succeed in getting off the stores. Capt. Hampton says you are in great want of a field piece to further your operations. One shall be sent you as soon as it can be had from Virginia."

Although Greene had lost a battle, he was master of North Carolina. He felt genial and expansive. "Our prospects are flattering in Virginia. They are not discouraging here, but I must refer you to Captain Hampton for particulars," he told Sumter. "Prosecute your operations as expeditiously as possible, and may glory and success attend you."

General Greene chased the British Army as far as Deep River. There he halted, for Tarleton, in spite of his mangled and swollen hand, held with his dragoons until they had destroyed the bridge. Satisfied with having driven the British from central North Carolina, Greene encamped at Ramsay's Mill. There he changed his entire campaign. He could not subsist his army in pine barren already gleaned by the British. The North Carolina and the Virginia militia, having served their terms, were returning home. His army was too weak to fight should he overtake Cornwallis. "In this critical and distressing situation," he wrote General Washington on March 29, "I am determined to carry the war immediately into South Carolina."

Next day Greene wrote a confidential letter to Sumter, warning him that "the object must be secret to all except the generals." After recounting his distressing situation, he said, "All of these considerations have determined me to change my route and push directly into South Carolina." After requesting the Gamecock to call out his entire brigade, he continued, "I beg you will therefore give orders to Genls. Pickens and Marion to collect all the militia they can to cooperate with us."

Although the general had once lectured the Gamecock that states and not posts should be his objective, he had now become intrigued with the idea of capturing the little forts along the Congaree and the Santee. "I am in hopes by sending forward our Horse and some small detachments of light Infantry to join your Militia," he said, "you will be able to possess yourself of all their little out posts before the Army arrives."

Although their return to South Carolina would leave Virginia open to invasion by Cornwallis, Colonel Lee had urged this movement upon Greene. The Virginian still regretted his recall from the Santee and the chance for glory in capturing the river posts, and when Greene promised to send forward his horse and light infantry, Lee begged to be allowed to join the Swamp Fox. With Greene's approval, on April 4 Light Horse Harry set his Legion marching toward Snow's Island. His move was timely.

After having chased the Gamecock from the High Hills, Lord Rawdon had decided to crush the Swamp Fox. During his conference with Colonel Watson, he had instructed the colonel to march immediately into Williamsburg. With a corps consisting of Colonel Henry Richbourg's Loyal militia, Colonel Harrison's provincials, two fieldpieces, and his own regiment, Watson could overwhelm Marion's brigade. Upon his return to Camden, Rawdon conceived a pincer movement. He ordered Colonel Welbore

Ellis Doyle and the New York Volunteers to move to the east, slip down the Peedee, and attack Marion's rear.

The plan was simple, and each commander accepted it with confidence. Early in the morning of March 5 Watson set out toward Kingstree. His troops moved with alacrity, and in late afternoon they formed a bivouac below Nelson's Ferry. But that evening Captain Zachary Cantey spotted their campfires, sensed their objective, and dashed away to warn Marion.

The Swamp Fox was already above Murry's Ferry, moving slowly toward his rendezvous with Sumter. From Cantey's estimate of the size of Watson's corps, Marion realized that the Gamecock had escaped and that the enemy's forces had been concentrated to destroy him. Now he must fight. He could not run toward Snow's Island, for flight would abandon the Whigs to Tory vengeance. By break of day he was astride Ball, already riding along the Santee road. At Wiboo Swamp, a narrow pass about halfway between Murry's and Nelson's, he ambuscaded his troops. After his men had posted themselves in thickets and behind cypresses and gums, he waited for the enemy.

In midafternoon of March 6, 1781, John Watson Tadwell-Watson reached the Wiboo. With a Guardsman's courage he decided to force a passage over the causeway. Using his two fieldpieces, he drove back Peter Horry's horse. Then in hand-to-hand fighting, fierce and bloody, his men drove Marion's militia from the Wiboo and sent them reeling back. Fighting bravely as they retreated, Marion and his men finally reached Lower Bridge over Black River. This was the gateway to Williamsburg. But there the troops of Major James were fighting for home and hearth. They defended the bridge so vigorously that Watson called off his attack and retreated to the plantation of John Witherspoon.

For the next two weeks Marion conducted a superb guerrilla campaign against the invaders. The Swamp Fox was angry. While he had been assembling his men, Colonel Hugh Ervin had sent Captain John Postell to Georgetown to exchange several prisoners. Although Postell carried a flag of truce, Captain John Saunders ordered his men to seize him. Saunders charged Postell with violating the parole he had signed after the fall of Charleston.

During the fighting along the Santee, Marion wrote a letter to

Watson, complaining about the detention of Postell. As heated letters began passing between them, the Swamp Fox wrote, "The hanging of men taken prisoners, and the violation of my flag will be retaliated."

"Men like his Majesty's troops, fighting from principle for their country, with heart full of conscious integrity, are fearless of any consequences," replied Watson.

Back and forth flew angry letters, pleading, threatening, citing military precedents, and quoting international law. As Marion fought with pen, his men used the sword, waylaying and bushwhacking and sniping. After two weeks on Black River, on March 28, 1781, Watson sank his dead in a rock quarry and retired toward Georgetown.

The Swamp Fox gave chase. For thirty miles his horsemen insulted and harassed the fleeing British. As Watson's troops were fording Sampit River, only nine miles from Georgetown, the Carolinians struck his rear guard. After a hot fight, ended by British grapeshot, Watson loaded his wounded on wagons, abandoned twenty dead, and plunged across the ford. Marion and his victorious troops camped beside the Sampit.

While the Swamp Fox and his ragged partisans were defending Williamsburg from Watson, the Gamecock lay in the New Acquisition. Outwardly he was content. After Mary had lived for a month with the Barnetts, recuperating from the terrible ride, he had settled her in a house confiscated from Captain Ezekial Polk, who had maintained his defection from Thomson's rangers. With several women servants who had followed her from the plantation, she was well attended, comfortable, and as happy as circumstances permitted. She was a little worried over Tom, almost thirteen years old and begging to be allowed to join the militia. He was already in the Gamecock's camp on the Catawba, eager, inquisitive, and observant. In after years he boasted of having seen Captain Hampton leaving in search of Greene and returning with the exciting details of the battle of Guilford Courthouse.

Inwardly, however, the Gamecock was smarting. He had failed in his campaign down the Congaree and the Santee. He was convinced that if Marion had been alert and co-operative they might have succeeded against the river posts. Without knowledge of the bloody fighting caused by his ramble, on the day that Marion was driving Watson across the Sampit, Sumter wrote him a long and powerful letter:

NEW ACQUISITION, 28th March, 1781

Dear Sir:

It was exceedingly mortifying to me, after so much pains taken to be deprived of a conference with you, a circumstance much to be lamented, as both individuals and the publick are consequently much injured thereby. Your advice and assistance in framing, digesting and laying down a proper plan of operation against the enemy in future, might have produced the most happy events. My unfortunate failing herein and withal finding contrary to my expectation, that you had neither men, or surplus of any kind, and the force I had with me but small and from many causes decreasing, rendered my retreat at once both necessary and difficult. I find that the disorders are prevalent in your Brigade, which have for some time past been practised on the frontiers with such avidity as to threaten the State with inevitable ruin. To obviate which evil as far as possible, I have adopted measures truly disagreeable, such as can only be justified by our circumstances and the necessity of the case. But it is clearly my opinion, unless this or a similar method be immediately carried into effect, that neither the State or the wealth thereof, will be in the power or possession of the deserving citizens after a few weeks. The dissoluteness of our pretended friends, and the ravages committed by them, are as alarming and distressing, as that of having the enemy among us. It is therefore necessary immediately to discriminate who are enemies, and who are real friends; the former treated as their baseness and perfidy authorize, the latter to be known only by their conduct, that is, by bearing arms and doing duty, when thereunto required by proper authority, and in case of refusal or neglect, both person and property to be treated and dealt with accordingly. Nothing can be more unwise or impolite than to suffer all the wealth of our country to be so basely and unfairly appropriated, for the sole purpose of accumulating our misfortunes, and finally completing our ruin, when it is in our power at once to check, if not totally prevent the evils and disadvantages resulting therefrom; to which end I propose raising several Regiments of Light Dragoons upon the State establishment, agreeably to the enclosed sketch of a plan for that purpose. I therefore request that you would be pleased to cause to be immediately raised in your Brigade two Regiments agreeably thereto. I have also to request that you give orders and oblige every person with you to join their proper Regiments or Brigades, and that none of the enemy when taken be paroled, or set at liberty, but in cases of extreme necessity—that all the property captured or taken from the enemy be securely kept for publick purposes, except what is allowed to, and appropriated to, and for the use of the troops in service, agreeably to the terms proposed. Nothing can be more essential to promote the happiness and secure the peace and tranquility of the people of this country, than treating with the utmost severity, all persons, who, contrary to orders, and to the total subversion of all authority, take upon themselves to form parties to go a plundering, distressing the resources of the country necessary for the use and support of an army. I recommend that too great a number of servants, idle persons and led horses may not be suffered to follow the army. You will be pleased to let me know what your present strength is, and what you judge it may be ten days hence, what your views are, what is the situation of the enemy, and what position you think will most effectually tend to distress the enemy, by preventing their being supported with beef, cattle, &c.—which at Camden they stand in great need of. At present it is my desire that you should have a position higher upon Black River, which is very necessary to not only prevent the stock from being drove to Camden, but also to facilitate my plans and designs on the west side of the Wateree.—The more speedy your movements are, the better they will answer. The enemy are taking great pains to raise a number of horse, a circumstance that should by every possible means by prevented. If men were to turn out cheerfully, so that large bodies might pass through different parts of the country, it would at this time very materially injure the enemy. News from the army and northward I have no doubt you have had. I have just received accounts that Col. Clark with a party of Georgians and South Carolinians fell in with Capt. Dunlap of the Legion near Savannah River, killed and made prisoners the Captain and about 70 more out of 80—some add that Captain Dunlap was recruiting for the Legion. The Governour has probably mentioned something to you respecting some stores, they were stored up in Virginia and will be of but very little consequence when brought forward, as what little there was, has been much pillaged, the dry goods he requested you might have a part of, if you choose to take them. I am apprehensive that the whole will not be sufficient to clothe one Regiment. The day I received your letter, Col. Marshall joined me with about——men, chiefly North Carolinians, chiefly of—— Regiment that left the Waxsaws with him and deserted some days before. I doubt you will get but few out of that Regiment to join you until you are higher up, after our joining they might perhaps remain, if not too leniently treated; they are an untoward set of people. If Col. Harden is still with you, I think it advisable for him to come this way. General Pickens has gone to take command of his Brigade. Col. Harden may be wanted upon some particular occasion. I heartily congratulate you upon the happy advantage gained by Major General

Greene and the army under his command, over Lord Cornwallis, near Guilford Court House.

I am, dear sir, your most obedient humble servant,
THOS. SUMTER

N. B. I shall be happy to hear frequently and fully from you.—I shall make some movements in about six days. I write in so much pain as hardly to know my own meaning, or read what I write.

Since his train of defeats, the Gamecock had reflected deeply upon the military organization in South Carolina. The regular militia, required by law to serve only sixty days when called, lacked training, equipment, and *esprit de corps*. Courageous and valiant in combat, his volunteers were undisciplined, highly independent, and hungry for plunder. Although they came from their farms and mills upon being called, often, as in Marion's brigade, they assembled slowly, in small numbers, and unprepared for great enterprise. They constituted no force in being with which to threaten the enemy.

The Gamecock realized that it would take better troops than volunteers to rid South Carolina of British regulars. Since there was neither executive nor legislature in the state, and since the Continental Congress seemed to have forgotten the partisans, as senior brigadier general and therefore commander in chief, Sumter had decided to act by dictatorial fiat. He proposed raising several regiments of State Troops, each regiment to be commanded by a lieutenant colonel, with his major, and to consist of five troops of dragoons, each troop to have a captain, with his lieutenant, and a sergeant and twenty-five privates.

Sumter's scheme for paying the State Troops was simple. He would use slaves plundered from the Tories. Setting a value of four hundred dollars upon each prime slave, with one over forty or under ten counted as one-half, he devised a regular pay scale: colonel, three and and one-half slaves per annum; major, three slaves; captain, two; lieutenant, one and one-half. He would pay a private a fully grown slave for each ten-months enlistment.

In his scheme Sumter also promised each private a blue coat and two waistcoats, two shirts, two pairs of blue jeans, a pair of shoes and hose, a leather cap, and a woolen blanket. He would furnish each with a horse, equipped with bridle, saddle, and spurs, and a sword and a brace of pistols. In addition to his pay, each soldier would share in two-thirds of all plunder except slaves and military stores, the other third being reserved as public property. And as a special incentive for enlistment, he promised to give the family of each dragoon a half bushel of salt.

Both uniforms and accouterments for the dragoons came from supplies brought by the wagons sent to Newbern in December. While returning, the wagoners had fled into the northwest corner of North Carolina to escape the advance of the British. After Lord Cornwallis had encamped at Hillsboro, the teamsters moved stealthily southward and after an absence of three months and ten days returned to Sumter's camp in the New Acquisition.

Excited by these promises of high pay, constant action for the recovery of their homes, and a chance for military glory, several of Sumter's more aggressive and high-spirited officers began recruiting State Troops. Colonel William Polk went recruiting in North Carolina. Colonel Hill turned into the New Acquisition. Colonel John Thomas began beating around the headwaters of the Enoree and the Pacolet. Colonel Myddelton, with Richard Hampton as his major, headed down between the Wateree and the Congaree. Henry Hampton dismissed his regiment of volunteer riflemen and began enlisting dragoons along Broad River.

"Brother Wade will I believe also raise a regiment," Richard Hampton wrote his brother John. "Should you meet with any young men who are willing to turn into this kind of service, you may assure them that the terms will be strictly complied with." And he concluded, "We are all in high spirits."

Francis Marion studied Sumter's proposal. He knew that the large slaveholders lived in the Low Country. Many of them were Loyalists. In confiscating their slaves without due process of law the Whigs were introducing sinister elements of class struggle into an existing civil war. At its best Sumter's Law, as the scheme was finally called, was simple plundering. At its worst, in tearing apart Negro families, it was barbaric. The Swamp Fox considered the proposal inhuman and subversive of morality. He refused to raise two regiments in his brigade or to have anything to do with Sumter's Law. In a long letter he even challenged the dictatorial power of the Gamecock.

Others were neither so squeamish nor so high-minded. Pickens raised his quota of State Troops. Governor Rutledge gave his tacit consent to the measure. Even though a Quaker, Greene was realistic, perhaps expedient. He neither approved nor disapproved of Sumter's Law. "Although I am a great enemy of plundering," he wrote Sumter during the march toward Camden, "yet I think the horses belonging to the Inhabitants within the Enemy's lines should be taken away from them, especially such as are either fit for waggon or dragoon service." But he cautioned that there would have to be legal safeguards. In the confiscation of "any horses, or any kind of property, whether taken from Whigs or Tories, certificates ought to be given, that justice may be done hereafter."

After his bloody skirmish with Watson, General Marion lay in his tent beside the Sampit. He was weary, and his men were exhausted from riding and fighting. But during the night he was awakened by an express from Colonel Ervin bearing alarming news. While he had been fighting Watson, Colonel Doyle and the New York Volunteers had ridden into Williamsburg, dashed across Clark's Creek, and captured Snow's Island.

Before daybreak the Swamp Fox broke camp. All day his horsemen followed him back toward Williamsburg. In late afternoon they bivouacked at Indiantown. All were bitterly disappointed. They were downcast over the capture of their island stronghold and the destruction of their little store of military supplies. Even the Swamp Fox, his hands clasped behind his back, was pacing to and fro, trying to formulate new plans. Surely Sumter, Rutledge, and Greene had forgotten him and his ragged band of heroes.

As he stood under the oaks near the ruins of Indiantown Church, Marion asked Colonel Peter Horry to muster the men. "It is not for words to express what I feel when I look around upon your diminished numbers," he then began. He reminded his troops of the recent fighting, the thievery of the Tories, and the house burning of Wemyss and Tarleton. Could they return home after so much suffering?

"As God is my judge," cried the Swamp Fox, "if I could die a thousand deaths, most gladly would I die them than live to see my dear country in such a state of degradation and wretchedness!" As his men began to cheer, Marion exclaimed softly, "Well, now, Colonel Doyle, look sharp, for you shall presently feel the edge of our swords."

After swimming Lynches River behind the plantation of Major James, Marion set out in pursuit of Doyle. By evening his troops had reached Burch's Ferry on the Peedee. There ferryman Burch, a staunch Whig, told them a curious tale. Earlier that afternoon Colonel Doyle had camped near the ferry, but as his men rested a mysterious rider had dashed into his camp. After that Doyle had called in his troops, set fire to his tents and wagons, and galloped off toward Camden.

Surprised by this turn of events, Marion encamped and then lingered for several days at Burch's. There he heard more alarming news. Colonel Watson was even then crossing the Peedee at Britton's Ferry. Conjecturing that he would march up between the Peedee and the Little Peedee and call out Ganey's Tories, Marion sent Colonel Peter Horry to count the enemy as they passed through Britton's Neck. With his remaining troops the Swamp Fox crossed the Peedee at Mars Bluff and took a position on the sand hills in Wahee Neck.

Watson was a Guardsman, intrepid and aggressive. He was also a gentleman. On April 9 he bivouacked in the field around the home of Widow Elizabeth Jenkins. Knowing that the widow had three sons with Marion, he begged her to call them home. But she pluckily replied, "I only wish they were three thousand." Outargued, Watson asked her to have a glass of wine with him. "Health to King George" he proposed, and Mrs. Jenkins drank the toast. Then slyly she refilled the glasses. "Health to George Washington!" she cried, as she handed Watson's glass to him. He made a wry face, but he good-humoredly drank the toast.

In the afternoon, Watson moved about a mile and camped at Rae's Hill just across the Peedee from Snow's Island. Next day, with his corps augmented by Ganey's Loyalist militia, he marched to Wahee and encamped on Catfish Creek. He was eager to wipe out the humiliation of his defeats at Lower Bridge and Sampit River.

Low on ammunition, commanding only part of his brigade, the Swamp Fox was in no condition to fight. He decided to retreat. Calling in his field commanders, he asked if they would follow him in search of Greene's army or, if needed, even into the fastness of the Blue Ridge.

"Yes!" they shouted.

Before Marion could retreat, consternation struck the enemy camp. Ganey's Tories began fleeing in every direction. As the Loyalist militia squandered, Watson formed his regulars, wheeled his two fieldpieces into Catfish Creek, and began retreating toward Britton's Neck. Nor did he pause until his troops were again safe in Georgetown.

Marion was astounded. What had caused these mysterious flights of Doyle and Watson? As the men rejoiced in the swift turn of fate, Ensign Baker Johnson, a staunch Whig and trusted scout, galloped into camp. Noting the lathered horse, Gavin Witherspoon cried, "What news, Baker?"

"Fine news!" replied the scout. "I saw a great number of Continental troops, both horse and foot, crossing Drowning Creek." The detachment was already marching through the Loyalist settlements on Little Peedee, their fifes shrilling and their drums rolling, trying to sound like the whole Continental Army.

Soon after the report of Johnson, Captain James Conyers found the camp of the Swamp Fox and handed Marion a letter from General Greene. "This will be handed you by Capt. Conyers, who will inform you what we have contemplated," Greene had written from Ramsay's on April 4. "He is sent forward to collect provisions for the subsistence of the army, and I beg you will assist him in this necessary business. The army will march tomorrow, and I hope you will be able to be prepared to support its operations with a considerable force. General Sumter is written to, and I doubt not will be prepared to co-operate with us."

Light Horse Harry Lee and his legion were also returning to the Peedee, and a Tory forewarning of this had sent Ganey and Watson scampering. After sending scouts to guide Lee to Port's Ferry, Marion called in his men, recrossed the Peedee at Mars Bluff, and hurried through Williamsburg. After crossing at Port's, Lee followed him, and on April 14 the militia and Continentals encamped at Benbow's Ferry on Black River.

Having accepted Lee's advice to return to South Carolina, on April 7 General Greene marched from Ramsay's. He had also adopted Sumter's strategy. With his Continentals he would attack the enemy's main bastions at Camden and Ninety-Six. He would leave the river posts to the Carolina militia, Sumter to campaign on the Congaree, and Marion to sweep the Santee.

He sent Major Hyrne on ahead of the army "To see and consult with you, respecting the force you are likely to collect to aid our operations," he wrote Sumter. "If we can get provisions, and you can raise a considerable force to co-operate with us, I think we shall perplex the enemy not a little, and perhaps do them an irreparable injury."

"I should have five hundred ten months men in the field," Sumter replied enthusiastically. "Genl. Pickens men are much scattered; he will have but few out, that is in any short time. I expect four or five hundred will be ready to join you out of Genl. Marion's Brigade." Hyrne also reported that there would soon be two hundred South Carolinians and three hundred North Carolinians in Sumter's State Troops.

The prospect of action revived the fighting spirit of the Gamecock. He wrote Greene that his plans "would disconcert and injure the enemy more than any other you could have thought of. And you may rely upon my unremitted endeavors to promote and facilitate your designs." But even as he wrote he winced. "I am obliged to write in great haste," he confessed, "as by holding the pen long renders my hand useless."

Chapter 12 WRANGLING IN THE BRASS

GENERAL Sumter and Major Hyrne, who had served together in Georgia, enjoyed an amicable conference. Both understood the temper of the Whigs and Tories. From years of service both knew the Carolina roads, lines of river communications, and natural passes where a small force could be most effective. With Greene approaching Camden, the Gamecock agreed to move down the road over which Cornwallis had marched from Winnsboro, rouse the miltia, and cover the fork between the Wateree and Congaree rivers.

"You will collect your force with all possible speed," Greene wrote on April 14, confirming the agreement for Sumter to protect him on the west, "and endeavor to take a position, as mentioned by you to Major Hyrne, where you may be enabled to cut off, or interrupt the communication between Camden and the other posts of the Enemy, keeping it in your power to cooperate with, or *join* the Army, should the movements of Lord Cornwallis render such measures necessary."

The call to action was exciting. His spirit soaring in spite of the itching, festering sore in his shoulder, the Gamecock broke camp in the New Acquisition. With his newly formed dragoons, a few mounted militiamen, and a convoy of wagons he rode toward Broad River, collecting men and supplies. "The militia are coming in tolerably well," he informed Greene. Then he added a caution: "My movements are slow which I fear will be attended with many Disadvantages."

Sumter's march alarmed Lord Rawdon. Aware that the American Army was moving toward Camden and fearing a co-ordinated attack upon his front and rear, Rawdon set up a diversion by sending one hundred and fifty of his Loyalists to scourge the Waxhaws. These Tories plundered the settlement, fired the Presbyterian church, and murdered several Whigs. Sumter dispatched Colonels

Thomas Taylor and Henry Hampton to chastise the raiders. "But as they begun to retreat on Wednesday night," the Gamecock ruefully admitted, "don't expect they will be overtaken."

Angered by the raid, Sumter decided to retaliate by harassing the Loyalists in the Mobley and Sandy Run settlements. After sending his dragoons, who swept along the creeks burning and killing, he felt "upon the whole they have been pretty well scurged."

Sumter's scourging Tories alarmed Greene. "The animosity between Whigs and Tories of this State renders their situation truly deplorable," he maintained in his correspondence with General Washington and with the Continental Congress. "There is not a day passes but there are more or less who fall a sacrifice to this savage disposition. The Whigs seem determined to extirpate the Tories, and the Tories the Whigs. Some thousands have fallen in this way in this quarter, and the evil rages with more violence than ever. If a stop cannot be put to these massacres, the country will be depopulated in a few months more, as neither Whig nor Tory can live."

While Sumter continued moving slowly down Broad River, Greene began advancing rapidly toward Camden. "Lt. Colonel Lee is on his march from the Pedee to the Santee," he informed the Gamecock on April 15. Lee intended crossing at Nelson's and ascending the river road along the Congaree. "Perhaps you may make your movements cooperate with his and also those of Genl. Pickens."

As Greene advanced he kept in touch with Marion. "We are on our march for Camden, and shall be there next day after tomorrow," he wrote April 17. "I am greatly in the dark respecting the enemy's strength and situation in South Carolina, and also of Lord Cornwallis's motions. This last circumstance is of the highest importance to the safety of our army, and I beg you to communicate to me all the intelligence you can obtain, and take measures to get all you can."

Two days later Greene reached Camden. That afternoon an aide drew up a terse note informing Sumter: "The Army has arrived and taken a position within three Miles of Camden." Colonel Lee wrote in his *Memoirs:* "Here the American general confidently expected to be joined by Brigadier Sumter, in consequence of his instructions to that officer previous to his movement from Deep River."

Greene's position was safe enough. His army was equal to that of Rawdon and on the south he was protected by Marion and on the west by Sumter. Nevertheless, he was uneasy and wrote Sumter, "The Country is barren and promises us no hope of support. My greatest dependence is on you for supplies of Corn and Meal. Both of these articles are immediately wanted, and unless you can furnish me with them, it will be impossible for me to keep my position: I want to know very much your situation, and how you have disposed of yourself, so as to co-operate with our Army on any particular emergency."

The request for co-operation brought on a crisis. Sumter remembered that Greene had once assigned his troops to Morgan. Although still bitter toward the Old Wagoner, he had become reconciled and respectful to the commanding general. But co-operation with the army would mean the subordination of his corps to Greene, and subordination would end his freedom of action. "Brigadier Sumter held off, much to the surprise, regret, and dissatisfaction of the American general," said Light Horse Harry, "and very much to the detriment of his plans and measures."

Greene became impatient. "I wrote you a day or two ago of our arrival in the neighborhood of Camden, and desired to know your strength and situation, to which I have received no answer," he wrote Sumter four days later, scarcely concealing his irritation. "I long to hear from you that I may know how to take my measures respecting Provisions and other matters."

Poking on down the road beside Broad River, stirring up the Whigs and confiscating provisions from the Tories, Sumter was buoyant even if noncommunicative. Although determined not to subordinate the Carolina militia and State Troops to the Continentals, after Greene's plea for corn and meal, he sent Henry Hampton's dragoons and a train of wagons to collect food along the Wateree. "I mentioned by letter to Genl. Polk—and many others of the inhabitants of Macklinburg—what straits you were in for provisions," Sumter wrote in response to Greene's second letter:

"in consequence I am informed that twenty odd Waggon loads were very soon collected and were to start yesterday."

Used to the alacrity of his Continentals, Greene had little patience with the militia and was disappointed by Sumter's slow-dragging. "The militia in our interest can do little more than keep the Tories in subjection," he complained to General Washington. "General Sumter also engaged to have one thousand men in the field by the 18th, to operate with us, but the difficulty of collecting the militia, from the disagreeable situation of many of their families, has prevented their embodying yet in any considerable force."

As Greene worried, the Gamecock encamped on the Davis plantation about five miles below Lyle's Ford on Broad River. About midway between Winnsboro and Granby, he could cover both the Dutch Fork and the fork between the Congaree and the Wateree. This pressure, however, caused an unforeseen movement. Major Thomas Fraser had been beating through the Loyalist settlements on the Broad and Saluda rivers, enlisting dragoons from Cunningham's militia and the survivors of the regiments of Innes and Ferguson. Upon the approach of Sumter, Fraser and his South Carolina dragoons passed quickly down the road from Ninety-Six, crossed the Congaree at Friday's Ferry, and rode on to Camden.

Sumter's allowing reinforcements to slip into Camden annoyed Greene. "Since I wrote you I have critically examined the fortifications of this place and find them much superior to what I expected," he wrote Sumter on April 23. "The garrison from the best intelligence I can get is also much stronger than I expected; and I have had the mortification to hear yesterday that the South Carolina royalists had the Day before thrown themselves into the place from Ninety-Six."

The reinforcement of the British did not excite the Gamecock. "I lament not having it in my power to prevent Majr. Fraser's Detachment from getting into Camden," he replied with equanimity. "I have been under great perplexity; the Detachments from North Carolina & the upper Regmts. in the South have not yet joined me."

As Sumter waited for his militia, General Pickens rode into Camp Davis. He had no troops. The Gamecock assigned him Colonel Flagg's regiment, promised him four more, and sent him to stop such activities as Fraser's among the Loyalists around Ninety-Six. "My force is daily increasing," he then informed Greene. "I move slow for that purpose." He expected three well-appointed troops of horse who were marching from North Carolina. "I shall move on tomorrow," he said, "and the instant I am joined by these troops behind march for the Congarees with all possible speed."

After a joyful reunion of their troops at Benbow's Ferry, General Marion and Colonel Lee, with mutual confidence and admiration, began planning their first move. Marion wished to march immediately to Georgetown and attack Colonel Watson. But Lee demurred. He wished to operate nearer Camden in order that he might co-operate with Greene. So they compromised. On April 15 Lee sent Major Rudolph and his dragoons down the Santee with instructions to report every movement of Watson. Then with Lee's infantry and his militia the Swamp Fox marched rapidly to Wright's Bluff and laid formal siege to Fort Watson.

Lieutenant James McKay, the young officer to whom Rawdon had entrusted the command of Fort Watson, was brave and resourceful. He had food and ammunition, but he had to draw water from Scott's Lake. When Marion sent a detail of riflemen to guard the water front, McKay set his troops digging a well. On April 18 they struck water. When Light Horse Harry saw that the Americans could not starve McKay into submission, he decided to call for help. "I beg you will send down a field piece; it can get to me in one day and a half," he wrote Greene. "Five minutes will finish the business, and it can immediately return."

As Marion and Lee sat before Fort Watson, the Virginia cavalier radiated the optimism of a professional, but the Swamp Fox grew slowly morose and sour. Smallpox had broken out in his camp, and the militiamen without inoculation had deserted. Others were growing restless. When he called for additional militia trouble broke out in his brigade.

The leader of the contention was Major William Clay Snipes. During the fall Snipes had served valiantly, but he now wished to raise a troop of dragoons on Sumter's Law. "I am informed you are taking all the young men that I have ordered to join Gen'l. Marion to the southward," Colonel Abel Kolb, who commanded the militia on the upper Peedee, wrote Snipes. "I must beg leave to inform you of Gen'l. Marion's orders against such proceedings."

"I received yours," replied Snipes tartly on April 16, "and this will inform you that I have instructions from Genl. Sumter, who commands Genl. Marion, to raise men where I can, and as to Genl. Marion's orders, in this case it avails nothing."

Kolb sent a few militiamen to Marion, "though not the number you expect," he wrote on April 18, complaining that the active young men were deserting the militia for the State Troops. "As soon as I received your last orders, I immediately informed Lieut. Lyons, who I had ordered to join you with the young men that were to have been continued with you, of your orders, informing him that I thought the young men that were ready in turning out with him to join Gen. Sumter, would receive the same advantage by joining you, but this did not avail anything."

Colonel Kolb visited Lyons. "I asked him about the men that he had raised," he wrote Marion. "He said that he had sent them to Gen. Sumter and that he would send every other man of the Regiment that he could recruit to him."

Marion immediately wrote Sumter. He complained about Sumter's interference in his brigade. He pointed out that the recruiting, so damaging to the militia, was being done by Snipes in an attempt to form a regiment of State Troops. He pointedly rejected Sumter's Law. He again challenged Sumter's dictatorial authority, and he threatened to appeal to Governor Rutledge.

As Lee watched Marion's dejection increase, he wrote a confidential letter to Greene. "I wish you would write a long letter to General Marion," he said. "His services demand great acknowledgements, and I fear he thinks himself neglected."

Greene was enthusiastic about the efforts of Harry Lee. As soon as he received Lee's request for a fieldpiece, he sent forward a six-pounder under Captain Ebenezer Finley, with an escort of infantry under Major Pinketham Eaton. But the major got lost and wandered into the swamp along Black River. Finally he turned back toward Camden.

After waiting vainly for Captain Finley and his six-pounder, Marion decided to raise the siege. But Major Hezekiah Maham, an enterprising former Continental from St. Stephen's who had recently joined the brigade, suggested an ingenious way of reducing the fort. Improving upon the tower of rails that Sumter had raised at Granby, during the night of April 22 Maham built an oblong tower of logs cut from pine saplings. Before daybreak Marion had filled the crow's-nest with McCottry's riflemen.

As soon as it was light on the morning of April 23, 1781, Lieutenant McKay found the garrison of Fort Watson under fire from Marion's sharpshooters. His men could not reach the tower with buckshot. He raised a white flag.

For the first time since Sir Henry Clinton invaded South Carolina, the Americans had toppled a strong point. The militia and Continentals, working in harmony, had set a pattern for reducing the posts along the Congaree and the Santee. "The officers and men of the Legion and the militia performed everything that could be expected," Marion said in his report to Greene; "and Major Maham of my Brigade had in a particular manner a great share of this success, by his unwearied diligence in erecting a tower, which principally occasioned the reduction of the fort."

Before an express could reach Camden with Marion's report of the capture of Fort Watson, on April 24 Greene wrote the long letter requested by Lee. "When I consider how much you have done and suffered, and under what disadvantage you have maintained your ground, I am at a loss which to admire most, your courage and fortitude, or your address and management," he said with complete sincerity. "Certain it is no man has a better claim to the public thanks, or is more generally admired than you are. History affords no instance wherein an officer has kept possession of a country under so many disadvantages as you have; surrounded on every side with a superior force; hunted from every quarter with veteran troops, you have found means to elude all their attempts, and to keep alive the expiring hopes of an oppressed Militia, when all succour seemed to be cut off. To fight the enemy bravely with a prospect of victory is nothing; but to fight with intrepidity under the constant impression of a defeat, and inspire irregular troops to do it, is a talent peculiar to yourself."

After receiving Lieutenant McKay's surrender, Marion moved quickly upward and encamped at Bloom Hill, the plantation of Captain William Richardson in the High Hills. Here the Swamp

Fox was in a highly strategic position. He could move against Watson still resting in Georgetown or he could rush to support Greene at Camden.

"I congratulate you on your success against Fort Watson," Greene wrote Marion on the morning of April 26. "The articles of capitulation I highly approve of, and feel myself particularly indebted to you and all the officers and men under you, for their spirit, perseverance and good conduct upon this occasion."

Upon the encampment of Marion at Bloom Hill, Lord Rawdon decided that, in spite of his stores, strong fortifications around Logtown, and superiority in troops, his position had become extremely perilous. Should Greene call in Sumter with his eight hundred troops and Marion and Lee with their four hundred, the American Army would become overwhelming. He decided to fight.

About nine o'clock on the morning of April 25, 1781, Rawdon suddenly marched out of Logtown. Under cover of the woods along Pine Tree Creek the young Irish lord began forming his troops. He assigned battle stations to the Volunteers of Ireland, New York Volunteers, King's American Regiment, and several battalions from the 63rd and 64th regiments. From Coffin's New York and Fraser's South Carolina dragoons he formed a reserve. Then moving quickly forward, he surprised the Americans.

At the moment the Continental pickets fired the alarm, their camp was in confusion. Provisions had just arrived, and most of the men were cooking and eating. Others were laundering their clothes. Tired General Huger was bathing his blistered feet. Greene was at breakfast. But there was no panic. The Quaker general began calmly forming his defense. He sent his baggage to the rear. He ordered his artillery formed in batteries. And he then sent every battalion of the Delaware, Maryland, and Virginia troops to its proper place in a straight line across Hobkirk's Hill.

When the British infantry reached the foot of Hobkirk's, the American infantry stepped aside. Through the openings their artillerists began raking the advancing enemy with grapeshot. Rawdon attempted to capture Greene's cannon, but the defenders drove back Coffin's New York dragoons. At the crucial stage, as the

Volunteers of Ireland and New York Volunteers moved steadily uphill, Greene ordered his troops to outflank them and Colonel Washington to charge them in the rear. But the maneuver failed. The Americans were outflanked by the superior British line, and after circling through the fields between Hobkirk's and Logtown, Washington, as humane as he was brave, frittered away his chance by capturing and paroling a flock of nondescripts, such as surgeons, wagoners, and cooks. Exclaimed his fellow officers: "Tarleton would have cut them to pieces and charged into the enemy rear."

At the height of battle, as violence and slaughter mounted, Colonel John Gunby's First Regiment of Maryland gave way. Unable to stem the enemy advance, Greene pulled back his artillery, started his ammunition wagons to safety, and began collecting his wounded. He then began retreating slowly from Hobkirk's Hill. Late in the afternoon he went into bivouac on Saunders' Creek.

Although Greene had been defeated he was cheerful. "We were obliged to retire and give up the field," he told Marion, "though without material loss." Having withstood Rawdon's attack without breaking, the Americans were eager to fight again. "That we may be able to operate with more certainty against the post," he advised Marion, "I should be glad you would move up immediately to our assistance."

"General Greene wishes you to collect all your forces and join him immediately. His army is too small to maintain his ground before Camden, and therefore it becomes necessary that we should form a junction of our forces," Major William Pierce, Jr., Greene's aide, wrote the Gamecock on April 25. "The Enemy advanced out this Morning and gave us Battle. They drove us some little distance from the field, but we saved our stores and took a number of Prisoners."

Unware that Greene was fighting one of the decisive battles of the war, Sumter was quietly encamped on the Davis plantation on Broad River, dawdling, collecting supplies, calling in troops, and chasing small bands of Tories. "I find the country very bare of provision," he informed Greene on the day of battle, but he hoped to send meal and corn by Saturday. "The trouble and perplexity

I have had to get the militia are inconceivable—but I think them pretty well subdued."

Understanding Sumter's independent and imperious character, Greene knew that the Gamecock would evade his order to cross the Wateree and join him before Camden. So he again sent persuasive Major Hyrne to confer with the brigadier. The two old friends argued and argued. But Sumter refused to come under the immediate command of Greene. He thought that the militia would not greatly strengthen the Continentals. Their chief service was in rousing and stiffening the morale of the Whigs and awing the Tories.

"General Sumter has got but few men; he has taken the field and is pushing after little parties of Tories towards Ninety-Six," Greene wrote Light Horse Harry in predicting the failure of his emissary. "Major Hyrne is gone to him, if possible to get him to join us, but this I know he will avoid if he can with decency." After insinuating to Lee that the Gamecock was only a glory fighter, Greene concluded, "The posts upon the Santee and the Congaree should be our great object."

Although Marion had captured a post on the Santee, the discord between the Carolina brigadiers had not enhanced Greene's opinion of the militia. "You frequently hear great things of Generals Marion and Sumter," he had written Colonel Joseph Reed of Pennsylvania. These are "brave and good officers, but the people with them just come and go as they please." He now wrote a similar report to General Washington. "The conflict may continue for some time longer; and Generals Sumter and Marion, and many others, deserve great credit for their perseverance," he told the commander in chief; "but their endeavours rather seem to keep the contest alive, than lay any foundation for the recovery of these states."

His defeat cut far deeper than the writer would admit. "General Greene, theretofore soured by the failure of his expected succor from Sumter," said caustic Henry Lee in his *Memoirs,* "became for awhile discontented with his advance to the South."

After failing to persuade Sumter, Major Hyrne rode back to headquarters, now removed to Rugeley's Mills. He was discouraged and apologetic. Soon a courier arrived with a letter from Sumter. Emissary, courier, and letter were emphatic in that the Gamecock was determined not to bring his militia and State Troops into the American Army.

Sumter's recalcitrance angered Greene. He had expected obedience and co-operation, but he felt that he had received only promises and evasions. Angrily he decided that the Gamecock was a Carolina freebooter who subsisted his private army by plundering Tories.

In his exasperation Greene began hinting at placing Brigadier General Thomas Sumter under arrest. Colonel Davie, now serving as an aide, quickly discouraged the idea. He knew most intimately the Gamecock, the officers and men of his militia, and the State Troops recruited and financed by him. With Governor Rutledge in Philadelphia, the General Assembly expired, and the courts in recess, General Sumter held the highest constitutional authority in South Carolina. He had the power of a dictator.

Besides, there were practical problems. Who had the right to arrest Sumter? Who would constitute a court-martial? Could Sumter be tried by Continental officers when he was not a Continental? Could Marion, Pickens, and some militia colonels try their commanding officer? The row with Morgan had shown that the militia were personally loyal to Sumter. An attempt to arrest the Gamecock would at best destroy the militia, without whose aid Greene would have to forget South Carolina. At worst, in a state already distressed by violence and civil war, it might lead to more bloodshed.

"General Greene was deeply disgusted with the conduct of General Sumter, who had repeatedly refused to obey his express and urgent orders to join him before Camden," said Davie; "to this strange and unmilitary conduct of Sumter, he justly attributed his incapacity to effect the complete investment of Camden; the loss of the action on the 25th; and the arrival of reinforcements under Watson to the enemy; and considering him as a mere Pandour, or freebooter, whose sole object was plunder, and who therefore, would neither act under him nor in concert with him. He would certainly have arrested him but from considerations arising from the state of the country at the time, and the hope that these rambling expeditions of Sumter might arrest the attention of the enemy, and be considered by them as connected with some plan of general operations, and thereby attract more attention than they really deserved."

Greene wrote Sumter on April 30: "Major Hyrne returned this morning, and soon after, Mr. Taylor arrived with your letter of the 29th." Without apparent malice, but resigning to the inevitable, Greene completely buckled under. "Both by the Major's report and your letter, I find you think it will be prejudicial to the public service, for you to cross the Wateree and join us," he wrote. "Our situation requires it; but as you press so many objections, and I am so desirous to rouse the people in that quarter, I have thought it most advisable to revoke the order, and leave you at liberty to prosecute your original plan."

Chapter 13 HASSLE OVER GRANBY

"I am glad you are so Circumstanced as to permit the Troops with me to Remain in this Quarter," Sumter replied to Greene's revocation of the distateful orders. Again his own master, he was cordial and optimistic, displaying more fire and drive than he had shown since the battle of Blackstock's.

Eager for another campaign against the river posts, on April 30 the Gamecock led his troops down to the Congaree. After bivouacking on the plantation of Loyalist George Ancrum, he sent Colonel Henry Hampton to dislodge the guard at Friday's Ferry. As soon as Hampton's dragoons had cleared the river, he crossed and threw a blockade around Fort Granby.

As his infantry began tightening their cordon around Granby, General Sumter turned to the neglected affairs of the South Carolina militia. In the doldrums at Camp Davis he had not answered the last two letters from General Marion, and consequently the Swamp Fox did not write him about the capture of Fort Watson. Tired, slightly piqued, and suffering from pain in his shoulder after the long ride, he began a rather brusque answer to Marion's complaint about Snipes and refusal to organize State Troops.

CAMP CONGAREE, April 30th, 1781

Sir:

I have received yours of the 18th inst. wherein you observe that you wrote me on the 6th, which letter is not lost, as you allege. You gave your opinion in that, it is true, with respect to raising troops upon the State establishment, which opinion it appears you have resumed, not from the ill policy of the measure, but because Major Snipes might have disobliged you. Whether he gave a cause of umbrage, I know not, he was acting by no particular direction of me. If he has transgressed he is amenable, and may, as an officer, be punished with great propriety, notwithstanding there is neither executive or legislative body in the State; yet I think their powers exist, and whoever denies it is dilating the almost mortal wound our laws have received, and directly admits what Major Snipes may have done to be just, or that what he prevented another from doing was unjust. I revere the citizen who is tenacious of the laws of his country. I lament their being so much abused. If I have done it, I think myself accountable and shall no doubt be called upon by the gentleman to whom you say you shall represent the matter, and if he is unacquainted with my motives and the step I have taken, should be happy to have his opinion upon that head. To his judgement and authority, I pay the greatest respect; but I have not a doubt but he and all impartial men, will applaud an undertaking which promised so much good to the United States, and this in particular; especially as it was the last and only measure that could be adopted for its security, or possession of, even the least part of it. As to the powers by which I act, they ought not to be called in question by any man, until gentlemen whom it might concern, had used proper means to obtain information. I am sorry the party you allude to is not likely to be taken. Gen. Greene wrote me a few days ago, that Col. Lee had made his appearance very near, so that he could take it in a few minutes with a piece of Artillery which he had sent him. Since which, I hear it is taken.

I am, sir, your most humble servant,
THOS. SUMTER

After defending his recruiting State Troops under Sumter's Law, the Gamecock relaxed in his camp at Ancrum's. With the siege of Granby going well, he became affable and expansive. His imagination began overflowing with action and strategy. His colonels, his spies, and his millers were busy. He was again the nexus in a web of military activity. Colonel Thomas had just scourged the Tories on Bush River in the Dutch Fork. In general the Loyalists were uneasy, deserting, seeking pardon. All of them will give up "if we can hold our ground a little longer," he wrote Greene in a long, gossippy letter.

The Hessians had gone to Charleston, except twenty-five who followed Major John Doyle into Camden. Major McArthur and his dragoons were quietly resting at Moncks Corner. "I have ten waggons on their way to you with meal, am doubtful they will meet with great difficulty in passing Catawba river," he said. If the general's commissary could meet his wagons on the Wateree below Camden, "I can send forward any quantity of meal that you may have occasion for."

As for dragoon horses, which Greene was frantically calling for, the state was bare except for the district around Ninety-Six, and he had requested General Pickens to secure some from there. There were many good horses high up in North Carolina. "I will use my endeavors to have some procured suitable for the purpose you intend them."

Three British vessels had arrived in Charleston. The sailors reported that Lord Cornwallis was still resting his army at Wilmington. Colonel Balfour was rebuilding the line of forts across Charleston Neck. McArthur was operating below Nelson's. Major Maxwell had three hundred men and two twelve-pounders inside Fort Granby. Good-naturedly, the Gamecock confided to the Quaker on May 4: "I mean to lie as close to the fort tonight as possible."

Sumter's refusal to bring his troops to Camden deranged General Greene's entire campaign. The American Army was in high spirits and capable of repelling an attack, but it was too weak to begin an offensive. So Greene rescinded his order for Marion to move toward a junction. On April 28 he suggested that the Swamp Fox move back fifteen or twenty miles. And "if you cross the Santee you can take all the posts upon the Congaree, and those posts that lie between Camden and the River."

Instead of crossing the Santee, Marion turned back toward Black River. The Loyalists beyond the Peedee had risen and murdered Colonel Kolb. After sending Colonel John Ervin and the Britton's Neck Regiment to punish the Tories, he waited, for his scouts reported that Colonel Watson had left Georgetown. Knowing that the Guardsman would try to cut his way into Camden, the Swamp Fox continued on pivot, ready to swing either north or south of the Santee. But John Watson was cunning. After slipping across Lenud's Ferry, he feinted toward Moncks Corner, as if retiring to Charleston. Then, with McArthur's Hessian dragoons riding as a screen, he began hiking toward Nelson's Ferry.

Learning of his enemy's stratagem, Marion quickly summoned Lee and headed toward the Santee. After crossing at Wright's Bluff on the afternoon of May 4, he tried to throw his troops in front of Watson. He was too late.

Sumter's scouts reported the approach of McArthur. As soon

as the Gamecock realized that Watson was marching close behind McArthur, he detached two hundred and fifty horsemen from Granby and sent them galloping toward the Santee. They were also too late. "Yesterday evening agreeable to the intelligence sent to you I was informed that Col. Watson was crossing the Santee at Buckenham's Ferry," Sumter informed Greene on May 6, in recording the Guardsman's escape. "I am not well informed of his strength, his men much fatigued and hungry."

Late on May 4 the Gamecock again wrote Greene. He had sent his agent back to Charleston for more detailed information about Lord Cornwallis. There should be an immediate attack upon Fort Motte, where Lieutenant Charles McPherson had only one hundred and seven men. In the morning he would send a detachment to Camden for the fieldpiece "which you are so obliging as to say I may have."

As he sat at Ancrum's, active, enthusiastic, and forgetful of his healing shoulder, with his horsemen raiding, gathering intelligence, and strangling Fort Granby, Thomas Sumter seemed again youthful. More like an inquisitive schoolboy than a brigadier general ruling a state he asked Greene: "If you have any thing from the Northward and not a secret, pleased to favor me with it."

While Sumter was enjoying directing the strategy in South Carolina, at Rugeley's Mills only forty miles away Nathanael Greene was suffering frustration. Knowing that both Watson and McArthur would throw their troops into Camden, thus giving Lord Rawdon a superiority, he made a surprising move. Abandoning Rugeley's, he crossed the Wateree seven miles above Camden Ferry. Because Sumter had outtalked Major Hyrne, evaded orders, and refused to bring his troops into the army, General Greene had now moved into a position to join the Gamecock. From his camp on the Wateree, Greene wrote him on May 4: "Last night intelligence arrived that Lord Cornwallis was moving up towards Cross Creek, and it is thought on his way to Camden.

"The movements of Lord Cornwallis will oblige us to collect all our regular force. You will be pleased to forward the letters which accompany this to Gen. Marion and Lt. Col. Lee," he said.

"I am glad to hear the people are joining you, but am afraid, it is a force little to be depended on as they will fall off from the first change of circumstances. I should be glad to know what force you have and what Genl. Marion can join us with," he continued. "We shall halt on 25 Mile Creek untill I hear from you, Lt. Col. Lee and Lord Cornwallis."

In need of horses for mounting scouts, foragers, and Colonel Washington's dragoons, Greene had become obsessed with the subject. He pelted Sumter, Marion, and Pickens with requests for mounts. "Do not fail to get us all the good Dragoon horses that you can, for we are in the utmost distress for want of them," he admonished the Gamecock. "General Marion I am told has a considerable number of them on which he has mounted Militia. It is a pity that good horses should be given into the hands of people who are engaged for no limited time."

Greene now became impatient. "Get all the good dragoon horses you can to mount our cavalry," he told Marion. The Swamp Fox evaded the command. But Light Horse Harry, his own dragoons splendidly mounted on thoroughbreds from Virginia, had seen the Chickasaw Reds that the militia had rustled from the Tories in the limestone region around Eutaw Springs. In his secret correspondence with Greene, he said that Marion could spare a number of blooded chargers.

"You would promote the Service greatly," Greene wrote Marion, his pen a little sharper after receiving Lee's note, "if you could furnish us with sixty or eighty good dragoon horses." The Swamp Fox had no dragoon horses, and he was too chagrined over Watson's escape to reply to Greene. Angrily he blamed his failure upon having to obey the general's orders and not having the freedom of action necessary for a Partisan. As they followed Watson's trail to Buchanan's Ferry, Lee was more philosophical. "Mortified with the result of their exertions," he said, "the disappointed commandants moved upon Fort Motte."

After Sumter's raid in February had shown the weakness of the post, Lieutenant McPherson had abandoned Belleville. Finding the new mansion of Mrs. Rebecca Motte, standing on Mount Saint Joseph and overlooking Buckhead Creek, strongly situated, McPherson seized and turned it into a bastion. He dug a fosse around Motte's, threw up an earthwork and erected a parapet, planted palisades and abatis, and mounted several cannon. He then dug a well and made Fort Motte the depot for convoys moving toward Camden, Granby, and Ninety-Six.

The capture of Fort Motte and the destruction of the fieldwork at Nelson's Ferry were prime targets in Sumter's strategy. "I dispatched your letter for Lt. Col. Lee as soon as it came to hand," the Gamecock reported to Greene on May 7, enjoying his liaison work. "Genl. Marion & Col. Lee arrived before the post at Mrs. Motte's yesterday forenoon."

As Marion settled his army around Fort Motte, Greene began fuming over horses. "Several times I have written you respecting dragoon horses," the general thundered at the brigadier. "We are in the utmost distress for the want of a number. I beg you will furnish us with all you can. I am told that the militia claim all they take from the Tories."

A Continental, relying upon his disciplined Continentals, Greene had little respect for the militia. He did not understand that the Carolinians, serving without pay, furnishing their own equipment, and providing their own transportation, felt justified in taking thoroughbreds from the Tories.

"I acknowledge that you have repeatedly mentioned the want of dragoon horses, and wish that it had been in my power to furnish them, but it is not, and never has been," the Swamp Fox grimly replied. "The few horses which has been taken from Tories has been kept for the service, and never for private property; but if you think it best for the service to dismount the militia now with me, I will direct Colonel Lee and Captain Conyers to do so, but I am certain we will never get their service in future."

As Marion wrote, he thought of the militia blockading, entrenching, and sniping around Fort Motte. He looked at the ragged, undisciplined citizens whom Greene wished to dismount. He knew that, confronted with Greene's orders, his men would merely slip bridles and saddles on the horses and abscond. "This would not give me any uneasiness," he wrote Greene, "as I have some time determined to relinquish my command in the militia as soon as you arrived in it, and I wish to do it as soon as this post is either taken or abandoned." And then he concluded gravely: "When Colonel Lee returns to you I shall take that opportunity in waiting on you, when I hope to get permission to go to Philadelphia."

Greene was shocked by Marion's threat of resigning from the militia and asking Congress for an assignment in the Continentals. He rushed persuasive Major Hyrne to Motte's to encourage the flagging Swamp Fox. "I shall always be happy to see you at headquarters," he wrote, "but cannot think you seriously mean to solicit leave to go to Philadelphia."

Then the Quaker general apologized to the Huguenot brigadier. "My reasons for writing so pressing respecting the dragoons was from the distress we were in," he declared. "It is not my wish to take the horses from the militia, if it will injure the public service. The effects and consequences you can better judge than I can. You have rendered important service to the public with the militia under your command, and done great honor to yourself."

"The movements of Lord Cornwallis will oblige us to collect all our regular strength," Greene again warned the Gamecock upon learning that the British Army had marched from Wilmington. Perhaps the Continentals would have to retreat from South Carolina. "I should be glad to know what force you have and what Genl. Marion can join us with. If our collective strength would warrant an attack upon Lord Cornwallis I should be glad to make it, for defeating him will be next to an entire recovery of the Country."

Sumter was still reluctant to join Greene. Popular, powerful, and unafraid, he wanted full scope to exercise his independent command. Leaving Ancrum's plantation, he crossed the Congaree and personally began tightening the cordon around Granby. "If you have thought proper to send a field piece," he told Greene, "I will endeavor to employ it to the best advantage."

The return of Lord Cornwallis was certainly a matter of moment, he thought, and he hoped his "Lordship will not come very rapidly upon us." The country through which he has to pass is against him in every respect. In the meantime the Americans should continue besieging Granby, take Fort Motte, and move against Ninety-Six. The capture of the posts would be a great acquisition and, the Gamecock said in tracing his own strategy, "would tend as much

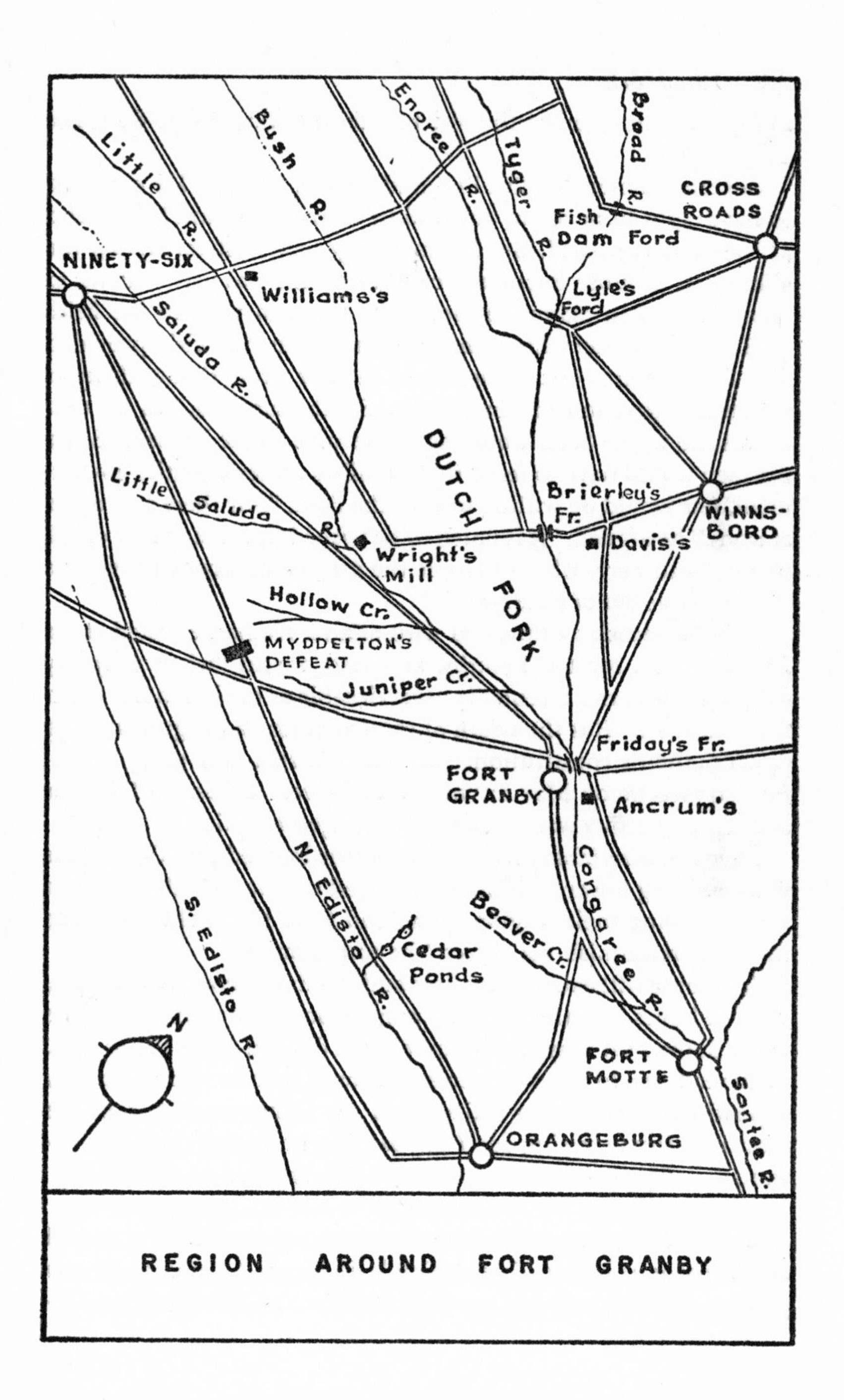

REGION AROUND FORT GRANBY

in my opinion to bring the war to a termination as the defeat of Cornwallis."

General Sumter had five hundred men at Granby. He expected to have eight hundred by the middle of the week and by the end at least one thousand. But because of general distress among the Whigs the number fluctuated constantly. He was even having to furnish bread to many families while the men were in the field.

"It is hard to say what number I could join you with, provided they had to march out of the State," Sumter wrote thoughtfully of Greene's suggestion of abandoning South Carolina, "as by that means the whole State would again devolve to the British." Since the men would have to leave their families under a hostile government, few would be willing to take the field. "For these and other reasons," he argued, "it is much to be wished that the enemy could be met with here, where there is the greater plenty of provisions than to move out of the State."

The Gamecock was pleased with affairs. He had enlisted three hundred men for ten months, and they would "when properly supplied with arms be equally as serviceable as the best horse upon the continent." But the strain of campaigning had begun wearing down Sumter's constitution. "My hand is still very stiff," he informed Greene on May 6; "my shoulder very uneasie & I fear as the weather grows warmer, shall be obliged to retire."

From fairly reliable intelligence Greene learned that Cornwallis was marching toward Virginia. "I am led to entertain this opinion from its being their original plan, and from the Earl's being too proud to relinquish his object," he told Sumter.

"If people will exert themselves and the Earl is gone Northward, I am in hopes that this Country may be once more unfetterd," he wrote Sumter on May 7. "But much will depend upon themselves. Be in readiness to join us if necessity should require it, but you may depend upon not being called from the Congaree but from the most pressing necessity; for I am as fully impressed with the advantages of your continuing there as you can be."

Restless and glum, during the afternoon of May 7 Greene waited in his marquee beside Twenty-five Mile Creek. As soon as he was positive that Watson had reached Camden, he decamped and retreated to Sawney's Creek. Still dissatisfied, he withdrew farther up the Wateree and posted his troops upon the ridges behind Colonel's Creek.

Next morning, as Greene had anticipated, after Watson had rested and accoutered his men, Lord Rawdon mustered his entire corps, crossed Wateree Ferry, and advanced toward Sawney's. Mistaking Greene's light infantry and horse pickets for the American Army, he threw his troops into battle formation and began inspecting the position. "I found it everywhere to be so strong that I could not hope to force it without suffering such loss as must have crippled my force for any future enterprise," he reported to Lord Cornwallis. "I therefore returned to Camden."

The unexpected withdrawal only heightened General Greene's anxiety. "Rawdon has now a decided superiority of force; he has pushed us to a sufficient distance to leave him free to act on any object within his reach," Greene told Colonel Davie. "He will strike at Lee and Marion." He then formed a desperate resolution. He ordered the army to march to Friday's Ferry. Distasteful as was the prospect, he would collect all of his force by joining Sumter.

Lord Rawdon was even more desperate. After retreating from Sawney's Creek, he conceded his position untenable. Cornwallis, under Tarleton's persuasion, had abandoned the Carolinas and was marching toward Virginia. Sumter on the Congaree and Marion on the Santee had cut all lines to Charleston. Reinforcements could break through from neither Ninety-Six nor Charleston. And Greene, with a powerful force, was hovering nearby, trying to collect enough troops for a decisive battle. And so, on May 10, 1781, Rawdon ordered his men to destroy their stores, burn the mills, release the prisoners, and fire the jail. That evening he abandoned Camden and began retreating toward Charleston.

"General Greene has this moment received information that the enemy have evacuated Camden," at eleven o'clock that night Major Pendleton excitedly wrote Sumter. The enemy would now abandon their posts at Augusta, Ninety-Six, and Congarees. "The General begs you will take such measure, if possible, as will prevent *Maxwell's* escaping."

The sudden crumbling of the enemy's main bastion did not change Greene's plan. "The Army was to have moved toward

Friday's Ferry tomorrow morning," said Pendleton. "It will move that way still, tho perhaps, by a different route and more slowly."

But Thomas Sumter was not at Granby. With more troops than Greene, he was independent. As soon as he had received the field-piece, without permission or disclosing his objective, he began a private campaign. Leaving Colonel Taylor to watch Maxwell, he rode quickly down to Orangeburg. The defenders held a strong position around the brick courthouse and jail, but he brought them to terms with a few rounds of grapeshot. "I invested this post yesterday evening at seven o'clock," the Gamecock reported to Greene on May 11; "and I have the pleasure to inform you that at seven this morning it was surrendered to the troops under my command."

With his flair for strategy, he recommended that Marion be disengaged at Motte's. He could then harass Rawdon and prevent his crossing at Nelson's. The evacuation of Camden was a favorable omen. There need be no doubt of the fall of the other posts. "That at the Congarees I think will be taken proper care of," he wrote. "No assistance will be wanted there to keep them close until I return with the troops and field piece."

To support Marion in the projected expedition, the Gamecock decided to scour the country between Nelson's and Moncks Corner. Off he rambled, his State Troops pursuing and scattering Tories from Wassamassaw to Dorchester. His wild incursion so frightened the Loyalists that for five days not a single friend of the King's dared crawl out of the swamps to the Royal Army.

After writing Sumter, Major Pendleton addressed an almost identical letter to Marion. He said that Greene now expected the evacuation of all the posts from the Savannah to the Congaree. He was marching the army to Friday's Ferry. "He begs you to take such measures as may prevent the garrison at Motte's from escaping."

The Swamp Fox began pressing his siege vigorously. But on the night of May 11 McPherson's troops began huzzaing. They could see the campfires of Rawdon's army twinkling in the High Hills. Relief was coming.

Marion then decided upon a desperate stratagem. On the morning of May 12, 1781, he sent Colonel Lee to ask Rebecca Motte's permission to burn her home. Courageously she replied, "If it were a palace, it should go." Handing Lee a bow and some arrows, a gift from the captain of an East Indian merchant ship, she calmly said, "This will serve your purpose."

While Lee's marksmen were shooting fire arrows into the roof of the mansion, Marion's militia were hurling burning lightwood. After igniting a ball of tar and sulphur, Nathan Savage threw it on the roof with a sling. Soon the shingles were blazing. McPherson's men tried to douse the flames, but when they started to climb the roof Captain Finley gave them a whiff of grapeshot.

"My first news, upon landing at Nelson's, was, that the post at Motte's house had fallen," Lord Rawdon reported to Lord Cornwallis. "It was a simple redoubt, and had been attacked formally by sap. Lieut. McPherson had maintained it gallantly till the house in the centre of it was set in flames by fire arrows, which obliged his men to throw themselves into the ditch, and surrender at discretion."

Soon after Rawdon's withdrawal from Camden, Greene sent troops into the ruined village. Then, as the army marched toward Friday's, he called an escort of dragoons and rode off toward Fort Motte. He wished to encourage the besiegers, to confer with Lee about future operations, and to visit and conciliate Francis Marion. He established headquarters at Widow Weston's near McCord's Ferry, and as soon as McPherson surrendered, he joined Marion and Lee at Mrs. Motte's.

With Quaker generosity and Huguenot cordiality, Greene and Marion settled their personal differences and forgot the row over dragoon horses. They talked strategy and ways of destroying the remaining posts. Marion wanted to descend upon Georgetown. Lee wished to capture Augusta. Greene was set to force Ninety-Six.

After a long and amicable meeting, Greene sent Marion down the Santee to watch and harass Rawdon. He ordered Lee to move up the Congaree to Granby. Then with an air of deep satisfaction over his war of posts, he rode on to join his army at Ancrum's.

With great address Henry Lee marched his victorious Continentals toward Granby. Arriving early on May 13, the ebullient Virginian took formal charge of operations. Soon his veterans began closing in upon the fort. Angered by Lee's brushing aside the militia, Colonel Taylor sent a messenger charging down to Orangeburg.

Thomas Sumter had set his heart on taking Fort Granby. "Notwithstanding I have greatest respect for Colonel Lee, yet I could wish he had not gone to that place, as it is a circumstance I never thought of; his cavalry can be of no service there, and may be of the greatest here," he wrote Greene with vehemence on May 14. "I have been at great pains to reduce the post, I have it in my power to do it, and I think it for the good of the public to do it without regulars."

Informed that Rawdon had successfully crossed the Santee at Nelson's, turned back toward Granby, and already reached Motte's, on May 15, 1781, Lee began negotiating with Maxwell. To get a quick surrender he offered overgenerous terms. The British officers would be accorded full honors. The garrison would be allowed to remove their accumulated plunder, even their horses. And Lee would furnish a guard to escort them to Lord Rawdon.

When Taylor's militia heard the terms and saw Lee's handsome troops parading in captured uniforms, they almost mutinied. They threatened to overpower the guards and kill the prisoners. They accused Lee of contumely toward the militia. They swore that he had hurried the negotiations only to cheat Sumter of the honor of capturing Granby.

Sumter was still at Orangeburg, and at three o'clock on May 15 he dashed off a note to Greene. "I have just received accounts that Lord Rawdon is moving upwards from Nelson's Ferry," he wrote. "This account I have no doubt you have received before now, I had several men reconnoitering that way, they have not been as attentive as I could have wished—Genl. Marion was in the evening near to the place where Rawdon was seen, which way he has gone I know not." Without any hint of the trouble ahead, he wrote manfully, "I am just going to the Congaree where I will act for the best as far as I am capable."

After galloping hard, on the morning of May 16 the Gamecock reached Granby. There he learned that Maxwell had surrendered. He heard the indulgent terms. He saw his angry troops. He was told that Light Horse Harry Lee had already marched toward Augusta.

Frustrated, stabbed anew in the wounds beyond healing, and both raging inwardly and outwardly contumacious, the Gamecock flew the pit. "I have been honored with your letter of yesterday's date," he wrote Greene. "I am convinced your reasons are cogent, and your observations exceedingly just; and it has ever been the first wish of my heart to promote and facilitate the public service.

"But with the deepest regret I find the discontent and disorder among the militia so great as to leave no hope of their subsiding soon.

"My indisposition and want of capacity to be of service to this country, induces me as a friend to it, to beg leave to resign my command, and have taken the liberty to inclose my commission, which I hope you will receive, as I find my inability so great that I can't, without doing the greatest injustice to the public, think of serving any longer."

Then bundling up his commission as brigadier general of militia with his letter of resignation, Thomas Sumter sent both documents across the Congaree to Nathanael Greene encamped at Ancrum's.

Chapter 14 FRUSTRATION BELOW NINETY-SIX

"WHAT ails these Carolina brigadiers?" thought Quaker Greene after a messenger had sped to Ancrum's with Sumter's resignation and commission. Within two weeks, at the moment of victory, when the British line against which the Partisans had struggled so valiantly was crumbling, he had received threats of resignation from the two generals chiefly responsible for the victory. Only four days before he had been at Motte's, apologizing over dragoon horses and stroking the rumpled fur of the Swamp Fox. Now he must cross the Congaree to Granby, apologize for the impulsive actions of Henry Lee, and smooth the ruffled feathers of the Gamecock.

Nathanael Greene was honest, conscientious, and sympathetic. He had witnessed the unparalleled efforts of the Carolinians. He understood the fierce pride of the Partisans. He knew the industry, courage, and suffering of Thomas Sumter. Almost singlehanded the Gamecock had aroused the Up Country. Throughout that section he had plagued the Tories and sustained the Whigs. He had organized more than a dozen militia regiments into Sumter's Brigade. He had recruited, armed, and financed six regiments of State Troops. He had harried the British from Nelson's Ferry to Rocky Mount, destroying Cardens, capturing Wemyss, defeating Tarleton, and even perplexing Lord Cornwallis. He had fed the Continental Army. And in the absence of Governor Rutledge he had borne the oriflamme of South Carolina.

As a Continental, General Greene had no authority to accept Sumter's resignation and commission. He could have forwarded the document to Governor Rutledge in Philadelphia and ignored the Gamecock until the governor had acted. Instead, after waiting overnight for the Gamecock to cool off, Greene wrote him a sincere and conciliatory letter.

Camp at Ancrams Plantation
May 17th 1781

The Honourable
Brigadier General Sumter
Dear Sir:

I take the liberty to return to you your commission, which you forwarded me yesterday for my acceptance; & to inform you that I cannot think of accepting it, & beg you to continue your command.

I am sorry for your ill State of health, and shall do every thing in my power to render your command, as convenient as the nature of the service will admit.

It is unnecessary for me to tell you how important your services are to the interest & happiness of this Country; and the confidence I have in your abilities; Zeal for the good of the service. Your continuing in command will lay the public in general and me in particular, under a very great obligation; & tho it may be accompanied with many personal inconveniences, yet I hope you will have cause to rejoyce in the conclusion of the business from the consideration of having contributed so largely to the recovery of its Liberty.

With Esteem & respect
I have the honour to be
Dear Sir
Your most obedient
Humble Servant
Nath Greene

The Carolina Partisans were patriotic, but they were also independent, jealous, and self-willed. Greene knew that there was friction between the Gamecock and the Swamp Fox. Both men were honorable, fearless, and strong-minded, but each wanted freedom of action. Marion consistently evaded Sumter's orders. Instead of going through military channels to the general, he always went over the head of the senior brigadier. To end this and to put the relations between Sumter, Marion, and Pickens on a proper footing, on the eve of marching to besiege Ninety-Six, Greene dictated a letter of policy confirming Sumter's command of the militia.

"You will continue your command of this place, & form and encourage the militia in all parts of the state," he wrote the Gamecock. And after a series of orders intended to mollify the intransigent brigadier, Greene concluded, "You will direct General Marion to take a position, & employ him in such manner as may most effectually annoy the enemy, & at the same time cooperate with us should the occasion require it."

To insure obedience to Sumter, Greene instructed Major Burnet to send the Swamp Fox a direct order. "The General has directed General Sumter to continue at this post to command and organize the militia," Burnet wrote Marion just as the army marched from Ancrum's. "You will be pleased to continue to harass the enemy and to receive General Sumter's orders."

As the State Troops had begun clamoring for the slaves promised them upon enlistment, Greene, although an enemy of plundering, decided to implement Sumter's Law. "Such of the negroes as were taken at this garrison," he wrote the Gamecock, "belonging to Tories or disaffected you will apply to fulfilling your contract with the ten months Troops."

Sumter's militia, especially Taylor's regiment, were still smoldering over Lee's Continentals' having seized the best clothing found in Fort Granby. To stop their grumbling, Greene ordered his quartermaster general to turn over the remainder of the captured arms and small stores to Sumter, which, he told the Gamecock, "You will apply as justice and the good of the service shall require."

Greene was now satisfied. He had made a truce with the Gamecock. He had quieted the clamor among the auxiliary troops and confirmed Sumter in command of the South Carolina militia. He was ready to strike at Ninety-Six. On May 18 he marched from Ancrum's and turned up the Saluda River. Before leaving he requested that Sumter level the old fortifications at Granby, Orangeburg, Motte's, and Camden. "You will carefully watch the motions of the enemy below this place," he instructed him, "and should they come out in force towards Ninety-Six, you will take such a route as to affect a junction with us at that place."

Completely mollified by Greene's conciliatory letter, Sumter returned to his command. With spirit and energy, even if worn and thin, he began campaigning. Soon he reported to Greene: "the works at Friday's ferry, Camden, Mott's, and Orangeburg I think tolerably well demolished."

After distributing the slaves from the garrison, he tried to satisfy his dragoons by stripping the plantations of George and

William Ancrum and seizing others from Andrew Lord. But traffic in human flesh is always a revolting business. His efforts left these horsemen unsatisfied and mutinous. They carried off an additional twenty horses, about a hundred cattle, and a like number of sheep. They then began indiscriminately seizing food, clothes, and medicine from the homes of the Tories.

To strike terror into the settlements of Loyalists along the Edisto, the Gamecock sent Colonel Richard Hampton and a regiment of reformed Orangeburg Tories dashing toward Charleston. Hampton swept down to Moncks Corner, on to Ashley River, turned at Dorchester, and returned by Round O. In covering about two hundred and fifty miles Hampton moved so rapidly that he picked up several British officers and almost bagged Colonel Balfour. "Upon the whole," said Sumter in praising Hampton's deportment, "it may be said his party has behaved well."

Although tattered and gaunt, the Gamecock now seemed indefatigable. Alert and nearly always in the saddle, he dashed in and out of his camp at Ancrum's, equipping and training his militia and State Troops. Many of his new men came in unarmed, and so he established an armory and set an artificer named McElroy forging swords. "I am glad," said Greene in giving Sumter permission to use the materials captured at Camden. "Nothing will strengthen the hands of the Country like measures for arming the people!"

On his seventy-mile tramp to Ninety-Six Greene decided that he needed some militiamen for guides, foragers, and entrenchers. Without consulting Sumter, he called out the regiments of Colonels Brandon, Hayes, Thomas, and Lyle. Brandon reported, but he said that Sumter had already ordered him to Ancrum's. "For particular reasons I have desired him to join us with all the force he can collect," Greene immediately wrote the Gamecock, fearful of again touching a tender spot. "I am sorry to break in upon your arrangements, but I flatter myself you will be persuaded it is for the good of the service."

The action "shore prevented me from making the necessary arrangements & inquiry into the State of these Regemts & the Temper and Designs of the people and has also curtailed my force very considerably," grumbled the Gamecock, "but as you have a call for them, I am Glad they was in the way of being Serviceable."

After separating from Greene at Fort Motte, Marion trailed the British down to Eutaw Springs. When Lord Rawdon retreated to Moncks Corner, he turned into St. Stephen's Parish. At Peyre's plantation, with its creeks and morasses, cypress trees and canebrakes, the Swamp Fox found another lair. After detailing Major Maham to watch Rawdon, he began building a camp reminiscent of his hide-out on Snow's Island. From his spies he learned that there were only eighty British and Tory troops in Georgetown. With his usual zeal and with unusual subordination, he requested Sumter to reinforce Maham. He then asked permission to surprise the garrison. To insure his request, he also wrote Greene: "Beg leave to go and reduce the place."

The Swamp Fox waited eagerly. Rawdon, worn and ailing, was resting quietly at Moncks Corner. There was no enemy activity elsewhere. The weak garrison lay so tempting in Georgetown! "Should be glad of the liberty of going against it," he pleaded with Greene the following day, "but will wait your orders."

Neither Greene nor Sumter was keen for the attempt. Both were equivocal. The Gamecock told the Swamp Fox to remain in St. Stephen's and await orders from Greene. He did, however, order Colonel Tate to assemble his regiment and join Maham.

"If the enemy are making no preparations to intercept the siege of this place or Augusta, and General Sumter don't think himself exposed in consequence of your moving to George Town, of which I have desired him to inform you, I have no objection to your making the attempt you propose," on May 26 Greene replied from Ninety-Six. "But if Lord Rawdon is making preparations for offensive operations which may interrupt the sieges now carrying on, or expose Gen'l. Sumter in his present situation, I would not wish you to make the attempt as that is but an inferior object."

Georgetown an inferior objective? Neither of his seniors understood Marion's burning desire to rescue the village in which he had spent his boyhood. The Swamp Fox knew that he could easily capture the post. Used to swift, independent action, he grew restless and rebellious. Suddenly he made up his mind. Crossing the

Santee at Murry's, he summoned his brigade to meet him at Cantey's Mount Hope plantation.

With his brigade at full strength, the Swamp Fox marched rapidly toward Winyah Bay. After a fifty-mile gallop, he reached Georgetown on May 28 and besieged the fort. All day his men cut trenches and opened regular approaches to the bastion. Their enterprise brought immediate victory, for about nine o'clock that night the garrison evacuated the town. Fleeing to their vessels, they dropped down the harbor to the bar.

"In my last I acquainted you of my intention of marching to this place," the Swamp Fox triumphantly reported to Greene on May 29. "I shall only stay to level the works when I will immediately cross Santee river, take post near Moncks Corner and wait your orders."

Francis Marion considered himself a Continental. His commission as commandant of the Second Regiment was older and, he felt, took precedence over his commission as brigadier general of militia. From General Greene he took orders, but he only co-operated with Sumter. The Gamecock resented his cavalier independence, and complained bitterly to Greene: "Soon after your departure from this, I received a letter from Gen'l. Marion wherein he expressed a Desire of going against Georgetown & said he had wrote you upon that head, upon which I mentioned that he would consequently follow your Direction, until which I requested he would Cover the Country, & prevent the Enemy from Ravaging it. He however proceeded against Georgetown."

Two days later the Gamecock congratulated Marion. "I am glad to hear you succeeded against George Town," he wrote tersely, "and that you think of passing the Santee soon."

Marion's capture of Georgetown drove the British below the Santee. "It gives me great pleasure to hear the enemy has left Georgetown," Greene said in his congratulations to the Swamp Fox. "After you have dismantled the enemy's works, you will collect your force, take the position you mentioned, and act in conjunction with General Sumter."

After capturing Fort Granby, Light Horse Harry Lee rushed over to Ancrum's for a long conference with General Greene.

Praised for his zeal and briefed in strategy, the Virginian set his newly outfitted Legion on the road toward Augusta. Three days later he joined General Pickens. Old friends, having operated together against Tarleton in Greene's retreat across North Carolina, they immediately began reducing Forts Grierson and Cornwallis.

Lee's Continentals and Pickens' militia invested Fort Grierson so closely that on May 22 Colonel Grierson tried to cut his way out. The besiegers killed or captured every member of his command. Then they concentrated against Fort Cornwallis. But Colonel Browne was resolute. At Savannah his South Carolina Loyalists had driven Marion's Second Regiment back from Spring Hill redoubt. With the same tenacity he now held Fort Cornwallis, and on June 3 when the American commanders summoned him to surrender he replied defiantly, "I have the honor to acknowledge the receipt of your summons of this day, and to assure you, that as it is my duty, it is likewise my inclination to defend the post to the last extremity." After two days more of bombardment, sally, and skirmish, Lee began constructing a Maham tower. Browne raised a white flag.

While Marion and Pickens were boldly uprooting the anchors of the old British line, General Greene was carefully pushing the siege of Ninety-Six. His infantry and militia were entrenching, cutting parallels, and making a formal approach to Star Fort. "I have nothing new," he informed Sumter on May 29. "Our approaches are going on but slowly."

Elsewhere there was excitement. On June 2 officers of the First Regiment in the prisoner-of-war camp on Sullivan's Island counted seventeen troop transports entering Charleston harbor. Lieutenant Colonel Pasten Gould had arrived from Cork with the 3rd, 19th, and 30th Regiments. Lord Rawdon could now relieve Cruger and reconquer South Carolina. "I shall march on the 7th toward Ninety-Six, having been reinforced by the flank companies of the three new Regiments," Rawdon informed Cornwallis.

"Just now received intelligence that the enemy has received reinforcements of near two thousand men," Alex McGregor, a former Continental and now a trusted spy, reported in a note to Marion. On the eve of joining Maham before Moncks Corner, the

Swamp Fox turned back to Cantey's. And calling in his swiftest courier, he rushed McGregor's letter to Sumter and asked him to relay it to Greene.

The Gamecock was unperturbed. After forwarding McGregor's report and a copy of *The South Carolina Gazette* to Greene, he forgot about them. Next day Marion sent a fuller account. "I am sorry to hear of a reinforcement having arrived," Sumter answered immediately; "have hopes it may not be so considerable as is suggested."

Greene was more disturbed. Even before receiving McGregor's note, he had intelligence of the arrival of Colonel Gould. He had also heard that Rawdon was rushing preparations to march to Ninety-Six. "Should the enemy attempt to penetrate the country," he wrote Marion, "I beg you to collect all the force you can and join Gen. Sumter."

With Cruger defiant and gallantly defending Star Fort, Greene determined to slow down the British advance until he could take Ninety-Six. With perfect confidence he ordered the Gamecock to fall in ahead of Rawdon and retreat slowly, skirmishing, scorching the earth, and removing provisions, cattle, and transportation from his line of march. "Collect all the force you can," he said firmly, "and give positive orders for Gen'l. Marion's force to join if the enemy attempt to penetrate the country."

Greene's assignment excited the Gamecock, and he responded quickly, "I will do all in my power to retard the enemy's March." He had about eight hundred men at Ancrum's. He had already written Marion, but the Swamp Fox had not replied. "He is at Murries ferry on the north side of Santee, is not moving up, as he has but few men, thinks to gather some more," Sumter fumed disgustedly. "I have given him positive orders to march with what he has."

The Gamecock's bad temper stemmed from suffering. Excitement, overwork, and hot weather had irritated his shoulder, and the ball received at Hanging Rock had never been taken from his thigh. "I am unfortunate enough to find my indisposition increases so fast as not to have any hopes from the Nature of it, to be able to remain with the troops many days longer," he finally admitted to Greene on June 11. "I shall endeavor to hold out until you are so disengaged as to take Measures in consequence of my withdrawing."

In the meantime Lord Rawdon was moving slowly, keeping his men concentrated and sending out few detachments. Convalescent from malaria, he was almost too weak to command, but like Sumter, he kept going from devotion to duty. His veterans, especially Watson's regiment, were worn out and sickly. His reinforcements were in even worse condition. Untrained and unequipped for campaigning in the Southern Provinces, they stumbled over the rough terrain, frightened by strange reptiles and tormented by chiggers, ticks, and mosquitoes. Still clothed in heavy woolens, they fainted from heat, and many died from sunstroke under the blistering, semitropical Carolina sun.

Rawdon's tardy movements confused the Americans. Sumter decided that the British commander was not marching to succor Cruger. Upon that assumption he changed his plans and prepared to move from Ancrum's toward Orangeburg. "If the last accounts of the enemy prove to be facts," he wrote Greene on June 14, "I shall this evening pursue my former intention, that is to march downward, with my whole force."

Greene agreed with Sumter. He could not believe that Rawdon would march an unsupported column through two hundred miles of hostile country, dogged by American militia and confronted by veteran Continentals. Cheerfully he replied, "I cannot persuade myself that the enemy mean to pay a visit to this place." Nevertheless he told the Gamecock, "Keep in front of the enemy."

Both Greene and Sumter hesitated, but Colonel Myddelton, encamped and making swords at McCord's Ferry, with his dragoons riding patrol around Orangeburg, soon corrected their misapprehension. His details reported the British advancing and the Tories flocking to the Royal standard. Quickly he sent his materials, workmen, and unarmed militia up country from the Congaree. "I am apt to think that the Enemy's Object is 96," he informed Sumter, "as the rout they take is directly for that place."

Sumter countermanded his orders to march downward. "There is scarce a doubt but 96 is the place of their destination," he informed Greene on June 16. "I am just moving upwards."

During the excitement the Gamecock sent for the Swamp Fox.

"I recommend that you call out three-fourths of your Brigade and move higher up the River," he first wrote. After Myddelton's report he wrote again: "I wrote you today that the enemy were upon the way to Ninety-Six. They go very slow. You may join me in time." And later in the day he wrote a third time: "The enemy are yet advancing, are some distance above Orangeburg, their force considerable."

Although Rawdon was moving along the road above the North Edisto, certain to cross the road to Augusta forty miles west of Granby and to continue along the sand ridges, Sumter delayed carrying out Greene's orders. Instead of throwing his whole corps of militia and State Troops ahead of the enemy, skirmishing, checking, and delaying their advance, he remained on the Congaree until Rawdon had come abreast of him.

In his siege operations at Ninety-Six, Greene found little use for cavalry. Consequently he ordered Colonel Washington's idle dragoons to return to Ancrum's. Sumter assigned some mounted militia and State Troops to Washington, augmenting his force to three hundred men, and rushed him off to operate ahead of Rawdon. He then sent Myddelton and Richard Hampton with their State Troops to hang upon the flank and rear of the British.

"With the remainder of the Troops I have crossed this River and shall fall upon your trail," he wrote Greene from Martin's Ferry on the Saluda. "I am now halted for Cols. Laceys, Taylors & Tates Regemts. to come up with me. As soon as they arrive I shall proceed on, with all speed. Genl. Marion is coming on & as provision & forage is provided for him, expect he will be up in three days."

When Sumter halted at Martin's, Rawdon encamped at the Cedar Ponds, morasses fed by springs bubbling from the sandy waste known as the Ridge. The two corps were now about fifty miles from Ninety-Six and more than twenty miles apart. Chafing because the Gamecock was making no effort to narrow the distance, Greene reminded him of the instructions "in my former letters."

Somewhat nettled, Sumter replied that he had sent out most of his horse. "The foot are very troublesome," he said, but "I will push them hard." He had only three hundred men with him on the Saluda, but he was assiduously trying to carry out Greene's orders. "The whole now chiefly detached," he said, "and is acting against the enemy as you wish & has been since they past Orangeburg."

To send small detachments against a concentration is to invite disaster. While the Gamecock was writing a defense of his tactics, misfortune struck. About ten o'clock on the morning of June 18, 1781, Colonel Myddelton caught up with the British rear marching between Juniper and Big Hollow creeks. The enemy turned back. Instead of wheeling and retreating, Myddelton prepared to fight. Instantly two hundred mounted infantrymen charged his front, while Fraser's dragoons attacked his flank and rear. Without swords for close fighting, the Carolinians broke and fled. "The whole dispersed," Sumter reported laconically. "The Colonel got off."

After his dragoons had cut up the State Troops under Myddelton, Rawdon sent them across the Saluda. Caught with his best troops scattered across the Ridge and "encumbered with rubbish," Sumter retreated hastily through the Dutch settlement to Wright's Mill. Completely outmaneuvered and too weak and far away to join Greene before Rawdon had cut his way into Ninety-Six, Sumter encamped. "I am very sorry that the post at Ninety-Six can't be reduced before the approach of the enemy," he wrote philosophically from Wright's. "The raising of the siege is a disagreeable circumstance, but in my opinion will not prove so disadvantageous as some may think it. If you can avoid a defeat, they are in a fair way to lose more than they will gain by saving the garrison."

The siege was going badly. By sap and mine the Americans had advanced to the base of Star Fort. Colonel Cruger, however, defended his post gallantly. When Greene built a Maham tower for his sharpshooters, Cruger piled sandbags above his parapet. When the Carolinians shot flaming arrows onto the roof, Cruger knocked off the shingles. Light Horse Harry's legionnaires captured the stockade defending the water supply. Cruger sent naked slaves through the dark to fill their pails at Spring Branch. With Rawdon only two day's march away, on June 18 Greene mounted two desperate attempts to storm the fort. In hand-to-hand fighting, Cruger's New Jersey Volunteers drove back the Continentals.

Next morning Greene raised the siege and began retreating toward the Saluda. "The General wishes you to halt with your troops at General Cunningham's plantation," Major Pierce hurriedly wrote Sumter on June 19. "You will be met there by this Army."

Inconvenienced, disappointed, and thoroughly angered by the Gamecock's apparent foot-dragging and failure to carry out orders, Greene reported to the Continental Congress, "The enemy passed him at Congaree before he got his troops in motion; afterwards he found it impracticable to gain their front."

Although chagrined, Greene then made a personal appeal to the Gamecock. "I am anxious to collect our force to enable us to give the enemy the most effectual opposition," he pleaded. "I beg you will march your troops and form a junction with us at the cross roads near the fort at Williams' plantation."

General Sumter did not go to the crossroads near Fort Williams. Instead he sent Colonel Polk to report his situation and explain his disobedience. His corps was scattered. After Rawdon's triumphant march, with the Tories riding and plundering and burning, the militia had gone to protect their homes. Every man in the regiments of Colonels Taylor, Tate, Winn, and Hampton had deserted. And worse still, because of vexation, strenuous physical exertion, and the sweltering heat, Sumter's shoulder had flared up badly. Exhausted and heartsick, the Gamecock could scarcely ride his charger.

While the American Army waited at the crossroads, Lord Rawdon paraded into Ninety-Six. For safety Greene drew back across Bush River. There he made a strategic decision. He would cross Broad River at Lyle's Ford, move back to Granby, and threaten to cut between Rawdon and Charleston. "You will continue in the neighborhood you are in," he wrote Sumter, "and collect and arrange the militia as fast as you can."

Nathanael Greene was humane. Even in his frustration he recognized the ordeal of the Gamecock. "Col. Polk informes me your health is getting worse, and your Wound more troublesome," he wrote with sympathy. "I am sorry on yours, my own, and the public's account."

Chapter 15 DEFEAT AT QUINBY

"I AM in hopes to see you in a day or two," Greene wrote the Gamecock from his camp on Bush River. Then after calling in Colonels Washington and Lee, who had been operating ahead of Rawdon, the general retired leisurely across the Dutch Fork and encamped on Indian Creek, a fresh, clean tributary of the Enoree.

Lord Rawdon quickly followed. Pausing at Ninety-Six only long enough to select his sturdiest and leave his ill and weary troops with Cruger, on June 23 he crossed the Saluda at Island Ford and headed across the Dutch Fork.

"The General would wish you to collect your force immediately, and march with all possible expedition to his assistance," Major Pierce wrote Sumter after Greene had decamped and begun retreating. "The Army will wait at Fishdam Ford upon Broad River."

The Gamecock responded quickly. With his rubbish, scattered companies, unfilled regiments, and disorganized corps, he crossed the Broad. Then moving toward the junction, he went into bivouac at his old camp on the Davis plantation. He was now only fifteen miles below the main army encamped at Fish Dam Ford. "Lament exceedingly that we have no better prospect of making a stand," he wrote, fully realizing that he could not furnish enough reinforcements to enable Greene to defy Rawdon. He also realized that the militia colonels in the lower territory of his brigade could not induce their men to march to the upper part of the state while the Tories were rampant. So he requested his colonels to call out their regiments and to join Marion in the High Hills. But, as he informed Greene, "I am apprehensive nothing of an extensive Nature will be in our Power."

In spite of the disorganization in his militia Sumter was optimistic. He believed that a move toward Granby would draw Rawdon downward and that Cruger would then evacuate Ninety-Six. "If any movements downward should be thought necessary I beg leave to say the sooner it took place the better it would be." And then as a soldier the Gamecock concluded, "I am moving toward the Cross Roads, where I shall be happy to receive your further commands."

With Rawdon rapidly approaching, Greene abandoned his camp at Fish Dam Ford and began retreating toward Charlotte. He planned to stop at the crossroads near Sandy River. Should Sumter join with enough men, he would turn back and attack the British as soon as Rawdon crossed Broad River. "His Lordship encamped last evening beyond the Enoree," Major Burnet informed Sumter; "his troops are greatly fatigued & without bread."

The Gamecock joined Greene at the crossroads. He brought the State Troops, but very few militiamen. He also brought news of two strategic developments. Lord Rawdon, fearing to march his exhausted troops farther, had turned back upon reaching Duncan's Creek; and General Marion, with part of his brigade, had reached Ancrum's. After a long conference it was decided that Sumter should move back toward the Congaree, again call out his brigade, and take command of Marion's militia and the Continental dragoons under Washington and Lee. He should then move between Rawdon and Orangeburg.

"It was my wish to have fought Lord Rawdon before he got to Ninety-Six, and could I have collected your force and that of Gen. Sumter and Pickens, I would have done it, and am persuaded we should have defeated him, but being left alone, I was obliged to retire," Greene wrote Marion on June 25 from his camp on Sandy River. "Gen. Sumter is preparing for a maneuvre down in the lower part of the State, and he will require your aid to bring it into effect. You will therefore call out the force you can and cooperate with him in any way he may direct."

"Sumter is on the march to the Congaree, and will prepare to go still lower down," Greene wrote Light Horse Harry on June 25, in calling his dragoons back from watching Rawdon. "Let your movements be correspondent with his, so far as you may find them consistent with the good of the service."

Greene was also optimistic. A detachment of Continentals had reached the crossroads and that afternoon Colonel Armstrong had marched in with the North Carolina regulars. "Sumter and Marion are collecting their forces," he confided to Lee. "If Pickens joins us with a considerable force it will be my wish to force Lord Rawdon to an action."

Thomas Sumter was independent, headstrong, and often contrary. After visiting Greene's field headquarters at Sims's ordinary, he rode off toward Winnsboro. He had seemed agreeable to his new task of rousing the militia, driving a salient into the Loyalist country beyond the Congaree, and preventing Rawdon's re-establishing a post at Granby. But he was worn and suffering and within a day's ride of his family. He felt that nothing would inspirit him like a visit with Tom and Mary. So he ordered his troops to move down to the Congaree and then he quietly set off to visit their home on Sugar Creek.

For a week, while Sumter remained with his family or visited old haunts along the Catawba, Greene and his army rested at Lee's crossroads above Winnsboro. On the evening of June 28, however, a British deserter rode into his camp, having come directly from Four Holes Swamp above Dorchester. He reported that a convoy of some three hundred troops with a large quantity of stores designated for Rawdon was moving slowly along the Edisto. Greene immediately ordered Washington and Lee to join at Ancrum's and move downward to intercept the convoy before it could reach Orangeburg.

Although unknowingly marching to battle, the Carolinians were poorly armed. The Gamecock knew that good morale stems from confidence and that confidence is inspired by superior equipment. Still hoping to maintain six regiments of State Troops, he now set up an armory in the New Acquisition, employed several artificers, whom he promised two slaves for a year's work, and set them forging arms. But steel was almost unobtainable, and he complained to Greene that "materials for making swords are extremely Scarce."

Greatly revived, the Gamecock was ready to set out on the long ride to Ancrum's. "I shall go by way of Waxsaws to Camden & meet with the Troops between the Wateree & Congaree," he said in sketching an itinerary that the couriers could follow. "I should have been happy in waiting upon you before my Return to the Congaree," he said manfully, hoping to explain his irregular behavior to the general whom he had left sitting at the crossroads; "but the want of arms and the doubts of the workmen at Camden not being well imployed induced me to go the nearest way to that place."

In the meantime, informed that Rawdon was moving steadily toward Granby with twelve hundred men, besides the reinforcement coming up through Orangeburg, Greene began forcing his own march toward the Congaree. Unable to handle his wayward brigadier by threats or orders, he turned to pleading. "I doubt not many advantages will result from your visiting the upper Regiments; but I fear the opportunity for striking the Posts at Monks Corner and in that Neighborhood is past," he wrote from Winnsboro on July 3, solemnly but without exasperation.

Greene feared that Rawdon planned to hold Ninety-Six, retake Augusta, and then seize Granby. "It is of the greatest importance that we prevent it if possible. For this purpose I wish to draw all our force together at or near Friday's ferry, and oblige the Enemy to give up the Post, fight us in detachments, or collect their force to a point." He knew that Marion was in the neighborhood of Friday's Ferry. Pickens was on the march and would join that day or the next. "If our force is separated we can expect nothing. If it is collected we can oblige the Enemy to keep theirs collected; and that will prevent their establishing their posts again; a matter highly interesting to these States, as I shall inform you when we meet, from the peculiar circumstances of foreign affairs. Having given you a state of matters," Greene continued entreating, "I beg you will form a junction with us as soon as possible."

Colonel Washington, in bivouac on Colonel Taylor's plantation near Ancrum's, reported that Rawdon had tramped into Granby about eleven o'clock on the night of July 2. "This is what I expected," Greene exclaimed in frustration in his second letter to Sumter on July 3; "not a moment's time is to be lost in collecting our force to that place; otherwise his Lordship will fix himself so firmly, that there will be no possibility of moving him."

"Had I the force sufficient to authorise an attempt without you, I would not delay a moment," he continued dejectedly; "but unfortunately for our cause I have but a shadow of a force, much less than you imagine. I write you thus plainly that you may not be deceived by common report." Then the general issued a direct order to the brigadier: "I wish you not to go by the way of Camden if it will delay you a single hour."

Greene's express caught up with the Gamecock at Hanging Rock. "I have just received your two letters," Sumter replied. And then with perfect nonchalance, without any compunction about not obeying the commanding general, he continued, "As it is your wish that I should not go by Camden—I am very sorry that I am so far advanced or that I have so much Reason to go that way, but upon account of some Arms and some Detachments that are gone on; & withal some Directions necessary to be given, together with the little difference it will make in point of Time with Respect to my joining you, induces me to proceed; which I hope, as Matters are, you will not disapprove of. Not a moments time shall be lost. You may Rely upon there being great reason for the Tyersum Round I am taking."

Next day Sumter rode on down to Camden. Finding things in great disorder, he spent the day completing the destruction of the fortifications, collecting material, and ordering out and arranging his troops. Learning that Rawdon had scarcely paused at Granby, but had wheeled away toward Orangeburg, and that Greene had pushed on across the Congaree, he decided to spend another day. "I intended to have set out this Morning for your Camp," he tardily reported to Greene. And then after reporting on the militia and State Troops, he concluded, "Shall therefore proceed to Marshalls Mill or Col. Taylors Camp near there, & wait your farther orders."

With Rawdon pulling away rapidly, Greene ordered the dragoons under Washington and Lee and the mounted militia under Marion to follow him, vexing, galling, and bushwhacking. With his infantry following slowly, he dashed ahead and on July 7 came to rest at Motte's. "You will please to collect all your militia and the remainder of the State Troops and follow on to give us support should it be necessary," he wrote Sumter.

And then without anger, but with a sense of complete helplessness, Greene turned away from the tardy brigadier. "Where this will meet with you I cannot tell," he wrote the wanderer, "and therefore leave you to take such route as you may think proper to bring you to a point of support in the shortest time."

Greene now slackened his drive against Rawdon, and there was lessening of tension and more orderly concentration. Sumter moved down to Russell's Ferry on the lower Congaree. He ordered the State Troops under Colonel Henry Hampton to pass the river, unite with the Continentals under Huger, and come under the immediate command of Greene. "If the Troops were now collected—I mean all the horse—I think his Lordship may be made very uneasie & forced to retreat," said the Gamecock.

With the regiments of Colonels Lacey and Winn already in camp, Sumter remained at Russell's until the arrival of the regiments of Colonels Hill and Bratton. "The whole would form a pretty detachment," he mused as he reported to Greene, "& you may rest assured I shall press forward with all possible dispatch the moment I am able to comply with what appears to be your Design."

Huger's men were short of provisions, and so, without waiting to find and consult Sumter, Greene called upon the regiment of Colonel Taylor to serve as foragers and purveyors. But knowing the sensitive nature of the Gamecock, Major Pierce wrote an apology for the general's trespass in the command of the militia. "The General was induced to send for Taylor's men because they were better able to serve this army from their knowledge of the country than any others." And then Greene's aide, attempting to prevent any possible friction, gave the Gamecock a hint of unlimited scope and power in the coming campaign. "No barriers will be thrown in your way to obstruct the execution of your plan, & our best wishes attend you for success."

Next morning Major Pierce sent a messenger to ask Sumter to furnish fifteen or twenty men "who may be acquainted with the Orangeburg road to reconnoitre the Country between that and the Juniper Springs." Scouts had just reported that Colonel Cruger and his troops, with those under Colonel Doyle, scattering contingents of Tories, and a migration of Loyalists had left Ninety-Six enroute to Orangeburg. Greene planned to throw his entire army between Cruger and Rawdon: "he therefore desires that you will hold yourself in the most perfect readiness to co-operate with us."

"The object is important and no delay can be admitted," Pierce warned the brigadier. At the same time he held out glory. "Much depends upon the success of our operations, and much credit will be the reward of those who exert themselves at this very interesting and important crisis. I again repeat to you that General Greene expects that you will hold yourself in the most perfect readiness to co-operate with this Army."

During this crisis Colonel Washington's dragoons were constantly patrolling the roads between Orangeburg and Charleston. A trooper ran down an express with dispatches for Lord Rawdon. From these Washington learned that Lieutenant Colonel Alexander Stewart and the 3rd Regiment were marching toward Orangeburg with medicines, provisions, and stores for Rawdon. Greene ordered Marion's brigade to intercept Stewart.

With four hundred horsemen the Swamp Fox moved rapidly but secretly. On July 6 he circled eastward of Rawdon's army so silently that he reported to Greene, "They have no idea of any force being near them." The British were exhausted, sick, and mutinous. "Their troops are so fatigued they cannot possibly move."

Before day on the morning of July 8 the Swamp Fox crept stealthily down the road between Orangeburg and Moncks Corner. He expected to meet the Buffs around every bend. But fate intervened. In unfamiliar country, Stewart missed the highway and marched along a seldom-used road. During early morning the two corps passed each other. Learning his ill luck at daylight, Marion sent Colonel Peter Horry back in pursuit. He overtook the convoy and cut out several wagons. But in spite of Horry's efforts, Stewart marched into Orangeburg.

Huger encamped the army on Beaver Creek, about halfway between Granby and Motte's. Here General Greene began concentrating his force. After the arrival of Washington and Lee, he called in Marion and Sumter. As the others came in, the Gamecock joined them, now fully co-operative and enthusiastic. Greene was highly gratified. For the first time since coming into South Carolina, with the exception of Pickens and his brigade, the American general had all of his field officers and their troops under his immediate command. He decided to march directly to Orangeburg and pick a fight with Lord Rawdon.

After marching all night to avoid the near-tropic sun, about nine o'clock on the morning of July 12 the army reached Turkey Hill Creek, a small branch of the North Edisto about four miles above Orangeburg. General Greene, escorted by the dragoons of Washington and Lee and accompanied by Brigadier Generals Marion and Sumter, promptly galloped off to reconnoiter the village. The generals found the enemy position exceedingly strong. The British Army was deployed around the brick courthouse, one wing resting against the jail and the other against the bridge over the Edisto. Realizing that Rawdon could probably hold his position until Cruger arrived, Greene decided not to attack. But he lay at Turkey Hill until six o'clock in the evening, provoking and insulting his foe, while his own sweltering and hungry troops chased up and down the creeks in search of frogs, turtles, and alligators. Content that he had offered to fight, he wheeled his army around and marched back to the plantation of Colonel Myddelton.

At Myddelton's, Greene held a council of war. He had been campaigning vigorously for six months, and now he wished to rest his troops. He wanted to save his Continentals from the heat and malaria of the Low Country. At the same time he wished to keep up pressure against the retreating British. After long consultation he decided to recross the Congaree and the Wateree and build a camp of repose in the benign High Hills of Santee. And he agreed to entrust the summer campaign to Brigadier General Sumter.

General Sumter now had his opportunity. He had always believed that it would stiffen the morale of the Whigs, win the vacillating and disaffected, and discourage the Tories should the troops of South Carolina win a magnificent victory. Thin and weak as he was, he accepted the challenge and the responsibility. Assuming command over Marion, Lee, and their horsemen, he began formulating bold plans. He decided to move downward some sixty miles, cut all the approaches, and then storm Moncks Corner.

With the largest and finest body of troops that he had ever commanded in the field, Sumter opened his campaign by deploying them in sweeping and characteristic fashion. He ordered Marion and the dragoons to dash ahead and seize the approaches. The Swamp Fox moved briskly. Light Horse Harry and his dragoons raced forward to secure Dorchester, his maneuver designed to prevent any help from Charleston crossing Bacon's Bridge and sweeping around the head of Ashley River. Colonel Henry Hamp-

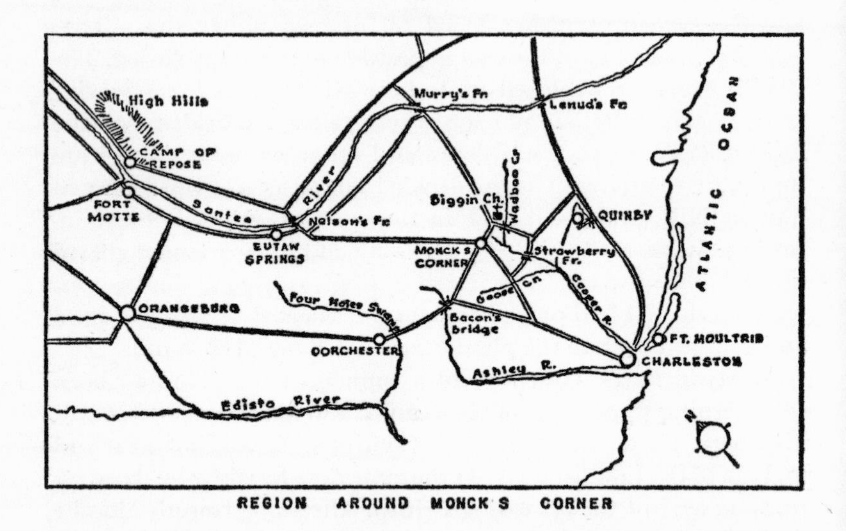

REGION AROUND MONCK S CORNER

ton dashed away to seize Four Holes Bridge and prevent reinforcement coming down from Rawdon. Colonels Peter Horry and Maham rushed down east of Cooper River to seize the passes and destroy the bridge over Wadboo Creek. And Colonel Wade Hampton charged across Goose Creek "to thunder even at the gates of Charleston."

While his dragoons galloped toward their objectives, Sumter and his mounted infantry moved slowly along the Santee. He ordered all ferryboats held in readiness for any emergency. "Every precaution has been and is still used in securing a retreat," he informed Greene. "It is a matter, Sir, that claims my earnest attention."

Reaching Eutaw Springs on July 15, the Gamecock camped on a plantation called The Rocks. Hearing rumors of an enemy contingent at Murry's Ferry, he sent a detachment against it. In the saddle again, with a powerful army under his command and with detachments moving in all directions, the Gamecock was confident. Although gaunt and suffering, he had no thought of failure. To Greene he confided, "I make not the least doubt but I'll give a good account of them."

Sumter had heard that "the Enemy have constructed some new works at Biggin." The rumor was true. After searching for a strong point to protect Moncks Corner, Colonel John Coates had selected the church of St. John's, Berkeley, situated on Biggin Creek about a mile and a half east of the village. Constructed of brick, with walls three feet thick, Biggin church could withstand any but the heaviest artillery fire. After throwing up some fieldworks, Coates ordered his 19th Regiment to move into the church.

As Sumter moved slowly down from Eutaw, his cavalry galloped rampant between Monck's Corner and Charleston. Lee reached Dorchester, whence the defenders had already fled, but he lost his momentum rounding up three hundred horses and sending off a wagonload of ammunition. Wade Hampton dashed up to Goose Creek Church, seized and paroled the worshipers, and carried off their horses. He rode down Charleston Neck as far as the Quarter House, frightening, capturing, and paroling. Maham partially destroyed Wadboo Bridge, fired two schooners moored alongside, and then turned back to watch Coates at Biggin church.

About five o'clock on the afternoon of July 16, as Colonel Horry's troops were resting, with many cooking and eating, Major Fraser and his South Carolina dragoons charged them. Surprised, but not thrown into panic, Lacey's riflemen broke the charge. Horry then rallied his men and drove Fraser and his Loyalists back to Biggin. Sumter was ecstatic. "Noble militia!" he reported to Greene. "What think you now of their charging British Dragoons with Rifles and pursuing them to their lines?"

Upon the repulse of his dragoons, Coates mustered his infantry and sent a detail to meet the charging militia. Horry immediately fell back to the main body. The Gamecock quickly formed his men behind a defile and waited until dark.

The British move was only a feint. Coates had orders to join Rawdon, but he now considered himself outmaneuvered. Believing that Sumter's corps had been sent forward to provoke a battle and that Greene's Continentals lay between him and Orangeburg, he decided to retreat to Charleston. About three o'clock on the morning of July 17, 1781, he destroyed his stores, fired St. John's Church, and headed down eastward of Cooper River.

Awakened by a sentinel's alarm, Sumter roused his men and started in pursuit. Sending Lee and Hampton ahead with the cavalry, the Gamecock followed with his infantry. Reaching Wadboo Creek, the dragoons found that Coates had completed the destruction of the bridge. After fording the stream, they returned to the chase. At the fork they discovered that Fraser's Loyalists had ridden toward Strawberry Ferry and that Coates and his infantry had taken the road to Quinby Creek. After a scouting detachment reported Fraser already across the Cooper, Lee hurried after Coates.

For eighteen miles under a broiling Carolina sun Lee chased the slogging British. He caught up with them at Quinby, just as their rear guard was throwing planks off the bridge. Captains Armstrong and Carrington charged across the chasm, but after a hot skirmish they wheeled off through the woods. Instead of pursuing them, Coates hastened on to Quinby, the magnificent plantation of the Shubrick family.

Soon after the skirmish General Marion galloped up with his mounted infantry. The Swamp Fox and Light Horse Harry moved forward to reconnoiter. They found Coates and his infantry drawn up around the Shubrick mansion, with a howitzer in front and his men ambuscaded in the houses and along the fences. They agreed that defenses were too strong for an assault without artillery and retired to await the coming of Sumter.

The Gamecock arrived in midafternoon. As soon as he spied the enemy, he was eager for battle. Marion and Lee begged him to wait until the arrival of Major Singleton and his six-pounder, but he was deaf to their arguments. Impetuous, all sweat and fury, he ordered the troops prepared for an attack by five o'clock.

A skillful tactician, Sumter deployed his regiments in an arc fronting Shubrick's. To his extreme right he sent Horry. Beside him he placed Myddelton, and then Polk, Taylor, and Lacey around in semicircle. To his far left he sent Marion and his brigade. And Lee and Hampton, with their dragoons, he posted in reserve.

At the Gamecock's command the Americans began advancing and firing. The British answered shot for shot. After a few minutes, as the firing grew hotter, some of Sumter's militiamen scrambled into the slave quarters. Protected but ineffective, they potted away for an hour. "My troops had some of those small woodings such as fences and a few small houses," he reported to Greene in explaining their ineffectiveness; "notwithstanding the distance was only 40 to 80 yards they did very little damage."

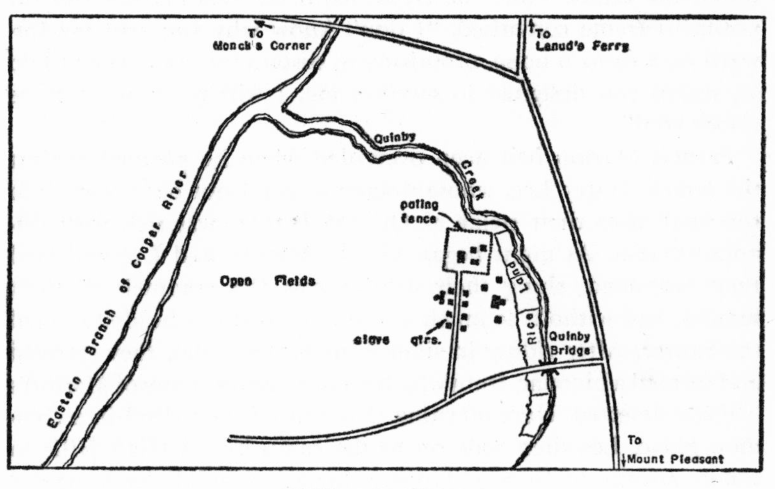

QUINBY PLANTATION

Seeing his attack bogging down in the face of enemy fire, Sumter ordered Colonel Taylor to cross the open field and seize the fence in front of the mansion. After a gallant charge, in which man after man dropped between the corn rows, Taylor reached the pickets. But in the pivotal moment before he could secure his position, Captain Scerrit drove him back with the bayonet.

Marion rushed forward from the left to sustain Taylor. As his men charged across the exposed field, they came under the fire of

British sharpshooters. Gallantly they fought, but after heavy casualties they began falling back. Even as they retreated, they kept up a well-directed fire.

"Not a man left his place until his ammunition was entirely exhausted, which compelled me to order a retreat," Sumter proudly reported to Greene. But as the militia retreated from Quinby, discord flared among them. They had been defeated badly. Old jealousies and animosities revived, and tempers kindled. The survivors swore that the Gamecock's courage exceeded his judgment.

After the retreat, Colonel Thomas Taylor found Sumter calmly sitting under a tree, meditating how to get more ammunition and renew the attack. "Sir," he cried, his hazel eyes blazing and his powerful frame convulsed, "I don't know why you sent me forward on a forlorn hope, promising to sustain me, and failed to do so, unless you designed to sacrifice me. I will never more serve under you!"

Francis Marion had been overruled when he pleaded against the attack. Harry Lee, whose dragoons could not be thrown into the fight after their strike at Quinby Bridge, was sick with disappointment. As night began to fall, Marion and Lee collected their wounded, slung their dead across the pommels of their saddles, and without so much as a sullen good-bye headed toward the Santee. After riding in silence for fifteen miles, they stopped and formed a bivouac, from which all but one company of Marion's brigade deserted. Next morning they buried their dead in a common grave. Lee then rode on to the camp in the High Hills to report angrily to General Greene. Marion crossed the Santee at Murry's and stopped at Cantey's plantation to discharge his one faithful company. He vowed that he would never again fight under the Gamecock.

Among Marion's dead was Francis Goddard, oldest son of Widow Elizabeth Jenkins of Britton's Neck. "When Cousin John returned and brought the news, it was like a dagger to my heart," said James Jenkins, Goddard's sixteen-year-old half brother. "And having heard that Sumter *would* go into battle, whether or not, live or die, I thought I could never forgive him."

Night fell at Quinby, and darkness ended the fighting days of

Thomas Sumter. The haggard man sitting alone in his marquee was but the shell of the magnificent commander at Hanging Rock. Suffering had left the chick of the blue hen only courage. In his last main, although the fighting was fierce, wing to wing and gaff to gaff, the Gamecock did not leave the pit crowing.

Chapter 16 END OF THE GLORY

"THE enemy were on the ground late yesterday," Sumter reported to Greene from his camp three miles above Quinby on July 19, 1781, "and had not gone 100 yards out, such is their apprehension." But Marion's withdrawal of his brigade, the possibility of enemy reinforcements coming by ship from Charleston, "together with Colonel Lee's marching off" made the Gamecock's position untenable. "Am moving up to Nelson's Ferry, but shall take a position 11 or 12 miles below. Men much fatigued & Horses quite broke down."

Fearing that Rawdon would send Stewart against him if he remained south of the Santee, Sumter crossed and encamped at Pierce's Pond in Great Savannah, "in order to refresh my people and renew their horses." But as soon as he passed the river, trouble broke out in his brigade. "Among other things was taken a Pay Master's trunk," he reported in an inventory of the goods taken from Coates; "it contained pounds of Species to the amount near 800 gold." From this windfall he impulsively gave each of his men a guinea. Such bounty to his own troops angered those of Marion and Lee. And worse, it set his State Troops clamoring for their back pay.

Desperate for something with which to pay these ten-month's men, the Gamecock began plundering. With characteristic high hand, on July 25 he sent Captain William Ransome Davis and a detachment of State Troops to Georgetown, with orders to seize and bring back to Great Savannah the slaves, horses, indigo, salt, and medicines of the Loyalists. The invasion of his militia district angered Marion; "but suppose I must submit," he snorted. Greene was also irritated, but he was realistic. "General Sumter's taking the goods of Georgetown was certainly wrong," he said, "but it is now too late to prevent it."

In his camp of repose in the High Hills, General Greene was

planning his fall campaigns. Since his return to South Carolina he had developed great confidence in General Marion. He had noted with growing distress that Colonel Lee was becoming moody and restless. He had also noted that General Sumter, exhausted, malarial, and tortured by his festering wound, had become quick-tempered and despotic. Undoubtedly the militia in his brigade were annoying, but the basic troubles with the Gamecock were the State Troops and Sumter's Law.

"I have already recommended to General Sumter to get all the state troops to join the army," Greene told Lee with his usual insinuations, "but be assured it would prove so fully my opinion of a certain person, to give such an order, as not only to prevent further exertion, but even opposition; and it is uncertain how far disappointed ambition may carry a man."

And yet, with the ailing Gamecock still commanding the State Troops, as well as his brigade, it was necessary to placate him. On July 27 Major Burnet relayed Greene's order "that he has received intelligence that renders it necessary for you to take your position at the Congaree, and remove all the grain from the south side of the river." Sumter ordered Myddelton and Henry Hampton to move the State Troops to Ancrum's. From Great Savannah, where he was expecting the return of Captain Davis, the Gamecock then wrote Greene, "I think to do myself the honor of waiting upon you in a few days." He had not ridden with his dragoons: "Indisposition interfering too much."

Captain Davis' robbing the Loyalists of Georgetown and hauling the plunder to Sumter's camp on Great Savannah brought on a fearful retaliation. On August 2, without warning, Captain Manson, who commanded the privateer *Peggy,* came up from the bar and began bombarding the village. When the Whigs ran for cover, he sent his Tory sailors ashore to fire the stores and warehouses. They set the torch to forty-two private dwellings. As these burned, Manson shelled the streets to prevent fire fighters extinguishing the flames.

In the meantime Governor Rutledge, who had spent the summer in Philadelphia begging Congress for aid, had returned to South Carolina. He reached Camden on August 1 and then rode on to Greene's headquarters in the High Hills. As he listened to reports of distress in Georgetown, the governor realized that with the British driven back around Charleston, the country was in a state of civil war. He decided to stop the vicious cycles of plundering, retaliation, and reprisal terrorizing both Whigs and Tories. As his first official act, he issued a proclamation against plundering.

Rutledge's proclamation was like a gaff through the heart of the proud Gamecock. In outlawing the system of paying State Troops, the governor discredited the power and integrity of their commanding general. With wounded pride, and too ill to ride his horse, Sumter demanded and took a coach that Captain O'Neale of Lee's Legion had borrowed from Widow Wright to bring some wounded soldiers from Biggin. He paused in the High Hills for a conference with Greene and Rutledge, but he received little satisfaction. In Camden he sold the carriage, mounted his horse, and rode off toward the Waxhaws.

Rutledge immediately sent Lieutenant Colonel William Henderson, former commandant of the Sixth Regiment, to assume command of State Troops. Henderson found the dragoons camping on the ravaged plantation of Andrew Lord, unpaid, fearful, and mutinous. "On my arrival to take command of them I found them the most discontented men I ever saw, both men and officers," Henderson reported to the governor. "The thirst after plunder that seems to prevail among the soldiery makes the command almost intolerable."

Upon Henderson's arrival at Lord's he was handed a note from Sumter. The Gamecock requested "that his troops should have a respite from service until the first of October." He also suggested "that the horses of the Brigade should be sent to the river swamp to pasture and committed to the care of detachments of militia."

William Henderson was normally cool and urbane, even under fire, but when he read the memorandum, his temper flared up. "Have I come here only to furlough a parcel of troops," he cried, "and that when the enemy is at our doors? And their horses to be guarded by militia? No readier way to dismount them could be devised!" He immediately reported Sumter's request to Greene. "With expectations of seeing at least four or five hundred men fit for the field, I came to take command of the *brigade* of State troops, but I find General Sumter has played the *old soldier* with me, for

I have not been able to collect quite two hundred fit for action, and they in a most shattered condition."

"I received your favour of the 14th, inclosing General Sumter's order for disbanding his brigade, for I can consider it in no other light," replied Greene in a rare flash of anger. "What can be his reasons for such an extraordinary measure, I cannot imagine: nor can I conceive, how he could think of taking such a step without consulting me, or obtaining my consent for the purpose. If he supposes himself at liberty to employ those troops, independently of the continental army, it is time he should be convinced to the contrary."

General Greene had always made allowances for Sumter's health, pride, and independence. For the sake of harmony he had overlooked the Gamecock's whims and actions. But disbanding Sumter's brigade would leave the country open to Tory ravage and the Continental Army exposed to British attack.

"It would be little less than madness, to grant the indulgences General Sumter requires, when the enemy are in motion in every part of the state, and all our regular force, including the state troops, so much inferior to theirs," Greene said in countermanding the order. "I have the public good, and the safety of the good people of the state, too much at heart to think of such a measure."

Both Continental and militia officers were outraged by Sumter's bungling. Light Horse Harry Lee, bitter and sarcastic, gave the *coup de grace* to the faltering Gamecock. "General Sumter is become almost universally odious," he confided to Greene. "I lament that a man of his turn was ever useful, or being once deservingly great, should want the wisdom to continue so, and to preserve his reputation."

Although often cantankerous and completely inflexible when bearded, Thomas Sumter could be attractive, winsome, and even boyish. After stopping briefly in the New Acquisition to visit Mary, he crossed the border into Mecklenburg. As he rode toward Charlotte, free of the tensions of command, he relaxed and his health began to improve. His enthusiasm revived. More like the Gamecock before Hanging Rock, he began collecting clothing, forage, and provisions for the Continentals. He rode on to visit his brother William in Burke County.

Greene had found it almost impossible to haul manufactured goods from the North without having them captured or plundered. As a relief Governor Rutledge decided to establish factories in the South. He asked Sumter to locate possible sites, and in pursuing this mission on August 23 the Gamecock reached Salisbury. A week later he was in Salem. "Upon examination found the Moravian town would not answer my Design as there was neither houseroom or workmen to be obtained there. Neither was there at Salisbury," he reported to Greene.

Although willing, Sumter was still too unwell to accomplish much. "By sickness and moving about, have not had much done, but have procured a considerable quantity of leather, shoes, homespun, and ready made shirts," he said. But he was resolute and cooperative. "I am far from harty but riding agrees very well with me, together with the air and water might prove rather an advantage to me in point of health," he concluded. "If I should be honoured with your Commands they shall be as fully complyed with as may be in my power."

Since neither buildings nor workmen for establishing armories and factories could be found in central North Carolina, Governor Rutledge suggested that Camden would be a more suitable location. Sumter, then, began his return down the Catawba. He spent the first weeks of September with Mary. "I have it to lament that my present indisposition renders me incapable of carrying the whole of your requisition into execution, being scarce able to sign my name," he wrote Greene humbly from her residence on Sugar Creek on September 19; "but rest assured that everything in my power will be done to promote your designs."

William Harden lived on a plantation near Beaufort. During the winter, stirred by Sumter's raid down the Congaree and Marion's campaigning along the Santee, Harden began rousing the Whigs along the Coosawhatchie. He visited Marion, accepted commissions for himself and his officers, and recruited a regiment. He also persuaded Colonel Isaac Hayne, who had taken protection, to enter the field again. While Marion besieged Fort Watson,

Hayne asked him for commissions for the officers of a regiment to be recruited along the Edisto.

Harden and Hayne then cut a swath through the Tories of southeastern Carolina. Bold but incautious, on June 5 Hayne swept down the road from Dorchester, reached the outskirts of Charleston, and carried off Brigadier General Andrew Williamson, the Indian fighter who had defected to the British. Incensed at the capture of turncoat Williamson, Colonel Balfour ordered Major Fraser and his South Carolina dragoons to bring in Hayne. Fraser surprised and captured Hayne in uniform, bearing arms, and in command of a squadron of militia. Balfour decided to make an example of the popular hero. On July 27 a court-martial presided over by Major Andrew McKenzie identified Hayne, confirmed the details of his taking protection and subsequent revolt and capture, and turned their findings over to the senior British officers. Acting under directions left by Cornwallis, Colonel Balfour and Lord Rawdon sentenced Isaac Hayne to be hanged.

The hanging of Colonel Hayne on August 4 caused a wild uproar. Rankling at the injustice to an officer whom he had commissioned, Francis Marion swore that he would hang every officer whom he should capture. Greene forbade such reprisal, saying, "I don't intend to retaliate on the Tory officers, but the British."

The Swamp Fox was cunning. Learning that Fraser and his hated Loyalists were harassing the Whigs beyond the Edisto, he slipped silently across the country and on August 30 hid his men in a swamp along the road to Parker's Ferry. When unsuspecting Fraser rode into the ambush, Marion's sharpshooters stacked men and horses on the causeway.

"The General with his gallant little corps of partisans attacked and beat upward of three hundred British and Hessians, killed twenty men dead on the field; wounded about eighty; also killed and took forty horses," Greene said in his general orders of September 5. "This action does much honor to General Marion and men under his command."

Francis Marion had settled the score at a hundred Tories for Isaac Hayne.

With the approach of autumn came changes in the British administration. Malarial, suffering from the heat, and worn out by two years of vigorous campaigning, Lord Rawdon had resigned the field command of the British Army. Balfour assigned the command to Colonel Stewart. Eager to succeed where Rawdon had failed, after sending Major John Doyle scouting along the Santee, Stewart moved up and pitched camp in the hills south of the Congaree, nearly opposite the camp of Greene in the High Hills.

As the two armies lay watching each other, Greene received cheering news from Virginia. General Washington was mounting a combined American-French campaign against Lord Cornwallis. He had already deployed LaFayette, Wayne, and Von Steuben. Count Rochambeau was waiting with a French corps at Newport and Count de Grasse was bringing a still more powerful force up from the West Indies. The commander in chief suggested that Greene resume offensive operations to prevent Balfour's sending reinforcements to Cornwallis.

In compliance Greene broke camp on August 22 and, afraid to attempt crossing the Santee in front of Stewart, moved over the flooding Wateree. A week later he crossed the Congaree at Howell's Ferry. He then began slowly advancing while Stewart backed down the Santee some forty miles to Eutaw Springs.

Greene marched leisurely on to Motte's. From there he called in Marion and sent Lee and Pickens to scout the enemy. On September 5 he bivouacked on the Laurens plantation, seventeen miles above Eutaw. Here he paused for a day, refreshing his troops and formulating his tactics. After organizing his army for attack, he moved on down the Congaree Road to Burdell's Tavern, only seven miles from the springs of Eutaw.

At four o'clock on the morning of September 8 Greene marched from Burdell's. He had divided his army into four columns and assigned each column its place in the coming battle. Colonel Henderson, with the State Troops and Lee's Legion, led the van. General Marion, in command of the militia of North and South Carolina, was second in the line of march. Major General Jethro Sumner came next with the Continentals. And Colonel Washington brought up the rear with his dragoons.

The American advance surprised the British. After momentary confusion Stewart pushed forward a detachment of infantry with orders to hold the enemy. He then began posting his troops across the Congaree Road. On his right he placed Major Majoribanks, with his flank battalion posted in front of Eutaw Creek. In the center he posted Colonel Cruger with his New Jersey Volunteers and the 3rd Regiment of Foot Guards. On his left he placed the 63rd and 64th regiments, their flanks in air, but supported by the cavalry under Major Coffin. And he stationed Major Sheridan and the sharpshooters from the New York Volunteers in the brick house of Patrick Roche.

After clearing the skirmishers from the road, Greene opened his attack. Colonel Henderson fought gallantly, but he was finally toppled from his horse, severely wounded. Marion continued the advance with his militia, and their steadiness astonished both the Continentals and the British. After they had fired seventeen rounds and exhausted their ammunition, the Swamp Fox drew them off in good order. Sumner's Continentals then struck the center of the British line, but Cruger's New Jersey Loyalists held, fighting back in desperate hand-to-hand combat. The battle swayed along the center until the Marylanders delivered a terrific volley. Cruger began falling back, but Stewart rallied his troops and re-formed his line in front of Roche's house.

During this critical evolution of the British, Greene ordered Colonel Washington to drive Majoribanks from Eutaw Creek. Washington charged. Striking the bushes in front of the creek, the dragoons veered to their right. As they galloped parallel to the British line, they began tumbling from their saddles. Drilled by a sharpshooter, Washington's horse crumpled, pinning his rider beneath him. As the colonel lay helpless, a British infantryman lowered his bayonet and charged. But recognizing the prostrate American, a British officer shouted for him to spare the life of Washington.

Under Greene's relentless drive the British line began retreating again, this time through the field, through their own camp, and into the woods beyond. But instead of continuing the attack, Greene's hungry, thirsty troops stopped to pillage. When they began feasting upon the enemy's food and drink, their officers lost control of them. As his army turned into a mob, Greene ordered a retreat.

Major Coffin hurled the British dragoons upon the milling Americans, but in vicious fighting Colonel Wade Hampton drove them back with the State Troops. Soon afterward Greene rallied his troops in Roche's woods, collected his wounded, and started slowly back toward Burdell's Tavern. From there he crossed the Santee and again went into camp in the High Hills.

Stewart claimed a victory. Nevertheless it was Pyrrhic, for his army was so shattered that he burned his stores, threw a thousand guns into Eutaw Creek, placed his wounded under a flag, left his dead unburied, and began retreating toward Moncks Corner. At last the British had been driven from central South Carolina.

For the number of troops engaged, the battle of Eutaw Springs was one of the bloodiest of the Revolution. Stewart had some twenty-three hundred men, and Greene commanded about two thousand. "We took five-hundred prisoners, included the wounded that they had left behind," Greene said in his report to the president of the Congress; "and I reckon that they had not less than six hundred killed and wounded."

Greene lost some five hundred and seventeen in killed, wounded, and missing. The Carolinians lost heavily, the militia and State Troops having twenty-five killed, one hundred and eight wounded, and eight missing. Among the prominent officers wounded were General Pickens and Colonels Henderson, Myddelton, and Washington. Colonel Washington was also a prisoner of war.

The wounding of gallant Colonel Henderson brought the indisposed Gamecock slowly back into active service. He was still with Mary at Ezekial Polk's on Sugar Creek, and eight days after the battle he received a long account of it from Greene, emphasizing the heroism of Sumter's troops, especially that of the State Troops under Wade Hampton.

Without a sign of envy Sumter immediately congratulated Greene for the glorious victory. The splendid showing of the American Army, with intelligence that a French fleet had reached the Chesapeake and begun co-operating in General Washington's campaign against Cornwallis, "gives me infinite pleasure, even at a time when anything else is incapable of affording me the least."

Sumter was indeed gravely ill. But tortured and suffering, he put duty above self and tried to do everything in his power to carry out Greene's orders. During the summer Colonels Shelby and Sevier had promised to furnish seven hundred Backwater Men, and now Greene wished them to proceed to Charlotte. He sent their orders to Sumter. Calling in couriers Thomas Hunter and John Milling, the Gamecock dispatched them over the Blue Ridge. He then reported, "I have to lament that my present indisposition renders me incapable of carrying the whole of your requisition into Execution, being scarce able to sign my name."

Greene believed that Lord Cornwallis, confronted by General Washington and Count Rochambeau, would abandon the Chesapeake and retreat through the Carolinas. Fearing the return of Cornwallis, he sent Colonel Lee to seek help from the Congress. In North Carolina, Lee sent Major Rudolph and a troop of dragoons to reconnoiter Wilmington, and in Virginia he turned aside to join in the siege of Yorktown.

Soon after Lee's departure, with his usual escort of dragoons, Greene rode from the High Hills and headed toward Charlotte. After entering the New Acquisition, he stopped at Polk's for a friendly visit with the Gamecock. They talked of the fall campaign and the reduction of the six regiments of State Troops.

Reaching Charlotte, Greene was disappointed in finding none of the troops promised by Sevier and Shelby. But upon his return to headquarters in the High Hills he found encouraging news. Lee reported that Washington and Rochambeau were carrying the fight to Cornwallis. Suddenly the Revolutionary War reached its climax. On October 19 Lord Cornwallis surrendered.

Nine days after the surrender, couriers with dispatches from General Washington reached the High Hills. Rutledge immediately forwarded the news, with his congratulations, to Marion and Sumter. The Americans began celebrating. At Cantey's plantation, near Murry's Ferry, General Marion gave a ball for his officers and their ladies. During the excitement, as ill as he had been, Sumter crawled out of bed, put on his old uniform, and galloped off toward the High Hills.

The Gamecock's arrival at headquarters surprised both Greene and Rutledge. The presence of the senior brigadier also created a problem. Both the general and the governor had decided that

Francis Marion, quiet, courageous, and adored by his troops, was the better general to handle the militia. What could they now do with Sumter?

After the capture of Lord Cornwallis, Greene had decided to break the British overland communications by moving down and encamping between Charleston and Savannah. So they decided to protect Greene's advanced base by posting Marion in the east and Sumter in the west. On November 5 Rutledge asked the Gamecock to march his brigade and the State Troops to Orangeburg, establish a post, and prevent Loyalists in the upper districts from communicating with the British in Charleston.

Without complaint Sumter took the assignment and early on November 11 crossed the Santee. Next morning he dispatched Major Bluford with part of the State Troops to bring in Captain Henry Giessendanner, the leader of the Germans still loyal to George III, a king sprung from their duchy of Hanover. Bluford failed, and, unfortunately, Major Moore with the remainder of the State Troops stumbled into five hundred Tories under Colonel William Cunningham, then on his infamous Bloody Scout, in which he killed fifteen hundred Whigs between the sea and the mountains. Bloody Bill Cunningham routed Moore, and all the following night shivering survivors crept into Sumter's camp at Harrisperger's plantation eight miles east of Orangeburg.

Sumter was discouraged by his defeat. Still sick and despondent, he turned upon his troops. "The Militia I have are trifling, consisting of the worst men and arms in the Brigade," he complained. "Neither is the State Troops equal to what I expected."

"I am sorry that Major More fell into the Enemy's ambush," replied Greene, who had just broken camp in the High Hills. Lee's Legion was already across the Santee. Marion had also crossed at Murry's Ferry. Greene begged the Gamecock not to retreat. "If you think you can give the Enemy a deadly blow by General Marion joining with part or all of his party," he advised, "please inform him."

"I have this day wrote to General Marion and sent a proper officer to confer with him on several points," replied Sumter after dispatching Major Bluford to St. Stephen's; "and when this officer returns, I shall be enabled, to form a proper judgement of the propriety of an attempt of this Nature."

As for the Tories in Orangeburg, they were so loyal to the House of Hanover that even after Governor Rutledge's proclamation of pardon to all save a few Loyalists, they still refused to break their allegiance. Cried the Gamecock, "Nothing but the sword will reclaim them!"

Greene bade the Gamecock keep his sword in its sheath. Quaker morality and military expediency determined him to use kindness to draw the Loyalists from the British. "For though we have great reason to hate them," he said, "and vengeance would dictate one universal slaughter, yet when we consider how many good people must fall in doing it, we shall find it will be more to our interest to forgive than to prosecute."

Some fifteen hundred of these Loyalists lurked in the swamps along the North and South Edisto. Sumter dared not try to dislodge them with his weak brigade. Instead, he told Greene, "Agreeable to your desire will endeavor by every possible means to induce the Tories to withdraw from the British."

Since coming to South Carolina, Greene had become increasingly horrified at the cruelties of the civil war between the Whigs and the Tories. "I lament the confusion and inhumanity which takes place; the daily scenes of the most horrid plundering and murder, which can only be accounted for by the great length to which personal animosities are carried, and the want of civil authority."

After Greene had moved down and established a winter camp at the little Colleton village called Round O, Rutledge decided that the time had come for re-establishing civil government in South Carolina. He called for the election of a General Assembly. On November 23 he sent writs of election to his brigadier generals and asked that they be distributed through the militia districts.

Sumter distributed the writs, but he did not announce his candidacy for a seat in the General Assembly. He was too busy conciliating Tories. After dispersing two small bands, he pleaded with the remainder to lay down their arms. By December 13 forty had come in. As the time set by Rutledge's proclamation neared expiration, more and more deserted the British. By December 22 three hundred had surrendered. So confident was the Gamecock in their fidelity that he enlisted a hundred in his militia.

"The post you hold and that of the Four Holes are exceedingly distressing to the Tories and must soon break up their whole nest," Greene said encouragingly. "Go on with the good work of trying to bring them in. It will save the lives of so many People, and perhaps hereafter they may prove good citizens."

But the Gamecock was suffering and resentful. Luring Tories out of Edisto swamp was not satisfying. He knew that he was receiving unequal treatment and that Marion had now become the favorite of Greene and Rutledge. After condemning the Gamecock's basis for the State Troops, Rutledge had given Marion permission to recruit two regiments of dragoons, to be commanded by Colonels Maham and Peter Horry. Over the protests of both Marion and Sumter, in order to save the expense of feeding their horses, Rutledge had dismounted the South Carolina militia. In concurrence with the governor, Greene had then ordered the six regiments of State Troops reduced to two, one infantry and one cavalry.

As the date of the election drew near, Greene cordially but tactlessly inquired of Sumter: "Do you intend to get into the General Assembly, and have the approbation of the House upon the measures taken to raise the State Troops? Nothing like the present time when gratitude is warm and danger not past, to get business of the sort approved?"

The question seemed to indicate that Sumter should use cunning to have the General Assembly approve raising State Troops on Sumter's Law. For the next ten days the Gamecock nursed his wounded pride. "You asked if I did not intend to get in the General Assembly: It is probable I may serve if elected, but as I never have solicited any public appointment, I can't think of doing it now," he then wrote proudly.

"Notwithstanding I have the Matter you have Mentioned very much at heart, but if men are lost or Callous to every sentiment of Gratitude & Justice My weak Reasonings although found'd on the Strictest equity will not prevail; however I shall be prepared to Make a true & fair Representation of Matters to the house. Perhaps the Result may prove favourable. I have nothing to urge upon my own account more than to Comply with the promises Made to the Troops—if they are paid & I am Sensured My expectations will not be disappointed."

Sumter then turned upon the inequity of dismounting the militia and reducing the State Troops. "I would most cheerfully adopt Such Measures as would tend to lessen the public expenses and encourage and enforce others to submit whenever it May be attempted upon sound principles," he continued. "I therefore beg leave to observe that the State Troops was Raised as light dragoons, of course Mounted and Should have been equiped as such—but has been hitherto totally neglected by the public, which has never the less been submitted to without much murmuring, but when they see themselves dismounted—Notwithstanding they was promised the use of their own or public horses, and at the same time Chief of the Militia upon Service in the State, My Brigade excepted and suffered to do duty as horse or Mounted infantry, Gives cause to think, to spare the public expense is Not the Reason for their being Dismounted."

As the Gamecock wrote, his pride and anger rose and he became eloquent. "The Militia of my Brigade also think themselves Much injured by being obliged to perform a two months & ten days tour of duty on foot, Not even suffered to Ride from home & send their horses back when at the same time they are told that Gov. Rutledge suffers other divisions of the Militia to do duty as horse or Mounted Infantry, & Remain but one Month in the field before relieved," he cried. "If this be the Case, they Certainly Complain with propriety —and such partialities Cant fail to prejudice the Service exceedingly, and I find has been the Cause of desertion having been so prevalent—it is with Regret I have to acknowledge that the public is poor but nevertheless is very liberal, if not profuse upon many occasions, upon the whole it is with design & not through inability, and has been ludicrously treated insomuch that he who would any longer submit to it Might Justly be Charged with Meanness & pusillanimity."

Thomas Sumter neither forgot nor forgave. Without seeking nomination, he was elected Senator by his faithful admirers in Camden District. Sullen and sulky, he remained in Orangeburg with his troops waiting for the convening of the General Assembly.

After winding up the affairs of his command, on January 2, 1782, he made his final report on the pacification of the Tories. "As the Assembly is to set soon," he wrote simply, "I beg leave to quit this place."

The Gamecock bade farewell to the backwoodsmen whom he had aroused, enlisted, trained, and led for eighteen months of guerrilla warfare. He had partaken of their hardships. He had felt their suffering. He had witnessed their heroism. He had seen them charge British regulars with home-made swords and squirrel rifles. He had seen their brothers and cousins and friends lying stark on fields of battle. And so, as he said good-bye, his emotions overflowed. "In my last I took the liberty to ask leave to withdraw from this place upon private Business or rather to prepare to attend the Assembly," he wrote Greene with dignity. "I hope to be indulged, and beg not to be honoured again with any of your commands until a proper enquiry can be made whether I am worthy of them."

Chapter 17 MEMBER OF THE ASSEMBLY

BRIGADIER General Thomas Sumter rode slowly through the gray woods and somber plantations below Orangeburg. As the war approached its end, he was without command. The hero who first had roused the Carolinians after the fall of Charleston was going home to wait for the General Assembly to approve or to censure his conduct. His peers in the legislature might impeach him, but South Carolina could never repay him for his suffering. All he wished was vindication for his struggle to preserve the independence of the militia and his actions in raising State Troops.

Ill and discouraged, he lingered for two weeks at his home on Great Savannah, resting, recuperating, and enjoying the attentions of Mary. Conscious of public duty, however, he rode over to Jacksonboro to take his seat in the General Assembly. He found the Assembly a reunion of veterans. With him in the Senate were Colonel William Thomson, Colonel Hugh Horry, Colonel Thomas Taylor, and General Francis Marion. The House was like a muster of Sumter's brigade. Among members were General Andrew Pickens, General William Henderson, and Colonels Thomas Brandon, Wade and Richard Hampton, William Hill, Edward Lacey, James Lyles, John Thomas, and Richard Winn.

On January 18, 1782, Governor John Rutledge addressed the General Assembly. With great ability he reviewed the war, praised the veterans in the Assembly, and recommended legislation for the rehabilitation of South Carolina. "Since the last meeting of the General Assembly, the good people of the State have not only felt the calamities of war," he said, "but from the wanton and savage manner in which it has been prosecuted, they have experienced such severities as are unpractised, and will scarcely be credited by civilized nations," he began.

Rutledge sketched Clinton's invasion of South Carolina and

Lincoln's surrender of Charleston. He then continued, "The loss of that garrison, as it consisted of the continental troops of Virginia and the Carolinas, and of a number of militia, facilitated the enemy's march into the country, and their establishment of strong posts in the upper and interior parts of it; and the unfavourable issue of the action near Camden induced them vainly to imagine, that no other army could be collected which they might not easily defeat. The militia, commanded by the Brigadiers Sumter and Marion, whose enterprising spirit and unremitted perseverance under many difficulties are deserving of great applause, harassed and often defeated large parties; but the numbers of those militia were too few to contend effectually with the collected strength of the enemy."

After thus passing lightly over the heroic struggles of Sumter and Marion, Rutledge placed the highest encomium upon the campaigns of General Greene. "I can now congratulate you, and I do so most cordially, on the pleasing change of affairs which, under the blessing of God, the wisdom, prudence, address, and bravery of the great and gallant General Greene, and the intrepidity of the officers and men under his command, has been happily affected —a general who is justly entitled, from his many signal services, to honourable and singular marks of your approbation and gratitude."

Turning to the subject of the militia, Governor Rutledge asked for reorganization, under a new set of laws. He wished the burden of service equally shared. He wished good order and strict discipline. "Certain it is, that some of our militia have, upon several occasions, exhibited instances of valour, which would have reflected honour on veteran troops," he said in rather faint praise of the volunteers who had fought under Marion and Sumter. "The courage and conduct of the generals whom I have mentioned, the cool and determined bravery repeatedly displayed by Brigadier Pickens, and, indeed, the behaviour of many officers and men in every brigade, are unquestionable testimonies of the truth of this assertion."

What of the Tories? Should they be admitted to the rights and privileges of citizens? "It is with you to determine whether the forfeiture and appropriations of their property should now take place," said the governor.

Rutledge's attitude was symptomatic. For years Carolinians had been either Whig or Tory. With the Tories defeated, disgraced, and excluded from voting or holding public office, the Whigs were now absolute. But there were signs of a new alignment. Since the founding of South Carolina, local government had been in the hands of the planters and professional men around Charleston. But the war, with its resultant change in the social and political structure of the state and with the emergence of local heroes, changed the basis of representation. For the first time, members from the Up Country were equal in number to those of the Low Country.

Before the convening of the Assembly there were rumors of an impending struggle between the sections. There would be two candidates for governor. The aristocratic party, centered in the Low Country where many large property holders and members of families had taken protection from the British, planned to support Ralph Izard. The democratic legislators from the Up Country, where the civil war between the Whigs and Tories had been fiercest, planned to run Thomas Sumter.

Nothing came of the move. Both groups voted for General Christopher Gadsden. When the old veteran declined, they chose Congressman John Mathews. The president of the Senate, in recognition of the heroic part that Sumter and Marion had played in recovering the state, sent them to inform Mathews of his election and to inquire when he wished to be sworn in as governor of South Carolina.

Among the first bills to come before the Assembly was one for paying the State Troops. Led by the colonels in Sumter's brigade, the House of Representatives ratified the terms upon which the Gamecock had enlisted his ten-months dragoons. The House also recommended that Governor Mathews be empowered to confiscate four hundred slaves from the Tories and turn them over to General Sumter for distribution among his troops.

General Marion had never acknowledged Sumter's Law. Fervent for conciliating the Tories, he fought the bill in the Senate. Sitting at the table of Governor Mathews, while the debate over seizing

Tory property was raging, the Swamp Fox raised his glass and cried, "Damnation to Confiscation!"

In spite of humanitarian appeals, the General Assembly began punishing Loyalists. They confiscated the property of the most violent and banished them from South Carolina. They amerced the minor Tories, the disaffected, and the turncoats by seizing 10 per cent of their property. Even so, the Assembly adjourned without completing any statutes for paying State Troops.

After listening to heated debates on confiscation, Sumter considered the inaction of the Legislature a censure of his actions. He felt that he could no longer hold a commission as brigadier general of militia from a state that had impugned his motives in recruiting dragoons. Hopefully he attended the sessions until February 26, the date of the *sine die* adjournment of the General Assembly. He then laid aside forever the shining gaffs of the Gamecock.

"Would you wish to have a part of the militia of General Sumter's Brigade?" Greene wrote Marion on March 1 with just a trace of regret. "I suppose you have heard of the General's resignation?"

After resigning his commission as brigadier general, Thomas Sumter returned to his plantation on Great Savannah. Situated only six miles from Nelson's, the busiest ferry on the Santee, his home had been the stopping place for friend and foe. The British had spared his house, but they had left everything else in ruin. His slaves were gone, his horses stolen, and his cattle slaughtered. But with the courage of an old campaigner he set to work restoring his demesne.

Although the war dragged on around Charleston, Squire Sumter returned to his planting, speculating, and politicking. In the election for the General Assembly in the summer of 1782 he lost his place in the Senate. But his veterans rallied and sent him to the House of Representatives.

In the meantime Greene, with Marion, Pickens, and Brigadier General Henderson, now commanding Sumter's former brigade and State Troops, continued to press the British around Charleston. Finally they were victorious. On December 14 General Leslie evacuated the city, and Lee's dragoons, followed by Governor

Mathews, General Greene, and General Moultrie, took their place at the head of Wayne's entering Continentals.

To the anger of the Carolinians, Greene excluded the militia who had fought so heroically under Sumter, Marion, and Pickens. "The American regular army entered it in triumph," observed Moultrie bitterly in his *Memoirs:* "but our poor partisans were thought too irregular, too ragged of raiment to share this triumph. They were not too ragged to fight; only too ragged to show."

Proudly the General Assembly convened in Charleston in January, 1783. Among the first items on the agenda was a petition from Adam Summers and Annie Lord for payment for their property confiscated under Sumter's Law. Sumter immediately asked the Speaker to appoint a committee to inquire into his conduct since the fall of Charleston and into his disposal of Tory property that had come into his hands. But sentiment was changing on this controversial subject. Carolinians were trying to forgive and settle down to peace. Nothing came of his motion.

Members from the Up Country who had campaigned under General Sumter believed that his motives had been honorable and his means justifiable. They now rallied around him in a loose democratic party, and when the Senate and House met in joint session on February 15 to elect delegates to the Continental Congress, the Up Country democrats backed Sumter. After re-electing Henry Laurens and John Rutledge, the Assembly elected Ralph Izard and Jacob Read. On the next ballot it "appeared that Thomas Sumter Esquire had a majority of the votes of the Members."

The election of Sumter to the Continental Congress revived inherent controversy. As the session rolled toward adjournment, on February 26 without debate the Senate voted "That the thanks of this House be given to Brigadier General Marion, in his place as a member of this House, for his eminent and conspicuous services to his country." They also voted that a gold medal be given to him "as a mark of public approbation for his great, glorious, and meritorious conduct."

The supporters of Congressman-elect Sumter moved that a vote of thanks and a gold medal be given him. But the Gamecock had campaigned too independently, had acted with too high a hand under Sumter's Law, and had resigned from the army too often. Now he had emerged as the leader of the democratic backwoods. The motion stirred heated debate. Next morning, however, tempers had cooled, and the Senate resolved the controversial issue by voting thanks and medals to Brigadier Generals Huger, Pickens, and Sumter.

"If I have contributed to the relief of this lately oppressed State, the approbation of my Country is a full and ample reward," Sumter wrote in acknowledging the honor. "I never expected—I wished for no other. At a time when every opportunity hath been given to investigate thoroughly the motives and principles by which my conduct hath been regulated, to be honoured with so high a testimony of that approbation, is decisive, of the justness and correctness of my Views, and affords me a pleasure that is difficult to express."

With his public conduct at last vindicated, Sumter now turned to his private affairs. His plantation was just emerging from its devastation. He was heavily involved financially with Colonel Lacey, Captain Davis, and other veterans forming the Stateburg Realty Company. He was badly needed at home, for Mary was now sixty and her health had begun to fail. And so, in time for the General Assembly to elect his successor, on March 15 he declined his election to the Continental Congress.

South Carolina began slowly recovering from the devastation of war. In his address to the General Assembly in 1784 Governor Benjamin Guerard urged the reopening of schools and churches. He also urged the improvement of roads, bridges, and ferries. But the most urgent problem concerned veterans. Knowing that Sumter was still popular with the men of his brigade, the Speaker appointed him chairman of the committee on the claims of wounded veterans. The General Assembly had never completely settled the matter of Sumter's having paid the State Troops with plundered property. During this session the House voted that "General Sumter be considered as having acted with Honorable and upright Views, and highly Meriting the approbation of his Country, and that an ordinance be passed indemnifying him and the officers under his command."

The Assembly then passed a law exempting from liabilities of civil suit all officers who had seized private property for public use. Both Sumter and Pickens accepted exemption under the law. But on hearing his name read in the Senate, Francis Marion rose and disavowed exemption. "If I have wronged any man I am willing to make him restitution," he said. "If, in a single instance, in the course of my command, I have done that which I cannot fully justify, justice requires that I should suffer for it."

The Speaker appointed a commission consisting of Sumter, General Henderson, and Colonel Richard Richardson, Jr., to settle the demands of the State Troops. The burden of the settlement fell upon Sumter. He advertised for the veterans to bring their papers to stated meetings at Powell's Tavern in Stateburg. But there were so many delays and faulty statements that the matter dragged on for years. Not until 1794 did he finally adjust all the claims arising from his establishing the State Troops under Sumter's Law.

Where the ravages of civil war had been extreme, the Whigs remained bitter toward the Tories. Although Major Ganey spent the required six months on active duty under Marion, his neighbors along Catfish Creek drove him into North Carolina. When twelve Loyalists returned to their homes on Fishing Creek, night riders killed eight. Those in the High Hills were held in subjection by night-riding, horse-whipping vigilantes who, the Loyalists said, were headed by the Gamecock.

Gradually the Whigs stopped their punishment. Some exiles were allowed to return to their homes. Even Sumter forgave them as men deluded. He realized that Colonel Samuel Tynes, whom Marion had scourged at Tearcoat Swamp, was a man of integrity. Since Tynes was still a powerful influence among the former Tories, Sumter built a store at Land's Ford on the Catawba and made him his partner. By 1784 there was equal franchise, and after this gesture of reconciliation both Whigs and Tories voted to return Sumter to the General Assembly.

Sumter realized that rapid expansion would follow the return of peace. Veterans were clearing plantations, crossroads were turning into villages, and districts were being subdivided into counties. At a sheriff's sale in late summer he bought the *Ruins,* the house burned by Captain Campbell, and began rebuilding it.

Soon after that he purchased two quarter sections of six hundred and forty acres each near his plantation in St. Mark's. Then, like a land-hungry migrant from Preddy's Creek, he began plunging. By the end of the year he was surveying tracts of ten thousand, fourteen thousand, sixteen thousand, and twenty-two thousand acres. In three years, besides other large holdings along the Catawba, Sumter acquired one hundred and fourteen thousand acres in Camden District. As a commissioner, he helped lay out Claremont County, and without scruples about profiting from official acts, he placed the county seat at Stateburg.

The directors of the Stateburg Development Company laid out a town around the crossroads. Sumter built a store and became a partner in the mercantile firm of William Murrell and Company. He built a small hotel. And then, on his plantation north of Stateburg, Sumter built Home House, a magnificent fourteen-room house, set in spacious grounds and surrounded by trees, shrubs, and flowers.

During the meeting of the General Assembly in 1785 the representatives from the Up Country demanded that the state capital be moved from Charleston. They pretended that they wished a more convenient seat for the government, but in reality they wished to get the control of the state out of the hands of men from the Low Country. For the first time the democratic back country had power to force the change, and on March 10 a bill was introduced in the House to authorize the purchase of lands for new buildings. Next day the Speaker appointed Sumter, Pickens, and Colonel John Anderson as a committee to determine the most central location in South Carolina. After a four-day conference the committee reported that the center of the state lay in a circle thirty miles in diameter that cut through the High Hills, crossed the Santee just below the confluence of the Wateree and the Congaree, crossed the Congaree just below the mouth of the Saluda, and returned to the High Hills.

Since Stateburg lay within this circle Sumter began using his great influence to have the village selected as the site for the new capital. Never squeamish when fortune threw government lands or money his way, he became excited over the prospects of the Stateburg Development Company. When the question of purchasing land came before the House, the Speaker appointed Edward Rutledge, General Pinckney, and Sumter to confer with a similar committee appointed by the president of the Senate.

After hearing their reports, the General Assembly appointed a joint committee of Commodore Alexander Gillon, General Richard Winn, Colonel Richard Hampton, and Colonel Thomas Taylor to purchase lands for the capital. All of these except Gillon lived in the country between the Wateree and the Congaree. Instead of choosing Stateburg, as Sumter had expected, they decided to buy a part of the Taylor plantation across the Congaree from Granby.

When the committee announced its decision, Sumter began to argue with Gillon. Their hot tempers quickly flared, and the old veterans became personal. Gillon was touchy about his record at sea, and Sumter was sensitive about his resignations. Each impugned the valor and patriotism of the other, and they left the Assembly very angry. But neither sent a challenge. Next morning, however, contrary to the rules of parliamentary bodies, each entered the House armed with a short sword, two old cocks gaffed and pitted for a bloody main. But as they eyed each other and their hackles began to rise, Edward Rutledge sprang to his feet and began extolling the courage and patriotism of both. The incident closed. But the commissioners laid out the new capital on the Congaree and named it Columbia.

From the constant association with men like Princeton graduates Davie and Brownfield and the Oxford-educated Pinckneys, Thomas Sumter became acutely conscious of his own lack of formal schooling. Determined that young Thomas should have better training, he sent him to Liberty Hall. Hoping to provide similar schooling for the sons of his neighbors, in co-operation with the Reverend Richard Furman, an eminent Baptist leader, in the spring of 1786 he advertised the opening of a seminary at Stateburg.

At Liberty Hall Tom received a classical education, attaining some fluency in languages and polish in English. He then returned home. Entering his father's business, he was soon planting, speculating, and surveying large tracts of land, a single tract in the Cheraws that he acquired in 1793 containing ninety-three thousand acres. High-spirited and attractive, he became attached to a young woman, and on Christmas day, 1787, they became the parents of a daughter whom they named Louisa. Before the end of the liaison they had a son whom they named William.

"Thomas Sumter was the most honest and honorable man I have ever known," declared old Colonel James Chestnut. With two illegitimate grandchildren helpless and scandal-tossed, he now acted with rugged integrity. He fetched Louisa and William to Home House, gave them the name of Sumter, and although advancing in years began rearing them as if they were his own children. He forbade anyone's disclosing their origin and in no manner ever treated them with less respect than his legitimate grandchildren. And in all of this he assumed the burden, for Mary had suffered a stroke and during her last thirty years became increasingly helpless.

As Sumter grew wealthy, he became noted for his hospitality. His table was often surrounded by veterans. The Catawba Indians who had joined him at Clem's Branch were welcomed, as were Colonels Hill, Lacey, Taylor, Winn, and the Hamptons, especially Wade, already on his way to becoming the richest planter in the United States. In 1787, General Henderson, who had married the widow of Jared Neilson, died after leaving Sumter the executor of his large estate. The Gamecock was also generous to his family. Visiting Colonel William Sumter, his brother in Burke County, and finding him in debt, he bought and gave him a large plantation.

The veterans were rough, given to drinking and betting, practical jokes, and horse racing. Soon after the Revolution, Charleston and other towns established racecourses, and Stateburg boasted its track, the oval lying in the flat lands between the hills and the Wateree. Here Sumter's bay running horse *Stateburg* beat Colonel Washington's *Oronoco* for £100. His stallion *Ugly,* trained and raced by Wade Hampton, in 1791 defeated all of the two-milers at the New Market Course in Charleston. But more interested in breeding than in racing, after losing heavily with *Plenipo,* Sumter turned his racing stud over to Tom.

Old Colonel Burnley, with Sumter's boyhood friend Lucas,

brought down a string of Virginia thoroughbreds. He stopped at Sumter's for dinner and, noting the gentility of the other guests, inquired, "What shall we do with our old friend Lucas? Had he not better wait?"

"No," exclaimed Sumter. "He must be treated as my other guests."

During the dinner, as Lucas watched Sumter, remembering their days together at Ben Cave's, with their ball games and cockfights, he burst out, "General, don't you remember when we used to play pushpin on Sunday?"

"Ah," replied Sumter with a wry smile, "that was in our youthful days."

Reared near Preddy's Creek Baptist Church, Sumter liked the informality of the Baptists and was a warm supporter of the Reverends Samuel and Richard Furman. But with Mary and Tom, he was a member of St. Mark's. Upon the establishment of a chapel in Stateburg, he worshiped there. At the Easter service in 1788 he was elected to the vestry of the newly organized Episcopal congregation, and for the next twenty years he served as vestryman. With characteristic energy he began working for a new building, donating some of his village property as a site for the Church of the Holy Cross.

As he mingled with her political, agricultural, and industrial leaders, Sumter became interested in movements for the internal development of South Carolina. One of the first proposals was that of dredging a canal between the Santee and the Cooper, thus linking all Santee basin with Charleston. He was keen for the project. And when the Company for the Inland Navigation from Santee to Cooper River was established in 1786, with Governor William Moultrie as president and former Governor Rutledge as vice president, Sumter was elected to the board of directors.

Keenly aware of the possibilities of expanding trade, in 1787 he became a charter member of the Company for Opening the Navigation of the Catawba and Wateree Rivers. This was to be a tremendous undertaking, characteristic of his expansive imagination. By an ingenious system of dams, canals, and locks, the company hoped to link the Wateree-Catawba with the Watauga River in Tennessee and thus connect Charleston with the rapidly developing West. But Sumter always had a sharp eye. The company agreed to dredge Slave Landing Creek and to dig a canal to Stateburg.

During the years immediately following the Revolution, like the other sovereign members of the American confederacy, South Carolina assumed its right to control internal finance. In 1785 the Assembly had passed a bill ordering the printers of paper money to relieve the general depression. But the entire issue of £100,000 was to be lent for five years, the specie secured by property valued at three times the loan or gold and silver plate worth twice the loan.

Sumter protested the inadequate issue of paper money. In 1786 he had sponsored a bill calling for a larger issue. But the conservatives, who had benefited from deflation, killed the proposal. Again in 1787 he introduced a bill to authorize more paper money. The conservatives defeated the measure. But with ruin threatening the state, the General Assembly began serious attempts to arrest the depression. Because of Sumter's study of the credit structure, the Speaker put him on a committee to prepare a bill to do justice between creditor and debtor. He also put him on the committee to provide a new law on installments. As a step toward securing financial stability the Speaker finally appointed a committee to investigate and report on the feasibility of establishing a Bank of the State of South Carolina.

The other states of the Confederation were in similar economic straits, and interstate frictions indicated the necessity of a stronger central government. A meeting in Annapolis, growing out of the long feud between Maryland and Virginia over the oyster beds in the Chesapeake, turned into a convention to prepare a federal constitution for the United States. When the General Assembly met in 1788, most of the members were on hand to hear a reading of the proposed constitution. On January 10 Governor Thomas Pinckney called their profoundest attention to the document. The Speaker appointed Sumter a member of the committee to consider the governor's message. On January 16 the constitution was read, and for the next three days the Assembly debated whether or not to accept it. On January 19 Sumter's committee unanimously recommended that a convention be called either to ratify or to reject the proposed constitution.

As the leader of the democratic Up Country, Sumter opposed holding the convention in Charleston. By a vote of seventy-six to seventy-five the men from the Low Country won, and, on May 12, delegates met in the City Hall in Charleston. They immediately began debating acceptance or rejection. Led by Charles Pinckney, the delegates to the Constitutional Convention defended their work and strove for its adoption.

Thomas Sumter did not approve the work of these Federalists. He opposed the article allowing the President of the United States to be elected for two terms. He could not vote to give a central government the sole right to coin money and issue paper currency. An incipient states-righter, he wished no higher authority than the General Assembly and the governor. Hoping to arouse the electorate, he moved to postpone the decisions until the following October in order to follow the example of Virginia. Although his motion brought out heated debate, it failed, and the Federalists began to pick up support. Sumter continued his fight, however, and when Governor Pinckney called for his vote on adopting the constitution, he shouted, "No!"

After the convention had ratified the Constitution of the United States, that of South Carolina became obsolete. In his address to the General Assembly in 1789 Governor Charles Pinckney proposed calling a convention to frame a new constitution for the state. Still dreaming of making Stateburg the capital, while serving on a joint committee to consider the convention, Sumter persuaded the members to designate his village as the meeting place. But both House and Senate passed amended bills putting the meeting at Columbia.

Late in the season of 1789 Colonels Hill and Lacey, with nine other officers of Sumter's brigade, wrote Governor Pinckney, proposing that Sumter be commissioned a major general, given a handsome salary, and placed in command of the militia of South Carolina. Realizing that in military circles Sumter was a controversial figure, Pinckney referred their letter to the General Assembly. The president of the Senate appointed General Moultrie the chairman of a committee to study the proposal. Moultrie knew

Sumter's record: the committee reported unfavorably, saying that the elevation of Sumter would tend to create jealousy among officers of the militia.

But Thomas Sumter was resilient. Defeated at one place, he appeared at another, stronger than before. Repulsed at Rocky Mount, he carried the field at Hanging Rock. Rebuffed in his move to become a superior Adjutant General of South Carolina, he rallied the democrats in the General Assembly, and they elected him a member of the first Congress of the United States.

Chapter 18 CONGRESSMAN AND SENATOR

On his way to New York, Congressman Sumter paused at Stateburg. Mary was in her wheel chair, but otherwise healthy and comfortable. Tom, now on the eve of his twenty-first birthday, was managing his father's vast properties. Satisfied that all was well, with coachman and body servant, Sumter set off in his carriage in a style befitting a landed gentleman.

At Richmond, Sumter found that the Virginia legislature was still in session. "As soons as he stopped at a hotel, he sent up to the capital for Martin & myself who were members of the legislature there," said John Redd in describing the first meeting between General Sumter and General Joseph Martin since the jail break at Staunton. "He was highly pleased at meeting with us—particularly his old companion Martin, whom he had not seen for some twenty-five years. They called each other by the familiar names, Joe & Tom. Time passed rapidly & pleasantly while they talked of the events of their youthful days. Just before Sumter started (for he staid only a few hours) he asked Martin if he recollected the last frolic they had at Johnson's. Martin said that they had really has *so* many he could not. Sumter said he recollected it well, and should never forget it, for, said he, I lost all my money playing cards, & you loaned me five pounds. Martin said he had no recollection whatever of the transaction, and Sumter must be mistaken. Sumter said he *knew* he owed the money, and putting his hands in his pockets, he pulled out ten guineas and said he *should* take it."

Although Sumter admired George Washington, whom he had known in the Virginia militia, he did not arrive in time for his inauguration. Soon after that he took his seat in Congress and on June 8 rose to make his first speech.

"I consider the subject of amendments of such great importance to the union, that I shall be glad to see it undertaken in any manner," he said with the fire of a States Rights advocate. "I am not, Mr. Speaker, disposed to sacrifice substance to form; therefore, whether the business shall originate in a Committee of the Whole or in the House, is a matter of indifference to me, so that it be put in train. Although I am seriously inclined to give this subject a full discussion, yet I do not wish it to be fully entered into at present, but am willing it should be postponed to a future day, when we shall have more leisure. With respect to referring [it] to a select committee, I am rather against it; because I consider it as treating the applications of the State conventions rather slightly; and I presume it is the intention of the House to take those applications into consideration as well as any other. If it is not, I think it will give fresh cause for jealousy; it will rouse the alarm which is now suspended, and the people will become clamorous for amendments. They will decline any further application to Congress, and resort to the other alternative pointed out in the Constitution. I hope, therefore, this House when they do go into the business, will receive those propositions generally."

Sumter next spoke on the question of establishing a department of foreign affairs. "This bill appears to my mind so subversive of the Constitution," he cried, in attacking the proviso for the President's removal of the secretary, "and in its consequences so destructive to the liberties of the people, that I cannot consent to let it pass, without expressing my detestation of the principles it contains. I do it in this public manner in order to fulfill what I think to be my duty to my country."

As the members grew tired of the endless rounds of debate, there was a motion that Congress recess during October and November. In so short a time Sumter could not travel to South Carolina, attend to his affairs, and return to New York. "Our conduct in adjourning for so short a time, and leaving so much business unfinished, can never be approved by the people," he said in his laconic style. "Gentlemen talk of their private concerns; I do not think any member has made a greater proportional sacrifice than I have."

After a tour of the North, in the spring of 1791 President Washington made a tour of the South. As he approached Charleston, Sumter sent Tom with a letter inviting the President to visit Stateburg in the beautiful High Hills.

Dear Sir:

Being informed by my son that he will wait on you in Charleston at your arrival, I am happy in having the occasion of offering you the sincerest welcome to our state, together with my best wishes for your health and happiness, not only at present but in perpetuity.

In your travels you may yet remark the *traces of British devastation* and I am afraid, the pernicious effects of impolitic counsels and lax principles. But you will also discern a happy contrast to this representation, in the prospects of vigor and prosperity that are now budding from the unity of our American Governments, and which have been so strongly assured to us by the happy management which has characterised the first and most trying period of your Presidency.

I hope, Sir, this freedom will be excused, as I have been moved to it from considerations of the highest esteem and the warmest regard. And likewise to declare how happy the people of this quarter and myself should be made, by having an opportunity of receiving *one* amongst us, who is always thought and spoken of with most affectionate emotion.

We have been led to suggest our desire from a report of your having it in your intention to visit Columbia and Camden. The first lies opposite to Stateburgh, at 30 miles distance, and the latter at not more than 20; so that the deviation will be, perhaps, more trifling than the pleasure which the view of those Highlands may afford, which have been doubtless described to you.

Allow me, Dear Sir, to subscribe myself with the truest sentiments of respect and regard.

Your most obedient Humble Servant
Thomas Sumter, Senior

12th April 1791
Stateburgh

The President of the United States
Charleston

Washington stuck to his itinerary and on his return stopped in Columbia and Camden. After receiving a tumultuous welcome, meeting the political leaders, and listening to gracious speeches and flattering toasts—and privately jotting down memoranda about the barrenness of the Carolina sand hills—he drove on toward Mount Vernon.

In his long and stormy career Thomas Sumter was usually conciliatory and seldom held grudges. But he had never forgiven General Greene for his condescension toward the Carolina militia. In 1788 the Reverend William Gordon published in London a four-volume work entitled *The History of the Rise, Progress, and Establishment of the Independence of the United States of America*. Gordon had read Greene's private correspondence and from it quoted some unkind remarks about the Carolina Partisans.

Gordon quoted Greene's indiscreet observation in a letter to Colonel Reed of Pennsylvania: "Generals Marion and Sumter have a few people who adhere to them, perhaps, more from a desire and opportunity of plundering, than from any inclination to promote the independence of the United States." When Sumter read that and similar quotations, his wrath overflowed. He prepared a letter of quotations for his veterans. To them he exclaimed, "View this and suppress your indignation if you can."

Sumter's anger led to one of his few vindictive acts. The seeds of this were sown in the closing months of the Revolution when to get food and clothing for his troops General Greene became surety for John Banks and Company. After the war the grateful people of North Carolina, South Carolina, and Georgia rewarded Greene with handsome gifts of money and of land confiscated from the Tories. He settled at Mulberry Grove, some fourteen miles above Savannah. Soon afterward John Banks failed, and to pay his surety bond, Greene had to sacrifice his estate near Orangeburg.

In 1786 Greene died of sunstroke, and Widow Greene appealed to the federal government for financial relief. General Anthony Wayne, then a member from Georgia, carried her petition to the floor of Congress. When it came up for debate, Sumter opposed it. He thought that Greene's connection with Banks had been both unnecessary and unwise. He contended that the awards had been ample and sufficient. And then he launched into a tirade which he ended by quoting Greene's aspersions on the Partisans.

"These reflections are gross calumnies on, and misrepresentations of, the character of the people, which are invalidated by facts that then took place, and by the general tenor of the conduct of South Carolina throughout the whole course of the war," he said.

"I am sorry to differ in opinion with the gentleman from Georgia, and am therefore disposed to make sacrifices of my own feelings of past injustices, and will not suffer them to warp or bias my judgement; but will endeavor to decide in conformity with the opinions of the people of my State."

Sumter's sincerity endeared him to colleagues from all sections of the United States. Among his warm friends were James Madison of Virginia, Fisher Ames of Massachusetts, Elias Boudinot of New Jersey, General John Muhlenberg of Pennsylvania, and General James Jackson, the Georgian who had fought under him at Blackstock's. John Randolph of Roanoke even declared, "If I had to vote by proxy, and the welfare of the country depended on that single vote, I would make Thomas Sumter my proxy."

After his first term in Congress, Sumter relaxed, served on few committees, and seldom spoke. But he was constantly in his seat, listening and voting. His chief principles were limitation of federal powers, economy in government, and justice to the claims of veterans and widows of veterans. When the question of redeeming the Continental certificates issued during the Revolution came before the House, he voted to favor the original holder.

But Congress passed a law to repay the amount of the certificate irrespective of the holder. Many speculators, including Washington and cabinet members, began purchasing the certificates wholesale. Operating through William Murrell and Company, Sumter, too, began dealing in Continental paper, partly for trade and partly to accommodate needy veterans.

Rumors immediately spread that Congressman Sumter was speculating in script, indents, and certificates. Political enemies accused him of accumulating vast quantities of Continental paper at a few cents on the dollar, with foreknowledge that the federal government would redeem it at full value. The Up Country rose against him. In the election of 1793 Brigadier General Richard Winn, once Sumter's aide and commander of the reserve at Blackstock's, routed the aging Gamecock.

Involuntarily retired from public service, for the next three years Thomas Sumter devoted himself to private interests. He dissolved his partnership with William Murrell, speculated heavily in land, and fought numerous lawsuits. And he finished paying off the claims of the State Troops, an activity which brought him again in contact with the people. During the summer of 1796 he broke his rule of never seeking office and announced his candidacy for Congress. In a broadside challenging any man to show any intentional wrongdoing, public or private, he appealed for vindication. The appeal rallied the veterans, and in May, 1797, he was in Philadelphia for the opening of Congress.

This special session was the turning point in Sumter's political career. He had learned that listening and voting is not enough. A congressman must *represent* his constituents. And as Vice-President Thomas Jefferson began marshaling his democratic friends against Adams' Federalist party, Sumter joined the Jeffersonians.

Although convivial, Thomas Sumter was often solitary and lonely. In Philadelphia without Mary, he frequently spent the evening at the theater. Coming home one evening, he heard that fire had broken out in a building across the street. Even though well past sixty, he ran across and was one of the first to climb to the roof of Independence Hall.

One evening in the summer of 1798 Congressman Sumter went to the Circus Theater in Market Street. As he sat quietly on a front seat, rumors spread that President Adams was entering. Most of the patrons began clapping. As a Jeffersonian who did not greatly esteem Adams, Sumter remained quiet. A Federalist named Fitzhugh asked him why he did not clap. Sumter replied politely. A second rumor started the crowd clapping again. Seizing the congressman's hands and trying to strike them together, Fitzhugh asked brusquely, "Why don't you clap?"

Resenting the familiarity, Sumter retorted that he was not acquainted with his assailant. "Do you know who I am?"

"Oh, damn you, we know you and all your party," replied Fitzhugh. "I hope, in six months time, to see you all banished from the country."

When Adams finally arrived, Fitzhugh attempted to snatch off

Sumter's hat, inquiring harshly, "Why don't you uncover like the rest of us?"

Sumter refused to be drawn into a public brawl. But his friends knew that he was a man not to be meddled with, allowing no liberties and taking no insults. Next morning he took down the old sword he had received from Major Wemyss at Fish Dam Ford. He had a smith shorten and sharpen it and then called upon Mr. Fitzhugh. Fortunately, the gentleman had already left Philadelphia.

Nor was Sumter less positive at home. After the Revolution, John Scott and Yusef ben Ali squatted on his land near Home House. Scott was a tailor, a very useful man on a large plantation, and for years he served as bugler for the Claremont dragoons. But the dark complexion of the two North Africans brought up the question of their right to sit on a jury. His neighbors sent for the old Gamecock to say whether or not they were white. He strode into the meeting, laid his pistol on the table, and shook hands cordially with Scott and Ben Ali. Then turning to the gathering, he asked, "Gentlemen, are there any other questions?"

But by tradition and training neither Scott nor Ben Ali was a farmer. In the fall Sumter would harvest their scattering crops and store them in his own barns. When a neighbor asked his reason, he replied testily, "Damn it, they'd only waste it. I shall have to feed them anyhow!"

In the elections of 1798 General Winn again ran for Congress. Rivalry was fierce and rumors spread. A writer purportedly from Stateburg accused Sumter of being heavily in debt to the state and evading prosecution by "availing himself of his seat in Congress, by which his person is privileged." Sumter replied in a broadside. He denied the malicious charges. He was not afraid to trust his case to the voters. And he was re-elected by a majority of two-to-one.

During the first session he served faithfully, following the Jeffersonians in their attacks upon the Alien and Sedition Acts. On the opening of the Sixth Congress he received a single vote for Speaker. A few days later Speaker Sedgewick appointed him to the powerful Committee on Elections and Privileges. In the party caucus held at

Marache's Boarding House in the spring of 1800, he voted for the nomination of Thomas Jefferson for President.

Although the Federalists renominated President John Adams and then chose Charles Cotesworth Pinckney as his running mate, the inclusion of an old friend from the aristocratic Low Country did not impress Sumter. He hurried home to work for Jefferson. On his sixty-fifth birthday on July 14, his admirers gave a dinner honoring him. A committee presented a complimentary address in appreciation of his political conduct. "General Sumter, our representative in Congress," they cried in a toast, "the man who hath persevered in well doing."

General Winn soon announced his candidacy for Congress, and Sumter began vigorous electioneering. His political enemies again attacked him on money matters. As usual, rumors flew. The most widely circulated was that the Gamecock had decided to retire from Congress and run for governor. But in a hot campaign, made worse by torrid weather, Sumter again won a two-to-one victory.

During the expansion of courts and counties after the Revolution, a section was cut from old Camden District and named Sumter District. In 1800 the commissioners for the district decided to erect a courthouse and a jail. After a survey, with plans for a flourishing realty development, Tom Sumter persuaded the commissioners to locate the public buildings on his father's tract of 14,288 acres lying along Turkey Creek and Black River. Because of the great popularity of the old hero, the village which soon grew up around these was called Sumterville.

In November the Congress met in the new capital laid out along the Potomac. With Jefferson and Burr leading in the race for the presidency, the Federalists attempted to pass as much legislation as possible. Jefferson's Republicans were just as eagerly blocking it. Sumter opposed the reorganization of the Federal judiciary. He voted against erecting a monument to Washington.

After the ballots of the Electoral College had been counted, there was a tie between Jefferson and Burr, and election of the President was thrown into the House of Representatives. When the day for electing the President arrived, Sumter was too ill to be present. During all the excitement he lay abed, feverishly trying to get well. "Mr. Sumter being sick has not attended," observed

The National Intelligencer, "but will attend, at every hazard, the moment his vote can be of any avail."

Thomas Jefferson and Aaron Burr were inaugurated President and Vice-President on March 4, 1801. At last the democratic element in America had come into power. The Up Countrymen whom Sumter had led for twenty years had helped sweep Pinckney and the aristocratic party of the Low Country from the halls of government.

President Jefferson began rewarding his followers. He appointed Chancellor Robert Livingston minister to France. On March 24 he wrote Congressman Sumter: "I have cast my eye upon your son to be secretary to the Legation to France, if the appointment shall be acceptable to him, as I hope it will."

Thomas Sumter, Jr., now a thirty-three-year-old planter, with some of the ambition but not the fire and drive of his father, considered the secretaryship a splendid opening for a career in the diplomatic corps. Soon he was on his way to France. While waiting in New York for a ship, he visited the home of a friend. There he met pretty, vivacious Natalie de Delage de Volude.

Mademoiselle de Delage was the daughter of the late Marquis de Volude. At the outbreak of the French Revolution the Marquise had sent her to New York, and she had been attending the seminary of Madame Sénat. Among her school friends was Theodosia Burr, daughter of Vice-President Burr. Theodosia had recently married Joseph Alston of Georgetown, and Natalie was intrigued at meeting another handsome Carolinian.

Madame Sénat and Natalie were preparing to return to France, and Thomas arranged for passage on the same ship. "Young Secretary Sumter, on the passage to Europe, fell desperately in love with Miss Natalie d'Lage," gossipy old Horatio Gates wrote Burr. "They landed at Nantz, near her mother's chateau. The old lady is a furious royalist, and will not hear of her daughter's being married to a republican."

After a tempestuous courtship, republican love triumphed over aristocratic hostility. The Marquise announced the engagement of Natalie and Thomas. "Nothing could be more grateful to me than your proposed connection with Mr. Sumter," Vice-President Burr, to whom she was like a daughter, immediately wrote Natalie.

"I know little of him personally, but his reputation and standing in society fully justify your choice, and I pray you to assure him that I shall most cordially take him to my bosom as a son. With his father I have been long acquainted, and always respected him. We were fellow-soldiers during our revolutionary war, in which he acted a most distinguished part."

Party faithfulness had an even greater reward. President Jefferson appointed Senator Charles Pinckney his ambassador to Spain, and the elevation of Blackguard Charlie, as the Federalists derisively nicknamed the Pinckney who had led the Low Country democrats against Charles Cotesworth, left a vacancy in the upper house. Thrusting aside former Governor Rutledge, and without Sumter's candidacy or knowledge, since he was in Washington, the Jeffersonians in the South Carolina General Assembly elected him to the Senate of the United States.

Thomas Sumter was sworn in as United States Senator on December 19, 1801. He was now sixty-seven years old, but except for an occasional cold or touch of influenza he was always up and working. The older he grew, the less his old wounds troubled him, and at the age when most folk retire he was hale, vigorous, and agile. "I have seen him place his hand upon the pommel and spring from the ground into the saddle," said a neighbor, "and he was nearing seventy."

Senator Sumter accepted his new duties seriously. As a Jeffersonian he voted along strict party lines. He voted to repeal the judiciary act and abolish sixteen judgeships, the work of the Federalists in the closing hours of the last Congress. As a former leader of the militia, he voted to reduce the army and the navy. He voted to repeal internal revenue laws and lower the tariffs.

Upon his return to Stateburg, however, the Senator found his affairs heavily entangled, with judgments and lawsuits pending. With several stores on his plantations extending credit to all who asked but who refused to pay until sued, for years he had been in constant litigation. William Murrell had now won a suit for £260. A creditor had also attached a shipment of cotton assigned to Philadelphia. Only slight relief came when for $3,138 he sold five hundred and twenty-three acres of land at Great Falls on the Catawba to the federal government as a site for Fort Dearborn.

As one who had made his fortune speculating in land, the Senator was enthusiastic over Jefferson's purchase of Louisiana. But there were repercussions in the family. Secretary Thomas Sumter, Jr., became so violently estranged from Ambassador Livingston that he resigned and took passage for South Carolina. While awaiting the return of his son, with wife and daughter, Sumter spent the fall in the High Hills. The younger Sumter arrived in Charleston on the eve of the Assembly Ball, the greatest event of the social season, and remained for it. "The people of Charleston have paid Natalie every possible attention," Theodosia Alston wrote her father: "indeed much more than I ever received."

But young Thomas, with Natalie and daughter, was at Home House for Christmas. "I found every thing to make me happy except that my Father and Mother were a little unwell and that the absence of 2 or 3 years made it perceptible to me that they were declining in life," said Thomas. "My wife and child met with all the affection from them that I did and as this was rather a new thing to her from parents and exceeded any idea she could have formed of it you may think it made a lively impression on her sensibility. These marks of attention were not confined to our parents alone, but extended to all our friends, including even the blacks who all deserted the plantations as soon as they heard of our arrival to come and welcome us."

President Jefferson's known confidence in Sumter gave the old Gamecock great prestige in the Senate. He was placed on important committees, and aspiring younger members sought his advice and help. He was a staunch party man, but as John Quincy Adams recorded in his diary, he was one of the few Jeffersonians independent enough to oppose the will of the President.

At the age of seventy Thomas Sumter reached the zenith of his political power. As the leader of the Jeffersonians he dominated South Carolina. In 1804 the Federalists nominated Charles Cotesworth Pinckney, his old friend and fellow Carolinian, for President. Nevertheless, the General Assembly elected Paul Hamilton, a Jeffersonian, to the governorship. So great was the old Gamecock's popularity that the Assembly then elected Thomas Sumter, Jr., lieutenant governor.

Although he had often made the journey on horseback, with advancing years Sumter began traveling to Washington in his own carriage. Mary never made the trip, but occasionally other members of the family went with him. In the fall of 1804 granddaughter Louisa, a bright, attractive girl of seventeen, rode with him on her way to a finishing school in Philadelphia. At Wilmington Vice-President Burr overtook and continued with them to Baltimore. He wrote Theodosia that he found Miss Sumter a frank, sensible, and amiable young lady. "She plays on the piano in a style which may be called superior," he noted, "and has a most uncommon fine voice."

On their return home in 1805 Senator Sumter drove down east of the Blue Ridge. For the first time in forty years he visited the little settlement on Preddy's Creek. While visiting surviving friends and old scenes, he drove his granddaughter to the site of his boyhood home. Pointing to a meadow along Preddy's, he told Louisa, "I used to tend my mother's sheep there when I was a boy running around in my shirt tail."

Near Charlottesville, Sumter paused at the home of James Suddarth for a visit with his sister Patience. He enjoyed meeting his relatives and for remembrance gave each of the youngsters a shining silver dollar. From Suddarth's he sent word to Tom Jones, a boyhood crony, to invite all of their old friends to a dinner in the hotel at Charlottesville. All began well, with greetings, good wishes, and reminiscences. Then Jones, noting the well-dressed and distinguished-appearing Senator, asked mischievously, "Tom, do you remember those old leather breeches you used to dance in at your father's mill?"

Stung by public reference to the poverty of his youth, Sumter reddened. A man of high seriousness, without any badinage or repartee, instead of turning the joke back upon Jones he became sulky. In anger he drove out of Charlottesville.

As a veteran who had suffered greatly during the Revolution, Sumter resented British interference with American shipping during the struggle with Napoleon. He finally decided that war was inevitable. Upon his return to Stateburg, he invited all the young bachelors of the community to his home. After a sumptuous dinner, he made a fiery speech, reciting the aggressions of the English navy, asserting that this young nation would be compelled to fight the old enemy, and offering commissions in the army to those who wished to serve their country.

Meanwhile Jefferson's attempts to keep the United States out of war, especially the imposition of the embargo, seemed to be ruining his party as well as the country. In the spring of 1808 the Jeffersonians returned home in gloom. "Our irresolution during last winter had lost us the power of doing right by design and the chance of doing so by accident," Lieutenant Governor Sumter wrote a friend. Nevertheless, as party stalwarts the Sumters threw their support to Jefferson's hand-picked candidate, and in spite of the Federalist renomination of Charles Cotesworth Pinckney, they carried South Carolina for James Madison.

Regularity in a winning political party carries its rewards. Soon after his inauguration, President Madison appointed Thomas Sumter, Jr., Minister plenipotentiary to Portugal. Because of the Napoleonic war, the Prince Regent, later Dom John VI, had moved the Portuguese government to Brazil. And so in January, 1810, Minister Sumter, his wife, and their growing family sailed for Rio de Janeiro, but not before he had seen William Sumter safely enrolled as a cadet in the United States Military Academy at West Point.

The old Gamecock was now seventy-six, but on the opening day of Congress he was in his seat, hearty and active. During the session he answered roll calls, served on various committees, and voted with the administration. Upon adjournment he drove back to Stateburg and spent the summer entertaining and politicking. Although elsewhere his party lost heavily, in a final test of his popularity, on December 10 his friends in the General Assembly re-elected him to the United States Senate.

Thomas Sumter now faced one of his gravest decisions. He knew that he could probably remain in the Senate until his death. But the bullet that had entered his thigh at Hanging Rock had never been removed, and during the summer the old wound formed a painful abscess. Because he and Tom had spent so much time in politics, his vast holdings had run down, and his finances were in a deplorable state.

Mary was now eighty-seven years old and quite feeble. With Louisa married to James Murrell, the manager of Sumter's estates, and William at West Point, she needed someone to give her loving attention. Thomas had spent the last thirty-five years in military and legislative service, most of them away from home, and he now wished to spend the rest of his life with her. Therefore, with all of his ambitions achieved by re-election, the Gamecock wrote out his resignation, sent it to Governor John Drayton, and quietly settled down on his plantation in the benign High Hills of Santee.

Chapter 19 LAST OF THE GENERALS

As Thomas Sumter's political dominion faded slowly away, the mantle of political leadership among Carolinians fell upon John Caldwell Calhoun, a brilliant young legislator from the Up Country. Calhoun's rise symbolized the crisis with Britain. In the final struggle with Napoleon, British warships had blockaded European ports and begun seizing American ships and impressing their sailors, and Calhoun campaigned for Congress on a platform of retaliation and war. In Congress he quickly allied himself with Speaker Henry Clay and became a leader of the War Hawks.

Upon the declaration of war in June, 1812, aged veterans began a sentimental clamor for the seventy-eight-year-old Gamecock to get into uniform. Colonel Hill, as loyal as on the day he stood behind the boulder tossing flaming lightwood against the house at Rocky Mount, headed a committee to persuade him "to return to public life and mix again in the stormy scenes of politics and war."

As the times demanded a leader with firmness, prudence, and experience, Hill's committee begged permission to nominate Sumter for governor of South Carolina. The invitation was tempting, for the governorship would have crowned to the fullest possible extent the career of the unknown sergeant of militia who in 1762 had come to Charleston in the *Epreuve*.

But the old Gamecock had no desire to exchange the joys of his plantations in the High Hills for the cares of the governor's office in Columbia. So he left the family honor to Lieutenant William Sumter; the arousing of the people to militia generals Bratton, Brandon, Lacey, and Winn; the campaigning to Major General Wade Hampton; and the glory to General Andrew Jackson, a Carolinian from the old Presbyterian settlement on the Waxhaws.

After the war, having served with distinction in the campaign around Niagara, William came home proudly wearing the silver bars of a first lieutenant. In the spring of 1817 he was promoted to captain. But having decided to study law, soon afterward he resigned from the army.

Freed of worry, the old general slowly metamorphosed into the village character. Nearly always on horseback, he was all over the High Hills, visiting, gossiping, and arguing politics. The people loved him. Sumter had become a regular worshiper at High Hills Baptist Church. When he entered the building, so great was their veneration that the congregation always rose and stood while the ushers escorted him to a seat in the front pew.

The venerable Gamecock seemed to have regained his youth. He was often with the young folk, meddling in their love affairs, scolding, and joining in their games. "I have seen General Sumter playing ball," said a neighbor, in commenting on his playing fives at Manchester when he was past eighty; "it required very severe running and active exertion to get the ball, and there were very few young men, if any, who could get the ball before he did."

The years sped by. Thomas and Mary lived happily past their golden anniversary. Now ninety-four, Mary was cheerful, constantly attended by friends, neighbors, and especially by Louisa. But in the summer of 1817 heavy rains fell, the rivers swelled and flooded, and epidemics of malaria and yellow fever swept South Carolina. In late September she became ill with intermittent fever. She lingered until October 24. Next day Thomas watched her coffin lowered gently into the cool earth near Home House.

Disconsolate, but with his memories, Sumter closed Home House and settled on his plantation at Bradford Springs, about midway between Sumterville and Camden. Lonely and restless, in 1821 he moved three miles farther west and settled at South Mount. Here he came out of retirement. The panic of 1819, followed by drouths and floods and crop failures, had left him desperate for cash. Still resourceful and self-reliant, he turned the first floor of his home into a country store. Then with the avarice and tenacity of an octogenarian, he began hawking, bartering, and selling; and dickering, haggling, and buying everything from 'coon skins to cotton.

The younger Sumters rallied around the old patriarch. William, now a practicing attorney in Sumterville, assumed jurisdiction over his grandfather's legal affairs. By then the old Gamecock needed a lawyer. James Webb, a carpenter to whom he owed four hundred dollars for material and labor, had sued him for two thousand dollars' actual and punitive damages, alleging that in January, 1820, Sumter did "beat, wound, and ill-treat" him; and that William Sumter did cause the sheriff of Sumter District to arrest and falsely imprison him for ten months and did then seize and sell his property under a writ of *capias ad satisfaciendum.*

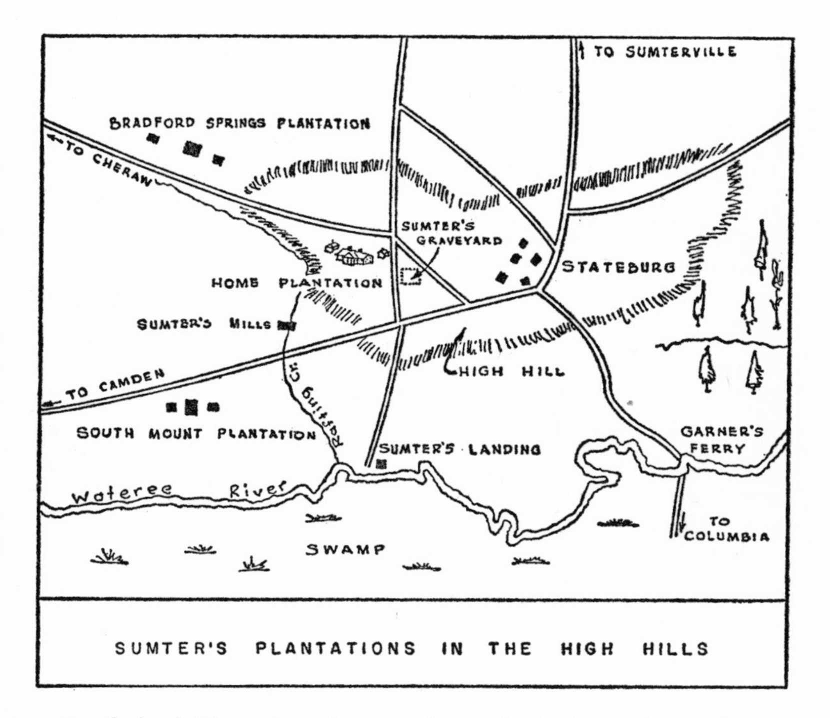

SUMTER'S PLANTATIONS IN THE HIGH HILLS

In their deliberation the members of the jury doubted that eighty-six-year-old Sumter did beat and wound the carpenter. They declared him "not guilty of trespass and false imprisonment." But in spite of William's eloquence they awarded Webb his bill, with interest, damages, and court costs.

After nine years as minister to Portugal, Colonel Thomas Sumter, Jr., now fifty-three and graying, had grown tired of diplomatic service. Worried about the health of Natalie, the condition of his father, and the education of his younger children, of whom their mother said, "They are quite Portuguese & really I am ashamed of their manner of speaking English," he decided to return to South Carolina. Upon Dom John's transfer of his court back to Lisbon, he resigned, and in the spring of 1821 sailed from Rio.

In his baggage Colonel Sumter brought a chest of curious Brazilian minerals for Thomas Jefferson. From Norfolk he forwarded them to Monticello, and the former President acknowledged the gift in a cordial note. "I lately learned with great pleasure that your father's health and activity continue wonderfully firm for his age," wrote Jefferson. "Be so good as to assure him of my constant and affectionate friendship."

Thomas, Natalie, and their seven children moved into Home House. After the excitement of the Portuguese court, they found Stateburg quiet and restful. He quickly fell into the routine of plantation life. She settled down in the petite society of the village, but as a devout Roman Catholic she took no part in church affairs. She spent her time entertaining, writing, and supervising her garden, planting domestic shrubs and flowers and importing others of exotic beauty. And whether in school or on vacation, the children frequently drove over to South Mount for a happy evening with their grandfather.

While Colonel Sumter had lived in Brazil, his plantation had been mismanaged, his finances had become entangled, and many of his unpaid bills had been protested. Nevertheless, Mrs. Sumter, who had not seen her mother for twenty years, began preparing to visit France. With the aging Marquise paying her expenses, in May, 1823, she sailed from Charleston. She took Annette Natalie, Brazilia, and Sebastian with her, and left Fanny, Mary, Thomas Delage, and Francis for their father to keep in school. "Mr. S. did not give me or send me any money," she wrote her friend Mrs. Mary Anderson in Stateburg. "You know it is what he fears the world would say."

In Paris, Natalie put Brazilia in a convent to learn English, introduced Annette Natalie into society, and began moving in the decimated post-Revolution circle of her mother's friends. "Nat is not much pleased, France is not what it was 50 years ago—except the theatres & some astonishing sights there is no pleasure, especially for a young girl," she wrote Mary Anderson; "there is still a little society amongst the old people of 60 or more, but as to all those that are younger you would find just as much pleasure in Charleston."

The Marquise bought Natalie elegant clothes and then took her to court. She presented her to King Louis XVIII. On another occasion the Marquise took her daughter and granddaughter to a private audience with Prince Charles de Bourbon, the heir apparent to the throne. Prince Charles took Natalie's hand and said, "Mr. Sumter must come here as minister." As Annette Natalie was unmarried, it was improper for her to visit the Prince. But he laughed and said jestingly, "She is only four years old."

The Marquise presented Natalie to the Duchesse d'Angoulême, daughter of Louis XVI and Marie Antoinette; and then to the Duchesse de Berry, widow of the oldest son of Prince Charles. "I was obliged to be presented at court or else it would have been very disagreeable to have met the Princesses at the parties," she wrote Mary with complete frankness. "I was invited there on account of my mother." With the Duchesse de Berry, however she had another bond. Prince Henri Charles was the same age as Sebastian, and the grandson of the millboy from Preddy's romped around the palace with the grandson of the Prince who became Charles X of France.

Natalie longed to have Fanny and Mary with her in Paris. The Marquise offered to "lend me the money, for she is so anxious to see them," she wrote, asking Mary Anderson to persuade Colonel Sumter to send their other daughters with Mrs. Raoul. "Do if you think it possible, beg him to do it," she urged. "Nobody knows what Mr. Sumter might do; you know that one day he is of an opinion and changes suddenly.

"I am not in want of money, my mother supplies me with everything & beside has given me one thousand dollars since I am here," Natalie wrote. "I am obliged to spend more than I would if I could say that my husband is embarrassed & that I am saving money, but my mother does not wish anyone to know it, and she always says to everyone that I brought a good deal with me & pay great many expenses in her house." But she asked Mary, "Do tell me also how all the lawsuits are going on & if there is any chance of having any crops & if Mr. S. pays any of the debts."

Did Natalie have a purpose in coming to Paris? "One of my cousins was saying to me yesterday—for they very naturally think I brought here Natalie to marry her—she asked me if I had anyone in view," she wrote Mary. After she had explained that the Sumter affairs were too embarrassed to hope for a dowry, her cousin replied, "For Nat that will not be necessary. She is very agreeable, and there are many young men of great fortune who will be very happy to be the grandson of your mother, for she will have to say only one word to the King, and he will have them placed in the Army or Corps Diplomatique."

As she wrote, Natalie thought of Fanny and Mary growing up in Stateburg. "If I was to choose I could marry them to men of birth, talent, and fortune," she confided to Mary Anderson. "But first they are not here, and next Mr. S. naturally would not like it; so even if I have an offer for Natalie I will throw cold water on it, for I will not do anything to displease him." And her tact was rewarded. Although Thomas wished his daughters to marry Americans, that fall he sent Fanny and Mary to join Annette Natalie and Brazilia in Paris.

But Annette Natalie, born in Paris and reared and educated in Brazil, had spent only seven years in the United States. She was more French than American and liked her grandmother's aristocrats better than her grandfather's democrats. Before leaving Stateburg she had come to an understanding with her father. He told her that she would be twenty-one before returning and able to decide for herself. She did. Before Natalie left Paris in 1825 she saw Annette Marie Natalie married to Comte Gabriel de Fontenay.

Just before sailing for New York, Natalie wrote Mrs. Anderson that "I should be followed by another intended son who means to become an American; this also has been a great cause of uneasiness, not on his account, for he is everything I can wish for Stephanie; but I am not sure of Mr. S.'s approval." He approved, and Fanny married Conte Guiseppe Agamemnon Binda of Genoa.

While Natalie was in Paris, visiting the court with her mother, attending parties with princesses, and marrying her daughters into nobility, Thomas remained at Stateburg, struggling desperately to untangle his affairs. With the country in an agricultural depression, he failed to do so, and in July, 1824, he borrowed twenty-five thousand dollars from his father. By giving a mortgage on fifty-two of his sixty slaves General Sumter borrowed the money from the Bank of the State of South Carolina.

Even though in financial straits, the Sumters were important. During the visit of the Marquis de Lafayette to America in 1824, the Freemasons of Camden invited him to lay the cornerstone for their monument to Baron de Kalb. As the younger Sumter had known Lafayette in Paris, the Masons asked him to serve on the committee to welcome the distinguished visitor. When the Marquis finally arrived in the following spring, they invited General Sumter to attend the reception. Pleading age and infirmity, he declined. Nevertheless, during the celebration the Masons toasted the old Gamecock as the Sword of South Carolina in the Revolution.

As Sumter grew older, tales about him grew wilder. The toasting and eulogizing became more frequent. In Sumterville on July 4, 1826, celebrants clinked their glasses and cried, "General Thomas Sumter! The active Partisan in our Revolutionary Struggle! While our district bears the name which honors it, his public services will remain fresh in our memory. May he live long to enjoy the blessings of old age!"

On the same day thirsty neighbors at Stateburg were toasting, "General Sumter, who in the most gloomy times, when scarce a ray of hope gilded the prospect, took the field at the head of a Spartan band, whose motto was Liberty or Death!"

After the toasts came tears. The depression began closing in upon the Sumters. William, whom the old general loved as a younger son, but whose education at West Point had fitted him for neither law nor planting, had mortgaged his plantation, his home, and even his hunting dogs. On the eve of foreclosure, he put a bullet through his head.

Colonel Sumter now tried to sell his seven-thousand-acre plantation, with slaves, houses, mills, gins, boat landing and warehouse, and even Home House. But times were hard and money scarce.

Finding no purchaser, he had to default on repaying the loan from his father.

Financing his son ruined Thomas Sumter. Poor crops, a low price for cotton, and heavy indebtedness made it impossible for him to float another loan. His creditors began hounding him. Like a guilty man the old hero sneaked off and hid out on one of his small plantations.

The Bank of the State of South Carolina, to which Sumter owed some thirty-five thousand dollars, began threatening foreclosure. Determined that the state should not beggar the Gamecock who had so nobly defended it, the voters of Sumter District petitioned the legislature to give him financial relief. Those in Kershaw District endorsed a similar petition, and the Kershaw grand jury made formal overtures to the General Assembly.

During the session of 1827 the president of the Senate and the Speaker of the House appointed a joint committee to investigate Sumter's financial status. The committee recommended that the Bank of the State be directed "to grant indulgence, free of interest, to General Thomas Sumter, upon his debt to the Bank, during his life, taking such steps as may appear expedient to them, to secure ultimate payment of the debt."

The Gamecock came out of hiding. In the following summer, with only Soldier Tom for companion, he set out on a sentimental tour of the scenes of his heroic exploits. He passed along the Wateree, stopping at Rocky Mount, Fishing Creek, and Hanging Rock. At Fish Dam Ford he pointed out the ravine where he had hid and shivered in November frost. He climbed the hill and stood again on the spot where forty-eight years before he had almost bled to death during the battle at Blackstock's. Most of his veterans were dead, but everywhere their sons and grandsons welcomed the old hero.

After his farewell tour, Sumter went into complete retirement. He became a legend. A young news reporter, sent to cover a trial in the magistrate's court at Bradford Springs in 1830, almost forgot his assignment when he saw the fabled Gamecock. "The trial was an interesting one, but a circumstance extraneous to the trial still more excited our feelings—that was the presence of the aged warrior and remarkable patriot, General Sumter, for a few minutes on the second day," he wrote. "We scarcely ever experienced greater satisfaction than when we pressed the hand which had so often wielded the sword of Liberty! The whole assemblage regarded the chief and statesman of other days with a common feeling of admiration, gratitude and enthusiastic attachment. He is now in his 97th year—has a healthy appearance—moves with activity and firmness of step—mounts his horse and dismounts with great ease, and is entertaining and instructive in conversation."

While the last surviving general of the Revolution was bidding farewell to the veterans of the strife between Whigs and Tories, another civil war threatened South Carolina. Smoldering indignation at the federal tariff laws, believed to be the cause of the long agricultural depression, flamed up and shook the constitutional foundation of the state. Led by Vice-President Calhoun, many Carolinians believed that their state had an inherent power to nullify the federal constitution. Heated arguments over that right divided the people into Unionists and Nullifiers.

During the struggle both parties listened vainly for the crow of the Gamecock. Pleading age and illness, he refused to enter the controversy. He declined all invitations to political rallies and dinners. Finally, in October, 1831, a letter appeared, purporting to be from the aged hero. It called upon the people of South Carolina "to endeavor to change a system of usurpations no longer in harmony with the spirit of our constitution."

Published in the *Pendleton Messenger* and reprinted in *Niles Register,* the letter circulated throughout the United States. In South Carolina it was greeted as if it were a message from the Delphic oracle. "The voice of the lion-hearted Sumter is heard again," wrote the editor of the Sumterville *Times and Gazette.* "He awakes from a slumber of forty years—the fire of his youthful patriotism rekindles in his bosom, and the spirit-stirring rally of the Revolution bursts from his lips."

How the Nullifiers exulted! "The South Carolina Gamecock—not too old to flap his wings and crow!" shouted fire-eating Major Waddy Thompson in a toast. "As the old cock crows may the young ones learn!"

After an alleged interview, the *Camden Journal* printed a sensational article on "General Sumter's Opinions." The writer proved him Unionist. Thomas Delage Sumter showed the article to his grandfather. The general's open letter denied giving an interview and repudiated the opinions. It was an absolute triumph for the Nullifiers.

They now tried to get the old statesman to attend their rallies and dinners. He refused to come out of retirement. Invited to a dinner in Sumterville for the delegates to an Anti-tariff Convention in Philadelphia, he declined. But he proposed a toast: "The year 1832—The period when the character of the State of South Carolina and of her inhabitants shall be fixed forever; when no middle course shall be open to them, and when every individual will either rank among the enemies of the liberties of his country, or else among those who have honored it!"

The triumphant Nullifiers wished to exhibit the Gamecock at their celebration of Washington's centennial. Governor James Hamilton, Jr., offered to send his horses and carriage to South Mount. Although Sumter had not been in Charleston for thirty-five years, he wrote to beg his friends to dispense with his company on the hundredth birthday of Washington, "who, though far my superior in everything else, was but little in age, and no more than my equal . . . in devotion to the cause of National Independence."

The Nullifiers of Sumter District wished to give a dinner in honor of their old champion. When a committee called at South Mount to invite him, they found that although his voice and hearing had begun to fail, Thomas Sumter was "sole manager of his planting and other interests—with all the faculties of his mind apparently as perfect, useful, and commanding, as they could have been in the meridian of life."

Sumter declined all invitations and lingered through the spring at South Mount. The High Hills were lovely with the fresh green of the oaks and hickories and maples. The air was warm and fragrant. On sunny days the venerable patriot rode through the ancient hills with grandson Thomas Delage. On the last day of May accompanied by Thomas, he rode eleven miles, stopping to inspect his farms and mills and shops. Exactly fifty-two years before he had fled along the same road just ahead of Tarleton's

Green Horse. As he looked back, Tom Sumter had come a long way from Preddy's Creek.

Having promised to ride again with Thomas, on June 1, 1832, the old Gamecock had his horse saddled early, and while waiting puttered around his garden and orchard. He pruned some yearling apple trees. About noon he sent his horse back to the stable and tottered into the house. Calling Jefferson, the body servant named in remembrance of glories past, he complained of being tired. As he was undressing for bed, he suddenly staggered across the room and slumped into a chair. His heart gave a final throb, and his magnificent white head rolled forward.

The funeral was simple. Both whites and blacks gathered at the graveyard near Home House. The Reverend Samuel Furman read some passages from the *Bible* and offered a prayer. The mourners broke into a spiritual. Then the pallbearers lowered his coffin into a grave beside that of Mary.

All South Carolina went into mourning. The people from the High Hills and beyond gathered in Sumterville for a memorial service. The Reverend Samuel Furman delivered the eulogy, showing God's providence in raising up Thomas Sumter to lead his people like another Moses.

The memorialists appointed a committee of nine members to solicit contributions for a monument. But men are mortal. Nature never forgets. From near the grave of Thomas Sumter grew an oak, gnarled and majestic, a symbol of the man whose atoms flowed into its fibers. In time the Carolinians remembered and inscribed above him in eternal granite:

This stone marks the grave of one of South
Carolina's most distinguished citizens,
THOMAS SUMTER.
One of the founders of the Republic.
Born in Va., Aug. 14, 1734.
Died June 1, 1832

He came to South Carolina about 1760
and was in the Indian Service on the

Frontier for several years before settling
as a planter in this vicinity.
Commandant of 6th Regt., S. C. Line,
Continental Estab., 1776-1778.
Brig. Gen. S. C. Militia, 1780-1782.
Member of Continental Congress, 1783-1784.
Member U. S. Congress, 1789-1793, 1797-1801.
U. S. Senator, 1801-1810

Tanto Nomini Nullum
Par Elogium

Sources and Notes

1. Sergeant from Preddy's

The primary sources of *Gamecock* are the letters of Thomas Sumter, Nathanael Greene, John Rutledge, Francis Marion, Henry Lee, William Henderson, Daniel Morgan, Banastre Tarleton, Lord Cornwallis, and many other American and British participants in the Revolutionary War. The majority of these is still unpublished. The *Memoirs* of Lee and the *Campaigns* of Tarleton, as well as the sketches, notes, memoirs, and histories of other participants are additional primary sources.

Secondary sources are extensive, the most important being the Sumter papers in the Draper collection left by Lyman C. Draper, Secretary of the State Historical Society of Wisconsin and author of *King's Mountain and its Heroes.* Draper planned a similar book about Sumter and his men and during forty years of research collected more than ten thousand pages of notes. These are now arranged in twenty-four manuscript volumes, marked Series VV, and preserved in the archives of the Society in Madison.

The sources for background are Christopher Ward, *The War of the Revolution,* edited by John Richard Alden, 2 vols., New York, 1952; and Sir Henry Clinton, *The American Rebellion,* edited by William B. Willcox, New Haven, 1954. Biographical information is from *The Dictionary of American Biography,* New York, 1937; *The Dictionary of National Biography,* London, 1921; Lorenzo Sabine, *Biographical Sketches of the Loyalists of the American Revolution . . . ,* 2 vols., New York, 1864; Francis B. Heitman, *Historical Register and Dictionary of the United States Army . . . ,* 2 vols., Washington, 1903; *Year Book: City of Charleston, South Carolina,* Charleston, 1893; Joseph Johnson, *Traditions and Reminiscences chiefly of the American Revolution in the South . . . ,* Charleston, 1851; and the unpublished muster rolls of the British regiments.

Maps used in tracing the campaigns of the Gamecock are Henry Mouzon, *An Accurate Map of North and South Carolina . . . ,* London, 1775; Robert Mills, *Atlas of the State of South Carolina . . . ,* Baltimore, 1825; and *South Carolina State Highway Primary System* and maps of the counties of South Carolina prepared and published by the South Carolina Highway Department.

The names of many towns, streams, and places have been changed since the Revolution. The original name has been used in *Game-Cock:* for instance, Cross Creek instead of Fayetteville and Drowning Creek instead of Lumber River. Modern spelling has been used, however; Charleston instead of Charles Town and Winnsboro instead of Winnsborough. In the main these spellings have come from the maps prepared by the South Carolina Highway Department.

The Santee River, formed by the confluence of the Congaree and the Wateree rivers, is the largest stream in South Carolina. Because of its size and location, with its vast drainage basin, it was of great strategic importance during the Revolution.

Accounts of the Sumter family and Sumter's youth are taken from Draper's manuscripts, especially volume 1VV. See also Anne King Gregorie, *Thomas Sumter,* Columbia, 1931. The story of Timberlake and Sumter among the Cherokees and in London is from Samuel Coles Williams, editor, *Lieut. Henry Timberlake's Memoirs,* Marietta, 1948. For the return of the Cherokees from London, see Draper, 2VV169. Sumter's appearance in Charleston is from *Journal of the Council of South Carolina.* Sumter's second visit to the Cherokees and capture of Des Jonnes is derived from Draper, 11VV330, 11VV335, and 11VV370, and from the *South Carolina Gazette,* March 19, March 26, April 30, and May 7, 1763. The account of Sumter's jail break is from Draper, 2VV80. Sumter's letter to Martin is in Draper, 1VV24.

Sumter is from "sumpter," a word which comes from Old French *sommetier,* which is derived from Latin *sagma,* a packsaddle. Sumpter designates an animal used to transport baggage, as a sumpter horse, and also a driver of such animals. In England in the thirteenth century sumpter changed from an occupation to a proper name. Family tradition says that the Sumpters came from Wales. Thomas Sumter spelled his name Sumpter or Sumter. On January 31, 1792, he signed his congressional pay voucher as Thomas Sumpter, but on March 2, 1792, and thereafter he signed it Thomas Sumter.

Louisa County once covered much of the piedmont region of Virginia.

Preddy's Creek flows into the Rivanna ten or twelve miles northeast of Charlottesville.

Joseph Martin became a noted Indian fighter, general of militia, and member of the legislature of Virginia.

Benjamin Cleveland became a famous hunter, Indian fighter, and militia leader. A hero of the battle of King's Mountain, after the Revolution he settled in the present Oconee County, South Carolina, and served as judge in Pendleton District.

Zachariah Burnley lived at Somerset in Orange County, Virginia.

Edward Braddock was commander in chief of the British forces in America. While leading an expedition against Fort Duquesne in 1755, he was ambushed and killed by French and Indians.

George Washington saved part of Braddock's army. Undoubtedly, Sumter knew Washington and perhaps served under him on the frontier.

Robert Dinwiddie, a Scotsman, sent to Virginia as lieutenant governor in 1751, attempted to prevent the French from occupying the Ohio Valley.

William Byrd III, of Westover on James River, was colonel of the Second Regiment of Virginia.

Henry Timberlake, from Hanover County, Virginia, served in the militia under Colonel Byrd. After escorting the Cherokee chiefs to England, Lieutenant Timberlake wrote his *Memoirs.* He did in London in 1765. Sumter was probably sergeant in Timberlake's company.

Stephen Holston, in search of free land in southwestern Virginia, built a cabin at the head spring of the middle fork of the stream subsequently called Holston River.

Samuel Stalnakres built a cabin nine miles west of that of Holston.

The Cherokee nation was concentrated in the Lower Towns, the Middle Towns, and the Over Hill Towns, all situated around the southern rim of the

Appalachian Mountains. The Lower Towns lay in northwestern South Carolina and northeastern Georgia. The Middle Towns were in northern Georgia and western North Carolina. And the Over Hill Towns were in western North Carolina and eastern Tennessee.

In 1760 Lieutenant Colonel Archibald Montgomerie and his Highlanders destroyed many of the Lower Towns. In 1761 Lieutenant Colonel James Grant, with twelve hundred regulars and a regiment of South Carolina militia under Colonel Thomas Middleton, destroyed many of the Middle Towns.

The Cherokees lived in cabins in neat villages, but their towns are difficult to identify. They gave the same name to several settlements, for example calling three places Chota or Echota, and having Great Tellico and Little Tellico, and Tomotley and Little Tomotley. The English wrote merely Chota, Tellico, or Tomotley. Modern villages with Cherokee names do not always occupy the original sites.

South Carolina leaders in the Revolution received their military training in the campaigns against the Cherokees.

Kanagatucko, head chief of the Cherokees, lived at Echota on Little Tennessee River. Because of his lameness, he was called Old Hop.

Attakullakulla, nicknamed Little Carpenter, was a peace chief, a powerful orator, and a friend of the English.

Adam Stephen, a Scotsman, became a military and political leader in Virginia.

Long Island in the Holston is now Kingsport, Tennessee.

Fort Prince George was on Keowee River in Pickens County.

Francis Fauquier, English colonial administrator, in 1758 became lieutenant governor of Virginia.

James Horrocks became president of William and Mary College in 1764.

Chief Wooe is usually called Wooe Pigeon, but *wooe* is Cherokee for *pigeon*.

Lord Egremont became Secretary of State in 1761.

Lord Eglinton was the former Archibald Montgomerie who led an expedition against the Lower and Middle towns of the Cherokees.

Thomas Boone was appointed governor of South Carolina in 1761.

Eutaw Springs, now in Lake Marion, was about six miles below Eutawville.

Congarees designated the community around the store of Chestnut and Kershaw between Congaree Creek and Congaree River. It is now Cayce.

Rabun Gap is in northern Georgia.

Nelson's Ferry was eight or ten miles below the place where U. S. Highway 301 crosses Santee River.

The word *ante* in Sumter's letter to Joe Martin is undoubtedly *aint* and *enter in again* seems to mean *reenlist*. Sumter was illiterate, but he had great capacity for self-education. He later became a vigorous, although ungrammatical, letter writer.

2. *Captain of Militia*

For background material see McCrady, *History of the Revolution in South Carolina, 1775-1780*, New York, 1902; and John Drayton, *Memoirs of the American Revolution . . .*, 2 vols., Charleston, 1821. See Joseph S. Ames, "Cantey

Family," *South Carolina Historical and Genealogical Magazine,* XVI. For letters of Drayton and Tennent and Richardson's report on the Snow Campaign, see Robert W. Gibbes, *Documentary History of the American Revolution, 1764-1776,* New York, 1855. See also Alexander Salley, Jr. *The History of Orangeburg County, South Carolina, from its first settlement to the close of the Revolutionary War,* Orangeburg, 1898, which contains "Colonel Thomson's Order Book—June 24th, 1775, to November 3rd, 1778." For Sumter's finances, speculation, and lawsuits, see Gregorie, *Thomas Sumter.* The story of Sumter's flight from debt comes from Draper, 11VV335 and 14VV29.

Long Canes Creek flows through Abbeville and McCormick counties.

Jack's Creek lies just west of Summerton.

Mount Hope plantation was near Greeleyville.

Sebastian Sumter wrote that the Jamesons had three children who died in infancy.

The Regulators were extra-legal groups who tried to regulate affairs in the back country just prior to the Revolution.

Moses Kirkland, an illiterate political and militia leader, lived on Saluda River.

Christopher Gadsden was a military and political leader during and after the Revolution.

Lord William Campbell was appointed governor of South Carolina in 1773 and tried unsuccessfully to keep the colony loyal to George III.

Colonel Richard Richardson came from Virginia, married Mary Cantey, and became the senior military leader in South Carolina, being promoted to brigadier general in 1779. He died in September, 1780.

Peter Horry, Hugh Horry, and Daniel Horry were from the Huguenot settlement on lower Santee River. Horry is pronounced O-ree.

Thomas Fletchall lived on Fair Forest Creek about five miles west of Union.

John Stuart was the British Superintendent of Indian Affairs in the South.

James Mayson was from the Ninety-Six Militia District (now Abbeville, Anderson and Edgefield Counties). John Caldwell was from the Upper Saluda District (Laurens, Newberry, and Union). And Ezekial Polk and Joseph Robinson were from the New Acquisition (York County).

William Henry Drayton was the most radical leader of the revolution in South Carolina.

John Drayton, son of William Henry, in *Memoirs of the Revolution,* wrote that Sumter held a captain's commission in Thomson's rangers, but "Colonel Thomson's Order Book" does not substantiate this claim. Colonel Richardson's appointing Sumter adjutant general indicates that he was a militia officer under Richardson's command.

The Council of Safety, consisting of thirteen members, was created by the Provincial Congress and given almost unlimited power.

Robert and Patrick Cunningham came from Virginia. Robert settled at Island Ford on the Saluda and served as magistrate. Patrick served as deputy surveyor. Moderates, they were driven into the Loyalist militia by the excesses of the Whigs.

The Dutch Fork lies between Saluda and Broad rivers. Most of the German settlers in Orangeburg, Lexington, and Newberry counties were Loyalists.

One tradition is that Colonel Fletchall hid in a cave; another is that he hid in a hollow sycamore.

Reedy River flows through Greenville County and into the headwaters of Lake Greenwood on Saluda River.

The capture of the Tory leaders was only a show of force by the Council of Safety. After a lecture by Laurens they were released for "the convenience of the electors" and for "the happy influence which it may have upon the peace and unity of the inhabitants."

3. Colonel in the Continentals

Background material comes from David Duncan Wallace, *The History of South Carolina,* 3 vols. New York, 1934; McCrady, *History of the Revolution in South Carolina, 1775-1780;* and Drayton, *Memoirs of the Revolution.* For the battle of Fort Moultrie, see William Moultrie, *Memoirs of the American Revolution so far as it related to the states of North and South Carolina and Georgia . . . ,* 2 vols., New York, 1802; David Ramsay, *The History of the Revolution of South-Carolina . . . ,* 2 vols., Trenton, 1785; Robert D. Bass, *The Green Dragoon: The Lives of Banastre Tarleton and Mary Robinson,* New York, 1957; and Robert D. Bass, *Swamp Fox: The Life and Campaigns of General Francis Marion,* New York, 1959.

For details of Williamson's campaign against the Cherokees, see Arthur Fairies, *Journal of an Expedition, in 1776, against the Cherokees . . . ,* Draper, 3VV162.

For the campaign in Georgia, see John Faucheraud Grimké, "A Journal of the Campaign to the Southward," *South Carolina Historical and Genealogical Magazine,* XII. In Draper, 18VV23, Sebastian Sumter wrote: "I had heard my father and grandfather, say that the reason he resigned his position in the Continental Army was, that the people could not be induced in the sections, from which he obtained his recruits, to serve under continental officers."

Isaac Huger was a Huguenot who served with distinction during the entire Revolutionary War. Huger is pronounced U-gee.

William Henderson, who came from Virginia, was a planter and merchant who lived south of Grindal Shoals on Pacolet River.

Lord Dartmouth, Colonial Secretary, advocated using force to suppress the unrest in America.

Sir Peter Parker, British naval officer, became Admiral of the Fleet in 1799.

Earl Cornwallis was educated at Eton and in 1756 became an ensign in the Grenadier Guards. In 1762, he entered Parliament; here he opposed the oppressive measures against the American colonies. In 1776 Lord Cornwallis came to America with British reinforcements. He advocated a strategy of capturing American seaports and then rallying the Loyalists. After his surrender at Yorktown, he was received sympathetically by the King and by the English people. In 1786 he became Governor General of India. His success in India was as great as his failure in America. He reformed the military and civil service and defeated Tippoo Sahib, Sultan of Mysore. Recalled to England upon the outbreak of war with France, in 1795 Cornwallis became Master General of Ordnance with a seat in the cabinet. In 1798 he was sent to Ireland as Viceroy and commander-in-chief. In 1802 as envoy plenipotentiary for Great Britain, he met Joseph Bonaparte and negotiated the peace treaty of Amiens. Sent out a second time as governor of India, Lord Cornwallis died at Ghazipur in 1805. He had been one of the most distinguished men of his generation.

Sir Henry Clinton was the son of George Clinton, governor of New York. After serving in the New York militia, on November 1, 1751, he became a lieutenant in the Coldstream Guards. After distinguished service in the army, he became a member of Parliament. In company with Generals Howe and Burgoyne, General Clinton came to Boston in 1775 and further distinguished himself in the battle of Bunker Hill. In 1778 he became commander-in-chief of the British forces in North America. After the Revolution he engaged in a heated controversy with Lord Cornwallis. In 1790 he again entered Parliament and in 1795 died while serving as Governor of Gibraltar.

Charles Lee, a British officer who settled in Virginia in 1773, was the second ranking major general in the Continental Army. Captured by Tarleton in 1776, he was exchanged and given another command. But he was found guilty of disobedience by court-martial after the battle of Monmouth and dismissed from the American Army.

Charles Cotesworth Pinckney, born in Charleston and educated at Oxford, was a political and military leader. After the Revolution he was the Federalist candidate for Vice President of the United States in 1800 and candidate for President in 1804 and 1808.

Thomas Pinckney, brother of Charles Cotesworth also born in Charleston and educated at Oxford, was a lawyer, statesman, and military leader. After the Revolution he was governor of South Carolina, minister to Great Britain, and Federalist candidate for Vice President of the United States.

John Rutledge, who studied law in the Middle Temple in London, was a political leader in South Carolina. He served as governor both during and after the Revolution. Washington appointed him Chief Justice, but his appointment was not confirmed by the Senate of the United States. From 1776 until 1778 Rutledge was President of South Carolina.

Andrew Williamson, a Scotsman who lived at White Hall near Ninety-Six, was leader in the Whig militia. Commissioned brigadier general in 1779, he signed a parole and refused to serve again after the fall of Charleston.

Essenacca was near Clemson.

Griffith Rutherford was a militia leader from Salisbury in the Yadkin Valley.

Anthony Hampton brought his family from Virginia and settled on lower Tyger River. His sons Edward, Henry, Richard, and Wade distinguished themselves in the Revolution. Wade, hero of the battle of Eutaw Springs, became one of the wealthiest planters in America.

Chattahoochee, Chestatee, and Hiwassee rivers flow from springs in north Georgia.

Tugaloo River forms the boundary of western South Carolina and Georgia.

Tawcaw Swamp was some eight miles below Nelson's Ferry.

Augustine Prevost, commander in east Florida, became major general in the British army. His brother was J. M. Prevost.

L. V. Fuser was an officer in the 61st Regiment.

Button Gwinnett, an Englishman who settled in Savannah, was a political leader and signer of the Declaration of Independence. In 1777 he became President of Georgia.

Lachlan McIntosh, born in Scotland, emigrated to Georgia with his parents. A member of the Provincial Congress and brigadier general of the Georgia

Continentals, he was removed from command after mortally wounding Gwinnett in a duel.

Samuel Elbert was a member of the Georgia Council of Safety. He commanded the Georgia Continentals after the removal of McIntosh. After the Revolution, he served as governor of Georgia.

Richard Winn, whose parents came from Virginia, lived on Little River in Fairfield County. After serving in the Continentals, he became a militia leader and rose to major general.

Thomas and Samuel Taylor came from Virginia and settled on Congaree River. Columbia is situated on the Taylor plantation.

Henry Laurens, merchant and planter, was president of the first Provincial Congress of South Carolina, of the Council of Safety, and of the Continental Congress. He was captured, confined in the Tower of London, and exchanged for Lord Cornwallis.

John Laurens, son of Henry Laurens, served on Washington's staff, was envoy extraordinary to France, and negotiated the surrender of Cornwallis at Yorktown. After a brilliant career, he was killed in a skirmish near Charleston.

John Faucheraud Grimké was a military, political, and judicial figure in Charleston.

Edmund Hyrne, who lived near Charleston, was an indefatigable officer in the Continentals.

Thomas Browne, a Loyalist of bravery and ability, became vindictive after being tarred and feathered by the Whigs of Augusta.

4. General of Volunteers

For background and progress of the Revolution, see Wallace, *History of South Carolina;* McCrady, *History of the Revolution in South Carolina, 1775-1780;* Bass, *The Green Dragoon* and *Swamp Fox;* and Banastre Tarleton, *History of the Campaign of 1780 and 1781, in the Southern Provinces of North America,* London, 1787. See also "Diary of Lieut. Anthony Allaire," Lyman C. Draper, *King's Mountain and its Heroes,* New York, 1881. For additional material on James Williams, see J. D. Bailey, *Commanders at King's Mountain,* Gaffney, 1926; Alexander S. Salley, Jr., editor, *Col. Hill's Memoirs of the Revolution,* Columbia, 1921; Maurice A. Moore, *The Life of Gen. Edward Lacey . . . ,* Spartanburg, 1856; and Samuel C. Williams, editor, "General Richard Winn's Notes—1780," *South Carolina Historical and Genealogical Magazine,* XLIII. For *Robert Wilson's Narrative,* see Draper, 16VV313-319. Letters from Colonel James Williams are in Robert W. Gibbes, *Documentary History of the American Revolution, 1776-1782,* New York, 1857. Gregorie is authoritative on Sumter's finances. For the story of the Gillespie brothers' naming Sumter the Gamecock, see Cecil B. Hartley, *Life of Major General Henry Lee . . . to which is a added Life of General Thomas Sumter of South Carolina,* Philadelphia, 1859.

Benjamin Lincoln, born in Massachusetts, became major general in the Continentals. After surrendering Charleston, he was exchanged and served in the campaign around Yorktown.

Count d'Estaing commanded a French squadron in American waters. In 1792 he was Admiral of France; in 1794 he was guillotined.

Mariott Arbuthnot commanded an English fleet in American waters.

Abraham Buford, after distinguished service in the North, was assigned the Third Regiment of Virginia Continentals and sent to reinforce the garrison in Charleston. His daughter said that his troops were fresh recruits, perhaps the reason for their failure in battle with Tarleton's veteran British Legion.

William Washington, cousin of George Washington, commanded the Second Continental Dragoons. After the Revolution he settled in South Carolina.

Francis Marion, a Huguenot from St. John's Parish, lived on Santee River. A veteran of the Cherokee campaigns, he was elected to the Provincial Congress and selected as captain of infantry. He became the commandant of the Second Regiment of South Carolina Continentals. After the fall of Charleston, he collected the militia in Williamsburg County and became the famed Swamp Fox.

Banastre Tarleton, son of the mayor of Liverpool, studied at Oxford and the Middle Temple. Forsaking law, he bought a commission in the King's Dragoon Guards and then came to America with Lord Cornwallis. He was one of England's greatest cavalry leaders. After the Revolution he served in Parliament twenty-two years, was promoted to general, knighted, and then made a baronet.

Johann Kalb, born in Germany, called himself Baron de Kalb after serving in the French army. In 1777 he was commissioned major general in the Continental Army.

Richard Caswell, a Marylander who settled in North Carolina and became a political and military leader, was elected governor of North Carolina in 1776 and again in 1785.

Henry Rugeley finally accepted a commission in the Loyalist militia. After he surrendered Fort Clermont to Colonel Washington without a fight, Cornwallis wrote Tarleton: "Rugeley will not be made a brigadier."

Murry's Ferry was near the place where U. S. Highway 52 crosses Santee River.

Anthony White commanded the First Continental Dragoons. Colonel White does not appear to have been with his regiment.

Nisbet Balfour, son of an Edinburgh bookseller, was lieutenant colonel of the 23rd Regiment, known as the Royal Welsh Fusiliers. He became a general of the army and member of Parliament.

Patrick Ferguson, born in Aberdeenshire, was captain in the 71st Regiment, better known as Fraser's Highlanders. He invented a breech-loading gun, and in *King's Mountain and its Heroes* Draper says, "He was regarded as the best rifle shot in the British army."

Brierley's Ferry crossed Broad River near Strother.

Sandy River flows through Chester and Fairfield Counties.

Rocky Mount lay below Great Falls and several miles east of U. S. Highway 21.

White's Mill was on Fishing Creek about ten miles west of Land's Ford across Catawba River.

James Williams, born in Hanover County, Virginia, was a miller, merchant, and planter who lived on Little River in Laurens County. The row between him and Hill seems to have grown out of each wishing to fight around his home and property.

William Hill dictated his *Memoirs* to his grandson and gave the manuscript to Sumter.

Tuckasegee Ford crossed Catawba River west of Charlotte.

King Hagler, murdered by enemy Indians in 1763, was chief of the Catawbas.
Hagler's Branch is west of Sugar Creek and Hagler's Hill is near Fort Mill.
Francis Rawdon, son of the Earl of Moira, was a college mate of Tarleton at Oxford. He became Earl of Moira and Marquis of Hastings. A friend of George IV, he became commander in chief in India.
Ramsour's Mill is Lincolnton, North Carolina.
Old Nation Ford was near the place where U. S. Highway 21 crosses Catawba River at Fort Mill.
Turnbull's order to Huck has been frequently printed. Huck has often been misspelled Hook or Hyuck.

5. *Gamecock of the Carolinas*

Background for Sumter's campaigns is from Wallace, *History of South Carolina;* and McCrady, *History of South Carolina in the Revolution, 1775-1780.* British movements are from Tarleton, *Campaigns;* and Bass, *The Green Dragoon.* Eyewitness accounts of the battles of Rocky Mount and Hanging Rock are from William R. Davie in John H. Wheeler, *Historical Sketches of North Carolina,* New York, 1925; Salley, *Hill's Memoirs;* Williams, "Winn's Notes"; and J. B. O'Neal, "Memoirs of Major Joseph McJunkin," *The Magnolia . . . ,* 2 vols., Charleston, 1842-1843. The account of the battle of Hanging Rock is largely from Sumter's letter to Pinckney, *State Records of North Carolina,* XIV; and a sketch by William Dobein James, Draper, 5VV115. Davie, Winn, and James name different sets of commanders at Hanging Rock, and their accounts are irreconcilable.
Horatio Gates was born in England, served under Braddock, and in 1772 settled in Virginia. In 1775 he was appointed adjutant general of the Continental Army and commanded the troops that defeated Burgoyne. After being relieved by Greene for his failure at Camden, he served under Washington.
William Richardson Davie was born in Cumberland, England; reared in the Waxhaws; and educated at Princeton. After distinguished service in the Revolution, he entered politics and in 1798 became governor of North Carolina.
Historians still dispute over the dates of the battles of Rocky Mount and Hanging Rock. The demand for surrender from "Winn's Notes," is dated July 31, 1780.
Rocky Mount is on the fall line and the country around it is strewn with boulders.
Hanging Rock derived its name from a large boulder towering twenty feet above the road from Camden to Salisbury.
Samuel Bryan, who lived on the upper Yadkin River, commanded the North Carolina Royal Militia.
The Prince of Wales' Regiment was completely destroyed at Hanging Rock.

6. *Debacle at Fishing Creek*

For the battles of Camden and Fishing Creek see Wallace, *History of South Carolina,* and McCrady, *History of the Revolution in South Carolina, 1775-1780.*

For details of the battle of Fishing Creek see Tarleton, *Campaigns;* Bass, *The Green Dragoon;* and Charles Ross, editor, *Correspondence of . . . Cornwallis.* Additional information is from O'Neal, "Memoirs of Major McJunkin;" D. G. Stinson, "Mrs. Susannah Smart," Draper, 9VV22; L. D. Spratt, in Draper, 11VV126; and Samuel Martin, application for pension, Draper, 10VV225. Sumter's letters to Pinckney, De Kalb and Gates are in *State Records of North Carolina.* The originals are in the Gates papers in the New York Historical Society.

Musgrove's house, the old ford, and a battle monument can be seen from the bridge over Enoree River on S. C. Highway 56 between Cross Anchor and Laurens.

Gilbert Town is Rutherfordton, North Carolina.

Charles Myddelton, whose plantation lay south of Congaree River, was well educated and soon became one of Sumter's aides.

British generals are also colonels of regiments. Lord Cornwallis was colonel of the 33rd Regiment, which was commanded by Lieutenant Colonel James Webster. An excellent soldier and humane officer, Webster died of wounds received at Guilford Courthouse.

Robert Crawford was a well-to-do planter in the Waxhaws. Tradition says that President Andrew Jackson was born on Crawford's plantation.

The battle ground at Fishing Creek can be seen from U. S. Highway 21 in Chester County.

The tradition of Soldier Tom's hiding the portmanteau with Sumter's papers and money is from Draper, 4VV142.

7. Gamecock and Swamp Fox

Background is from McCrady, *History of the Revolution in South Carolina, 1775-1780;* and Gregorie, *Thomas Sumter.* Material for the narrative is from Salley, *Hill's Memoirs;* Tarleton, *Campaigns;* Bass, *The Green Dragoon* and *Swamp Fox;* Draper, *King's Mountain and its Heroes;* and J. D. Bailey, *Commanders at King's Mountain,* Gaffney, 1926. See also Ross, *Correspondence of . . . Cornwallis,* and Joseph W. Barnwell, editor, "Correspondence of John Rutledge," *South Carolina Historical and Genealogical Magazine,* XVII-XVIII. For Sumter's report to Smallwood see Draper, 5VV76; the story of Sealy, Draper, 14VV92; and Sumter's treatment of Wemyss, Draper, 17VV221. The map of the battle ground at Fish Dam Ford was drawn from one by Colonel Winn.

Jonathon Roberts was captain in the 63rd Regiment.

Port's Ferry was about five miles below the place where U. S. Highway 378 crosses Peedee River.

Micajah Ganey, son of an English settler, lived six miles below Marion.

Indiantown, a community on S. C. Highway 261 about fifteen miles east of Kingstree, centers around Indiantown Presbyterian Church.

The Great White Marsh, near Whiteville, North Carolina, lies along the southern branch of Waccamaw River.

Isaac Shelby, son of Welsh settlers in Maryland, commanded the militia of Sullivan County, North Carolina, at the beginning of the Revolution. After distinguished service in the war, he settled at Boonesboro and became the first governor of Kentucky. In 1818 President Monroe offered him the post of Secretary of War.

William Lee Davidson, a Pennsylvanian who had settled in Rowan County, North Carolina, served in the Continental army around New York. Sent to the relief of Charleston, he found the city encircled by the British. Returning to North Carolina, he became active in the militia and was killed trying to prevent Cornwallis from crossing the Catawba at Cowan's Ford.

Abraham DePeyster, scion of a distinguished Tory family in New York, was a captain in Colonel Edmund Fanning's King's American Regiment.

Samuel Smallwood was a political and military leader in Maryland. After distinguished service under Washington, he marched southward with De Kalb and then served under both Gates and Greene. After the Revolution, he was three times elected governor of Maryland.

New Providence was just above the Waxhaws.

Drowning Creek is Lumber River.

Singleton's Mill was near the recreation grounds in Poinsett State Park.

Cowpens was the site of some rail cattle pens built by early settlers.

8. Victory at Blackstock's

Background for the battle of Blackstock's is from Wallace, *History of South Carolina;* McCrady, *History of the Revolution in South Carolina, 1775-1780;* Draper, *King's Mountain and its Heroes;* and Bass, *Swamp Fox*. The account of the battle is from Tarleton, *Campaigns;* Bass, *The Green Dragoon;* O'Neal, "Memoirs of Major McJunkin"; Salley, *Hill's Memoirs;* and the unpublished Cornwallis correspondence. For Captain David Hopkins's letter describing the wounding of Sumter see Draper, 12VV278.

William Blackstock's plantation lay near Cross Anchor in the western part of Union County. The map of Blackstock's was prepared by placing the troops of Sumter and Tarleton on a sketch drawn the day after the battle by Captain McDonald of the British Army and preserved in the unpublished Cornwallis correspondence. In October 1960 the author, in company with descendents of William and Mary Blackstock, visited the site, now in thick woods. So well was McDonald's map drawn that the visit revealed nothing except that the hills are much steeper than anticipated.

The 71st Regiment wore kilts and bonnets in summer and uniforms with red coats faced with white in winter.

Major John Money, a man of education and character, was aide to Lord Cornwallis. Tory newspapers praised Tarleton's rescue of Money.

Mary Dillard is usually given credit for warning Sumter. See Tarleton, *Campaigns,* and Robert Mills, *Statistics of South Carolina, 1826.* But Draper, *King's Mountain and its Heroes,* gives the credit to Jane Thomas, wife of Colonel John Thomas of the Spartan regiment.

Benjamin Few commanded militia from Georgia.

John Twiggs, commanding a regiment of Georgia militia, was senior officer under Sumter.

James Jackson was born in Devonshire, England, but at fifteen he emigrated to Georgia. He fought at Savannah, Cowpens, and Augusta. After the Revolution he served Georgia as governor and as United States senator.

Adam Goudelock was an early settler on the Pacolet.

Sumter maintained that Dr. Brownfield saved his life. Brownfield's son John married Sumter's granddaughter Brazilia.

9. Wounds beyond Healing

For background see McCrady, *History of the Revolution, 1780-1783.* The narrative is derived from William Johnson, *Sketches of the Life and Correspondence of Nathanael Greene . . .*, 2 vols., Charleston, 1822; Gregorie, *Thomas Sumter;* James Graham, *The Life of General Daniel Morgan . . .*, New York, 1856; Tarleton, *Campaigns;* and Bass, *The Green Dragoon* and *Swamp Fox;* as well as from the letters of Sumter, Greene, and Rutledge, *Year Book of the City of Charleston, 1899,* Charleston, 1900; "Letters to General Greene and Others," *South Carolina Historical and Genealogical Magazine,* XVI; and Barnwell, "Letters of John Rutledge," *South Carolina Historical and Genealogical Magazine.*

In 1787 Tarleton published his *Campaigns* to exculpate himself from blame for his defeat at Cowpens. His book brought on bitter controversy. Roderick Mackenzie, a fomer lieutenant in the 71st Regiment who had been badly wounded at Cowpens, attacked Tarleton in *Strictures on Col. Tarleton's history of the Campaigns of 1780 and 1781, in the southern provinces of North America,* London, 1787. George Hanger, former major in the British Legion, replied in *An Address to the Army: in reply to Strictures by Roderick M'Kenzie (late lieutenant in the 71st Regiment) on Tarleton's History of the Campaigns of 1780 and 1781,* London, 1789.

Henry Lee, nicknamed Light Horse Harry because of his service in the Continental cavalry, was born in Virginia. After graduation from Princeton he joined the Continentals and won the admiration of Washington. Sent to the Southern Department, he campaigned under Marion, Sumter, Pickens, and Greene. After the Revolution, he entered politics and in 1792 became governor of Virginia. He was the father of General Robert E. Lee.

Daniel Morgan, born of Welsh ancestry in New Jersey, settled in the Shenandoah Valley of Virginia. At the outbreak of the Revolution, he recruited a company of riflemen and served gallantly around Boston, on Arnold's march to Quebec, and at Saratoga. Promoted to brigadier general of Continentals, he served under both Gates and Greene. After the Revolution, he was active in Virginia politics and militia affairs. In 1797 he was elected to Congress.

Thaddeus Kosciusko was born in Lithuania. After graduation from the Royal College in Warsaw, he studied engineering and artillery in France. Coming to America with Lafayette, he was commissioned colonel of engineers in the Continental Army. Returning to Poland after the Revolution, Kosciusko led a rebellion against Russia.

Lord Cornwallis commissioned Robert Cunningham a brigadier general in the Loyalist militia.

Greene's attitude toward the South Carolina partisans aroused animosities that still rankle. Compare McCrady's attacks upon Greene and the defense of him by Wallace.

10. Rescue of Mary

Background for Sumter's raid down Santee River comes from McCrady, *History of South Carolina in the Revolution, 1780-1783*. The story of the raid is reconstructed largely from the letters of Sumter, Marion, Watson, and Rawdon in Gibbes, *Documentary History of the American Revolution, 1781-1782*. See also Johnson, *Nathanael Greene*, and the correspondence between Sumter and Greene, *Year Book of the City of Charleston*. For Marion's part, see Bass, *Swamp Fox*. For additional details see "Col. Robert Gray's Observations on the War in Carolina," *South Carolina Historical and Genealogical Magazine*, XI; "Levi Smith's Narrative," the *Royal Gazette*, April 13, 1782, Draper, 17VV44; traditions from Thomas McDill, Draper, 11VV178; pension statement of James Jordan who helped rescue Sumter's family, Draper, 11VV326; and Stinson, "Susannah Smart," Draper, 9VV22. For Tarleton's capture and treatment of James Bradley, see Bass, *The Green Dragoon*.

Snow's Island, a strip of land five miles long and two wide lying between Peedee River, Lynches River, and Clark's Creek, an alternate mouth of Lynches, is in lower Florence County. Marion used the island as a refuge from November, 1780, until March, 1781.

Fort Granby, built around the store of Chestnut and Kershaw, was at Cayce. The house, known as the Cayce House, stood until recent times.

Andrew Maxwell, a Tory from the Eastern Shore of Maryland, belonged to the Prince of Wales' Regiment. Because of his plundering, the Whigs considered him a common thief.

John and Welbore Ellis Doyle were from Ireland. John helped Lord Rawdon recruit the Volunteers of Ireland. He was brigade major at the battle of Hobkirk's Hill. After the Revolution, he was Secretary of War for Ireland and Secretary to the Prince of Wales. Welbore Ellis, younger but senior to his brother John, commanded the New York Volunteers in the absence of Colonel Turnbull. After a distinguished career in the British Army, he died while governor of Ceylon.

James Bradley, an ardent Whig and member of the General Assembly, lived at Salem in Sumter County.

Benbow's Ferry crossed Black River thirteen miles above Kingstree.

Charles and Thomas Fraser were Tories from the Low Country and connected by marriage with the Rutledges. Charles served as British intendent in Charleston and Thomas as major in the South Carolina provincials commanded by Lieutenant Colonel Innes.

Stirrup Branch is near Bishopville.

Robert Gray succeeded Robert Mills as commander of the Loyalist militia around Cheraw.

11. Founding the State Troops

Information on Sumter's founding the State Troops is derived largely from correspondence between Sumter and Greene, *Year Book of the City of Charleston;* and between Sumter, Marion, and Greene in Gibbes, *Documentary His-*

tory. For Marion, Watson, and Doyle, see Bass, *Swamp Fox*, an account derived from William Dobein James, *Sketch of the Life of Brig. Gen. Francis Marion*, Charleston, 1821; Peter Horry and Mason Locke Weems, *The Life of Francis Marion . . .*, Philadelphia, 1857; and letters in Gibbes, *Documentary History*. For Watson and Widow Jenkins, see James Jenkins, *Experience, Labours, and Sufferings of Rev. James Jenkins of the South Carolina Conference*, 1842. Sumter's scheme of paying the State Troops is from Richard Hampton's letter, Gibbes, *Documentary History*. For the uniforms and equipment that came from Newbern, see Draper, 11VV460.

For the battle of Guilford Courthouse, see Johnson, *Nathanael Greene;* Tarleton, *Campaigns;* Bass, *The Green Dragoon;* and Henry Lee, *Memoirs of the War in the Southern Department of the United States*, 2 vols., Philadelphia, 1812.

John Watson Tadwell-Watson was an officer in the 3rd Regiment. He built Fort Watson.

Ball was Marion's horse, so named because Marion took him from Colonel John Coming Ball after the battle of Black Mingo.

Hugh and John Ervin were leaders among the Scotch-Irish around Aimwell Presbyterian Church in lower Florence County. Hugh Ervin was the senior militia officer under Marion.

In his letter Sumter left blanks for the name of the regiment and number of men under Colonel Marshall.

Mars Bluff is the place where U. S. Highway 301 crosses Peedee River.

Sampit River flows into Winyah Bay just below Georgetown.

Burch's Ferry crossed Peedee River twelve miles below Mars Bluff.

Britton's Ferry across Peedee River, now Smith's Mill, is at the end of the boundary line between Williamsburg and Georgetown counties.

The author's boyhood home was on the same site as the house in which Widow Jenkins entertained Watson.

Catfish Creek lies just west of Marion.

12. Wrangling in the Brass

Historical background comes from Wallace, *History of South Carolina;* and McCrady, *History of the Revolution in South Carolina, 1780-1783*. The controversy between Sumter and Greene is derived from Johnson, *Nathanael Greene;* and especially George Washington Greene, *The Life of Nathanael Greene . . .*, Boston and New York, 1897. See William Gordon, *History of the Rise, progress, and Establishment of the United States of America . . .*, 4 vols., London, 1788. See also Lee, *Memoirs;* Bass, *Swamp Fox;* and Robinson, *Davie*. Additional material is from Horry and Weems, *Life of Francis Marion;* James, *Life of Brig. Gen. Francis Marion;* and Alexander Gregg, *History of the Old Cheraws . . .*, New York, 1867. Letters of Greene, Marion, and Sumter are in Gibbes, *Documentary History*, and letters between Greene and Sumter are in *Year Book of the City of Charleston*.

The Davis plantation was near Monticello in Fairfield County.

William Clay Snipes was brave and active, but also ambitious and contentious.

Hezekiah Maham, from St. Stephen's, was captain in the Fifth Regiment of South Carolina Continentals, but joined Marion after the fall of Charleston.

Bloom Hill was in Poinsett State Park.

Logtown was the British camp about two miles from Camden.

Pine Tree Creek lies southeast of Camden.

John Coffin, an officer in the New York Volunteers, was an active and gallant leader. Settling in New Brunswick after the Revolution, he was prominent in Canadian politics and rose to general of the British army. He married Anne Mathews of South Carolina.

Hobkirk's Hill is now in the town limits of Camden.

John Gunby commanded the First Regiment of Maryland Continentals. Greene blamed him for the loss of the battle of Hobkirk's Hill.

13. Hassle over Granby

For background, see McCrady, *History of the Revolution in South Carolina, 1781-1783;* and Gregorie, *Thomas Sumter.* Greene's side of the controversy with Sumter and Marion is from Johnson, *Nathanael Greene;* especially Greene, *Nathanael Greene;* Lee, *Memoirs;* and Robinson, *Davie.* Marion's siege of Fort Motte is from Bass, *Swamp Fox.* Letters between Sumter and Greene are from *Year Book of the City of Charleston.* Letters from Greene and his aides, Sumter, and Marion are in Gibbes, *Documentary History.*

Friday's Ferry, which crossed Congaree River between Cayce and Columbia, was run by Martin Fridig, a settler from Switzerland.

Major McArthur, who surrendered to Pickens at Cowpens, had been exchanged and had raised a regiment of dragoons, many of whom were Hessians.

Buchanan's Ferry, miscalled Buckenham's, crossed Santee River about ten miles below the confluence of Congaree and Wateree rivers.

Charles McPherson was a lieutenant in Cruger's battalion of DeLancey's brigade of New Jersey Loyalists.

Cross Creek is now Fayetteville.

Fort Motte stood on a site now covered by thick woods.

Sumter's "best horse on the Continent" probably means best cavalry on the Continental establishment.

Tarleton confided to Colonel John Hamilton of North Carolina that he had persuaded Lord Cornwallis to march into Virginia.

Colonel's Creek, Sawney's Creek, and 25 Mile Creek flow into Wateree River in eastern Richland County.

14. Frustration below Ninety-Six

Background is from McCrady, *History of the Revolution in South Carolina, 1780-1781;* Johnson, *Nathanael Greene;* Lee, *Memoirs;* and Bass, *Swamp Fox.* The letters of Sumter, Marion, Myddelton, and Greene and his aides are in Gibbes, *Documentary History* and *Year Book of the City of Charleston.*

Hampton's Orangeburgers were repentant Tories serving the six months required for rehabilitation.

Round O is on alternate U. S. Highway 17 between Summerville and Walterboro.

Star Fort, main bastion at Ninety-Six, is still visible.

After leaving Orangeburg, Lord Rawdon marched above North Edisto River, passed Batesburg–Leesville, and turned toward Ninety-Six. The Cedar Ponds are in western Lexington County. Juniper Creek is near Gilbert and Big Hollow Creek is near Batesburg-Leesville.

Historians have censured Sumter for not trying to prevent Rawdon's relief of Ninety-Six. When John Marshall was writing his life of Washington, he wrote Congressman Sumter, asking why he did not do so. Sumter did not reply. The truth seems to be that, although Sumter disliked Greene, he did his best. He was too ill to be active and had too few troops to be effective. He was probably ill of malaria as well as suffering from his wound.

Bush River runs through Newberry County, lying a few miles southwest of Newberry.

Lord Rawdon was undoubtedly suffering from malaria.

Thomas Polk, a Pennsylvanian, settled at Charlotte, North Carolina. Having become a political and military leader, in 1775 he served in the Snow Campaign. After serving in the Continental army, he resigned, but later served under both Gates and Greene.

Lyle's Ford crossed Broad River some two miles above the mouth of Enoree River.

15. Defeat at Quinby

Background comes from McCrady, *History of the Revolution in South Carolina, 1780-1783*. Material for the narrative is from Johnson, *Nathanael Greene;* Greene, *Nathanael Greene;* Lee, *Memoirs;* Jenkins, *Experience, Labours and Sufferings;* James, *Life of Brig. Gen. Francis Marion;* and Bass, *Swamp Fox.* Letters between Sumter and Greene are in *Year Book of the City of Charleston;* other letters are in Gibbes, *Documentary History.* Many unpublished letters of Greene and Marion are in the Clements Library. Colonel Taylor's remarks are from Draper, 16VV35.

There is some doubt as to Sumter's visiting Greene at Lee's Cross Roads. Johnson, *Nathanael Greene,* says that he did. Their letters sound as if they had met and made plans for the campaign.

Greene's "a matter highly interesting to these states" was information about the plans for the campaign which culminated at Yorktown.

Russell's Ferry crossed Congaree River about twenty miles below Columbia.

Alexander Stewart commanded the 3rd Regiment. Upon the return of Lord Rawdon to England, Stewart succeeded to the command of the British troops in South Carolina.

Beaver Creek flows into Congaree River about twenty miles below Cayce.

Four Holes Swamp runs through eastern Orangeburg County.

Bacon's Bridge over Ashley River is on S. C. Highway 165 about five miles below Summerville.

Wadboo Creek is two miles below Biggin church. S. C. Highway 402 crosses it at Wadboo Bridge.

Biggin church has crumbled, but the foundations are still visible.

Strawberry Ferry crossed Cooper River some five miles east of Strawberry.

Quinby plantation was near Huger in Charleston County.

16. End of the Glory

For the battle of Eutaw Springs and the trial and execution of Isaac Hayne, see McCrady, *History of South Carolina in the Revolution, 1780-1783;* Johnson, *Nathanael Greene;* Greene, *Nathanael Greene;* Lee, *Memoirs;* and Bass, *Swamp Fox.* The account of Sumter's actions is derived largely from the letters of Sumter, Greene, and Rutledge in *Year Book of the City of Charleston;* Gibbes, *Documentary* History; and Barnwell "Correspondence of John Rutledge," *South Carolina Historical and Genealogical Magazine,* XVII-XVIII.

Marion's letter reporting the battle at Parker's Ferry is in the *Pennsylvania Gazette,* October 24, 1781.

The paymaster's trunk captured at Quinby contained £720.

Widow Wright was the relict of Captain John Wright of Wassamassaw. During Hampton's raid on Goose Creek Church Captain Waugh of the 71st Regiment killed Wright. After Waugh surrendered, comrades of Wright killed him in cold blood, an incident for which the Americans apologized to the British.

William Harden, who had served in the artillery around Beaufort earlier in the Revolution, visited Marion in 1781 and afterward organized a regiment and began campaigning along the Edisto.

Isaac Hayne, a planter and industrialist who lived on Edisto River, took protection under the Articles of Capitulation of Charleston. When Sir Henry Clinton revoked these paroles, he signed another statement under coercion declaring his allegiance to King George. Contrary to their promises the British threatened him with confinement unless he consented to bear arms. Instead of joining the Loyalist militia, Hayne recruited a Whig regiment, obtained commissions for his officers from General Marion, and began campaigning boldly around Charleston.

A French war vessel captured the ship on which Lord Rawdon was returning to England. There was demand that Rawdon be returned to South Carolina and tried for his part in executing Isaac Hayne. The surrender of Lord Cornwallis, however, allayed passions.

Patrick Roche had married Martha Marion, a niece of General Marion.

Upon coming to America, Marquis de Lafayette landed near Georgetown, visited the Hugers, and then went northward to join Washington. Commissioned major general in the Continental army in 1777, in 1781 he was sent to oppose the march of Cornwallis through Virginia. After the Revolution Lafayette returned to France and had a distinguished political and military career.

After a distinguished military career, during which he was aide to Frederick the Great, Baron von Steuben came to America. He was appointed inspector general and given the task of training the Continental Army. After the Revolution he settled in Pennsylvania.

A soldier with a distinguished record, in 1780 Count Rochambeau was appointed commander of the French expedition to America. His forces were decisive in defeating Lord Cornwallis. In 1791 Count Rochambeau was marshal of France.

Count de Grasse commanded the French Fleet which entered the Chesapeake and prevented the British from relieving Lord Cornwallis at Yorktown.

William Cunningham, infamous as "Bloody Bill" Cunningham, was a cousin of Robert and Patrick Cunningham.

17. Member of the General Assembly

For background see Wallace, *History of South Carolina;* and McCrady, *History of the Revolution in South Carolina, 1780-1783.* For Sumter's finances, speculations, and land holdings, see Gregorie, *Thomas Sumter.* See also Johnson, *Nathanael Greene;* and Greene, *Nathanael Greene.* Bass, *Swamp Fox,* gives the story of the vote of thanks. For Sumter in Stateburg, see Thomas S. Sumter, *Stateburg and its People,* Sumter, 1939. For the story of Lucas see Draper, 2VV195.

John Mathews, who had served as ensign in the militia company of Captain William Moultrie and Lieutenant Francis Marion in the war with the Cherokees, was a member of the Continental Congress.

Alexander Gillon, a wealthy merchant in Charleston, was appointed commodore of South Carolina's small fleet. He failed in his mission to purchase frigates in Europe.

18. Congressman and Senator

Material for an account of Sumter in Congress and in the United States Senate is from Draper's manuscripts. See also Johnson, *Nathanael Greene;* and Gregorie, *Thomas Sumter.* For Thomas Sumter, Jr., and Natalie de Delage see Mary Virginia Sanders White, *Fifteen Letters of Nathalie Sumter,* Columbia, 1942.

For Sumter's grandchildren see Ames, "Cantey Family," *South Carolina Historical and Genealogical Magazine.* Thomas Sumter, Jr., and Natalie de Delage were married on March 20, 1802. Their children were as follows:

Annette Marie Natalie, born in 1803, who married Comte Joseph de Fontenay.

Stephanie Beatrice, born in 1805, who married Conte Guiseppa Binda.

Maria Thomasin, born in 1806, who died unmarried in Paris.

Paul Thomas Delage, born in 1809, who died unmarried at Stateburg.

Pauline Stephanie Beatrix, born in 1813, who married John W. Brownfield.

Francis Brasilimo, born 1815, who died unmarried.

Sebastian D'Amblimont, born 1820, who married Mary Butler Waties and Emma Bradley.

The account of Sumter and Martin is from Draper, 2VV83. Sumter's speech on Widow Greene's petition is in Draper, 8VV60. For Sumter's encounter with Fitzhugh see Draper, 11VV505. For Jefferson's letter see Draper, 11VV496. Sumter's visit to Preddy's Creek is in Draper, 18VV37; and his visit to Charlottesville in Draper, 2VV83.

The story of Sumter and his Turkish tenants is in Draper, 2VV87. Some letters from Sumter's grandchildren are as follows: Sebastian Sumter, 11VV332; Thomas Delage Sumter, 11VV339-342; and Louisa Sumter Murrell, 11VV351.

Sumter's letter to Washington, probably written by Thomas Sumter, Jr., shows an enormous growth in perception since the crude letter written to Joe Martin from Long Canes Creek.

Sumter's joining Jefferson's party set a political pattern for South Carolina that has persisted even down to the presidential election of 1960: adherence to the Democratic Party; dominance of the Up Country; extreme States Rights; and rugged independence of political domination.

The name *Sumterville* was changed to *Sumter* in 1855.

19. Last of the Generals

Material for the story of Sumter's last years comes from the Draper manuscripts. For a parallel account and especially for Sumter's tangled finances see Gregorie, *Thomas Sumter.* For Sumter's worship at the Baptist church see Draper, 2VV73; and Sumter's playing ball, Draper, 2VV87. For Sumter's sentimental journey to the battlefields see Draper, 14VV94; Sumter's visit to Bradford Springs court, Draper, 1VV5; and Sumter during Nullification, Draper, 8VV152-170. For Sumter's death see Draper, 11VV516; and Furman's eulogy, Draper, 8VV172.

Sumter would probably have been elected governor of South Carolina in 1812. The factions in the General Assembly became deadlocked and compromised by electing Joseph Alston, who had married Theodosia Burr.

Thomas Sumter, Jr., was colonel of the Claremont regiment of militia.

To Sumter's monument the Countess de Fontenay affixed a bronze plaque bearing the following inscription:

> To General Thomas Sumter
> who fought so gloriously for the
> Liberty of the United States
> in remembrance of his two grandsons
> Charles and Etienne de Fontenay
> who fought so heroically and died so nobly
> for the liberty of France in 1916
> Hommage du Vicomte de Fontenay
> Ambassadeur de France

Sumter said that he was born on Bastille Day.

Tanto . . . Elogium—Eulogy can add nothing to so great a name—is from the tomb of Machiavelli.

INDEX

DATE DUE
OCT 19 '72
NOV 13 '72
AP 17 '79
GAYLORD
PRINTED IN U.S.A.

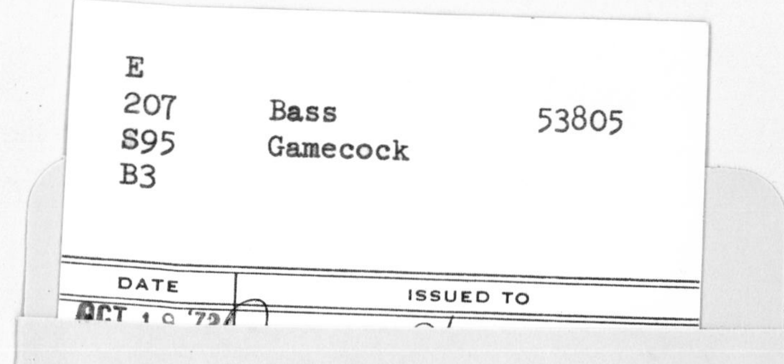
E
207
S95
B3
Bass
Gamecock
53805
DATE
ISSUED TO

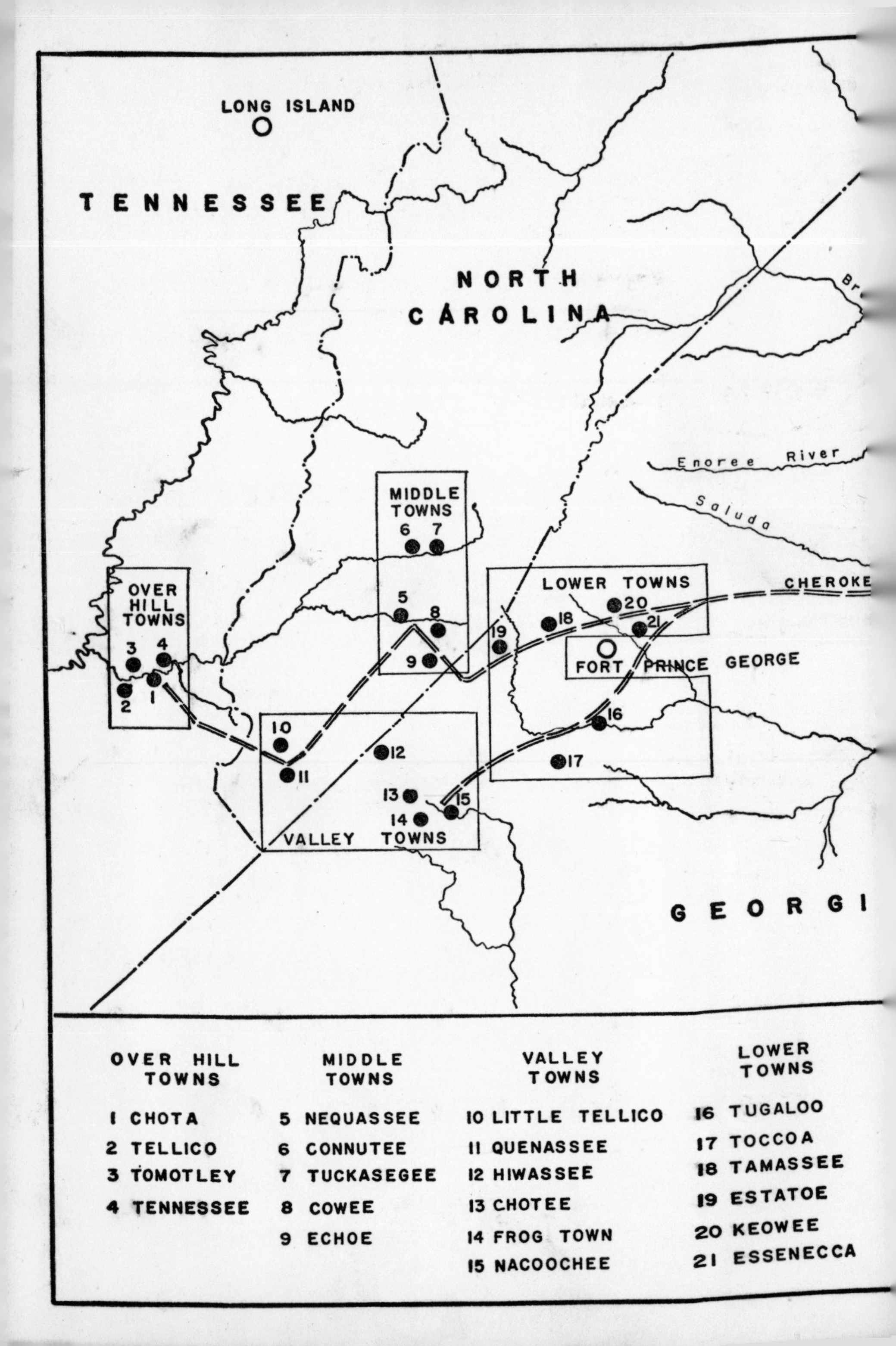
LONG ISLAND
TENNESSEE
NORTH CAROLINA
Enoree River
Saluda
Br
MIDDLE TOWNS
OVER HILL TOWNS
LOWER TOWNS
CHEROKE
FORT PRINCE GEORGE
VALLEY TOWNS
GEORGI
OVER HILL TOWNS
1 CHOTA
2 TELLICO
3 TOMOTLEY
4 TENNESSEE
MIDDLE TOWNS
5 NEQUASSEE
6 CONNUTEE
7 TUCKASEGEE
8 COWEE
9 ECHOE
VALLEY TOWNS
10 LITTLE TELLICO
11 QUENASSEE
12 HIWASSEE
13 CHOTEE
14 FROG TOWN
15 NACOOCHEE
LOWER TOWNS
16 TUGALOO
17 TOCCOA
18 TAMASSEE
19 ESTATOE
20 KEOWEE
21 ESSENECCA